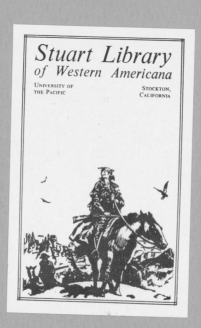

The Road West

Bertha S. Dodge, a professional writer with a
dozen nonfiction books to her credit, has most
recently edited and provided an introduction for
Marooned, an account of shipwreck and survival
on the Falkland Islands first published in 1829.

photo by Paul A. Quinn

The Road West

Saga of the 35th Parallel

Bertha S. Dodge

UNIVERSITY OF NEW MEXICO PRESS

Albuquerque

Library of Congress Cataloging in Publication Data

Dodge, Bertha Sanford, 1902–
    The road west.

    Bibliography: p.215
    Includes index.
    1. Frontier and pioneer life—New Mexico.
2. New Mexico—History. 3. El Morro National
Monument. 4. Overland journeys to the Pacific.
5. Southwest, New—History. I. Title.
F796.D62 1980   978.9   79-21051
ISBN 0-8263-0526-1

Contents

Illustrations follow page 144

Acknowledgments

This account of the road west attempts to present a bit of the history of our nation in terms of the people involved, many not of great individual importance yet adding up to a significant whole. Some of those westward movers were of rather limited literacy, while others may have had special axes to grind. Thus, a chronicle of such a movement demands as many personal documents as possible without, in general, personal correspondence to help. Journals and more private diaries there are—some published, some not, but in any case not easy to locate or to secure access to. None could have been located without access to libraries or without the help of knowledgeable librarians.

With every hope that I am overlooking no one who may have contributed to this work, which has been spread out over a considerable number of years, I must acknowledge appreciatively the following institutions and persons:

The Huntington Library, San Marino, California, which has graciously given permission to quote from William Floyd's Journal (HM 19334), penciled in a notebook carried during Beale's 1859 expedition.

The Library of the University of New Mexico, whose splendid western collections, notably the books collected by the late Senator Clinton P. Anderson, have helped immeasurably.

The Library of the New Mexico State University in Las Cruces, which has some pertinent material not available in the University of New Mexico Library.

The Bailey Library of the University of Vermont. Much work could be done here since, with Vermont the fourteenth state to join the Union, the file of government documents is almost complete. These include reports made by leaders of government-sponsored expeditions—reports which make excellent reading and are usually well illustrated, largely with lithographs, hand colored in some instances. Free access to the stacks housing such documents has made possible not only the frequent consultation of such reports but the locating of briefer and lesser items such as reports by officers in charge of western outposts. Much appreciated, too, have been the efforts of Ms. Sandra Pease, in charge of interlibrary loans at the Bailey Library, who has never failed to locate needed books and documents in other libraries and to secure them on loan.

The Library of Congress, which has made available microfilm of Beale personal documents and, further, answered queries concerning permission to quote both from the microfilmed material and from photocopied documents.

The illustrations herein assembled are, first, from the published lithographs made by artist R. H. Kern for two of the expeditions he accompanied before his tragic death in another such. The photographic copies of these (made from those in the Library of the University of Vermont) have been contributed by Dr. Frank V. Rich of Burlington, Vermont. The two Beale portraits are here included through the courtesy of the National Trust for Historic Preservation, which holds the copyright to the material. Thanks are here due to Dr. Vincent Ponko, Jr., Academic Vice-President of the University of Scranton, Pa., who suggested the pictures used and loaned transparencies made from paintings (in Decatur House, Washington, D.C.) to which the National Trust for Historic Preservation holds the copyright.

Family portraits of some 1858 wagon train survivors have been generously loaned, with permission to include them in this book, by descendants of two of those families. Hedgpeth portraits, taken in Missouri in 1858 before the start of the western trip, are loaned by Dr. Joel Hedgpeth of California. The Baley portraits are included thanks to the kind efforts of Mr. Mark Simpson of California (great-great-grandson of William Wright Baley), who also supplied much material on the lives of wagon train people after settling in California. This is a research to which he has devoted much time and effort, so that special thanks are due him for the sharing of this information as well as the contribution of family portraits.

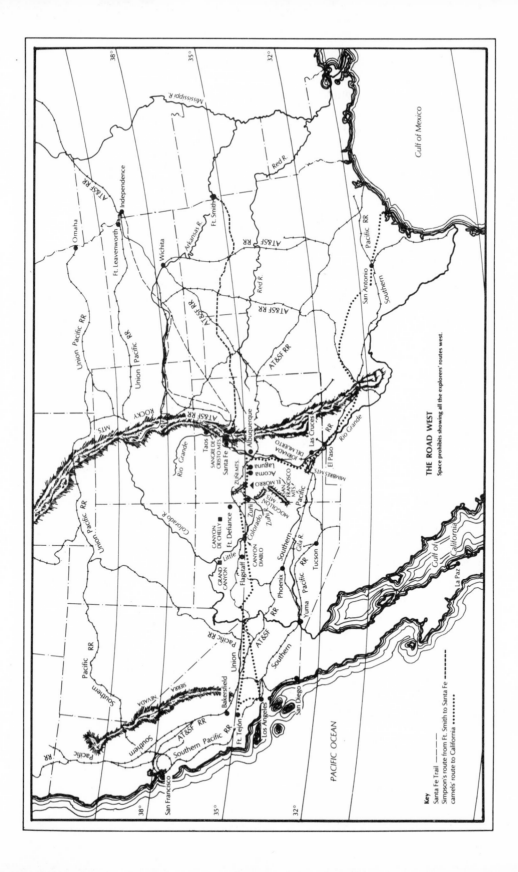

THE ROAD WEST

Space prohibits showing all the explorers' routes west.

Key

Santa Fe Trail —————
Simpson's route from Ft. Smith to Santa Fe ------
camels' route to California ••••••••

1

Pasó Por Aquí

It was a moment of larger historic import than men long appreciated when, on April 30, 1803, by the stroke of a pen and the
commitment to pay a sum totaling about fifteen million dollars, the
young United States expanded from the Mississippi River to the
borders of California. People who knew the lands near the river for
the sad malarial swamps many of those were, thought the money,
which the young republic could ill afford to spend, was being
thrown away to no good purpose. For others who had already been
illegally hunting and trapping in the newly acquired territory, that
purchase meant ever expanding legally permissible hunting and
trapping grounds (if legality meant anything to them). Politicians
were thinking in terms of an all-American Mississippi River, then,
as decades passed, of an ocean-to-ocean nation enjoying direct
ocean access to the profitable markets of the Far East. To all, it
spelled new opportunity not fully exploitable until roads of one sort
or another should make that opportunity so.

They started moving west—the hunters and trappers, the explorers, the roadbuilders, and, finally, after the discovery of those
glittering sands at Sutter's millrace in California, propertyless men
who saw themselves turning suddenly and fabulously rich by a few
turns of a spade. The routes they took were various, each having its
own supporters, each embodying special risks.

When the dust of controversy began to clear, there were four
favored, if contested, routes along which wagon roads and, presently,
railroads were to be built. These were: (1) the 41° parallel route,
which the Northern Pacific Railroad now approximates; (2) the 38°
parallel route of today's Union Pacific line; (3) the 35° parallel route

1

today followed by the combined Atchison, Topeka & Santa Fe and Central Pacific lines; (4) the 32° parallel Southern Pacific Route designed to link New Orleans to San Diego and on to San Francisco. None of these routes could have been realized without the adventurous men who explored them, the knowledgeable men who planned and supervised road construction or—and these we are too inclined to underrate—the run-of-the-mill people whose presence gave both urgency and support to the efforts of politicians (who, during the 1850s, were further spurred by increasing awareness of the tenuous nature of the bonds holding their nation together).

Exactly who were the persons who made such routes possible? Names of the planners and leaders are today known only to a handful of history buffs. The average passerby's name is rarely known to anyone save interested descendants. A notable exception is where the people themselves made an effort to escape oblivion by leaving a record of their passing. To this end there has served especially the sheer sandstone face of a New Mexican mesa that bears the descriptive name of El Morro ("The Headland"), and rises steeply above a surrounding sea of sand. It is topped by a layer of more durable rock, which has helped resist the weathering that might otherwise have erased the records left there.

What has made El Morro unique among the many flat-topped hills that soar skyward from the plains of western New Mexico, others of which also look out across the imaginary line marking the 35° of latitude, is the unusual attribute of a fresh water pool snuggling close to its base. Thus it became an objective of travelers in an otherwise too waterless land, a place where they could spend a relatively comfortable night and then, with morning's light, record their presence before setting forth toward the possible oblivion that might await them beyond.

For many, the initial impulse to make those marks may have been due to the fact that earlier men had already left theirs—the long gone Indians whose now lichen-dimmed petroglyphs may have conveyed meaning to their gods or to their ancient contemporaries but which even the Indians of the nineteenth century did not know how to interpret. Of now decipherable inscriptions, the oldest record activities of Spaniards who had appropriated the land, which they claimed in the name of a contemporary Spanish monarch and of an earlier Spanish Pope. Their frequently boastful comments, inscribed in the Spanish lettering and spelling of the seventeenth and eighteenth centuries, tell us not only their names but often also the reasons for their passing. Literate English-speaking later comers, equally uncertain as to what might await them beyond and perhaps unwilling that the records there remain exclusively in a foreign tongue and of a foreign civilization, added their names and, often though not often enough for us of today, the dates of their passing. Whatever their motives, the face of El Morro now gives a special, personal reality to the centuries of history represented there. Equally important, it also bears witness to the significant role played in history by average men who could not have been very average to face the risks and uncertainties of the route they had undertaken.

The Indians who drew the fascinating doodles on the rock were probably the same who once inhabited the fortress town whose ruins still adorn the top of that mesa. No one now knows who those Indians were. Modern archaeology might supply approximate dates but tells us little about the people who cut and fitted together thousands of rocks into walls which now are weathering back into formlessness. Toeholds gouged out of the sheer sandstone above the pool suggest a reason for the selection of that particular mesa from among the many others they might have chosen but which could have supplied water only in rain-filled depressions in the capping rock. It is not a land where any rain can be counted on.

Did failure of all water in an especially dry year drive those people forth? Did illness reduce their numbers to the vanishing point? Or did enemies finally manage to storm and seize their fortress? Whoever they were, wherever they went, whatever their reasons for abandoning the town they built with so much effort, their marks yet remain upon the rock and will probably remain there in protected places after the last vestiges of that town disappear altogether. Surely their ghosts still hover there looking down in disbelief and dismay at the ghostly throng of latecomers passing below.

There were, in any case, no living inhabitants in that town atop El Morro when, in 1540, the first of the alien latecomers—Spaniards in the band of Don Francisco Vázquez de Coronado—glimpsed it from afar. Certainly they could have seen nothing about that mesa, in a land of mesas, that might have suggested giving it a second glance. They were not looking for a tiny marginal village atop a mesa but for great fabled cities glowing with gold and silver and precious stones. They based their expectations on ancient legend plus recent reports of a credulous padre who had been previously guided thither by one Estevanico. Estevanico was a black Moroccan slave who had crossed that region as one of the pitiful remnants of the shipwrecked Narvaez Florida expedition. So the men of Coronado's band were persuaded that they were to find here seven fabled cities of Cibola, rivaling Mexico and Peru in wealth. Only one of the cities, now identified as Zuñi and within a few miles of El Morro, close to the thirty-fifth parallel, remains today. It was and is far from golden and is impressive only in the remarkable pueblo dwellings that rise story on story.

In 1540, the passing Spaniards were on their way from Zuñi to Ácoma, guided by Indians not along the relatively easy path to the north of El Morro but across notorious badlands to the south—"A horror to travel," a writer of our day described them, "thickly strewn with volcanic lava that is murderous to the feet of horses" and, of course, of men. The guiding Indians may well have thought thus to discourage further penetration of their lands by outsiders. Though most of the Spaniards in that band must have been having second thoughts about the black and barren land, some continued their penetration as far as the vicinity of today's Wichita, Kansas (Quivira), before turning back toward Mexico. And some of them—rather, their descendants—were destined to remain in New Mexico, holding lands there for the next two and a half centuries. They were not, however, destined to remain there in peace and comfort—to this El Morro bears multiple witness though, even so, far from complete.

We may assume that the route followed by Coronado's band from Mexico north, then northeast near the thirty-fifth parallel of latitude was frequented for some time. Possibly this was because it was first known, possibly because the Zuñi pueblos, as well as those of the Hopis farther to the northwest toward the Grand Canyon, lured friars dedicated to spreading Christianity among the heathen. Certainly El Morro's pool was an all but irresistible invitation for travelers to go that way.

Not until 1610, however, was there published an account of that area by a Captain Gaspar Pérez de Villagrá, who, in the year 1598, had acquired a too painfully intimate acquaintance with those lands. His "Historia de la Nueva México" tells in verse of his adventures when, in an October snowstorm—nothing unusual at that elevation—he had lost his way and fallen into a hole whence soldiers were to rescue him, starved and exhausted, some days later. Juan de Oñate, then governor of New Mexico, reported the incident: "Captain Villagrá arrived, being brought in by three soldiers who had gone to round up horses which the snow storm had scattered and found him almost dead at El Agua de la Peña" —the pool by the great rock—"without horse or arms, and not having eaten for two or three days . . . only the mercy of God prevented him from perishing." [14]

That governor was back near the same site in December 1599, but it was not until five years later that he was moved to cut there the first now decipherable inscription. "There passed this way," it reads, "Adelantado Don Juan de Oñate from the discovering of the South Sea, on the 16th of April, 1605." What it did not need to explain was that if Don Juan failed to reach home, this might inform his world that he had at least arrived at his aim of reaching the South Sea, today's Pacific Ocean. Actually, he had mistaken for this the Gulf of California—but a notable journey for all that.

Don Juan came from a family important in New Spain, as Mexico was then referred to. If his father, Don Cristóbal de Oñate, did not accompany Coronado when, in 1540, he set forth on his expedition of discovery into New Mexico, one of Don Cristóbal's horses made the trip, loaned but not donated to Coronado to avoid possible future accusations of bribery. And, as fate would have it, it was the horses that bore Coronado's troop into the new land that would have effects both more far-reaching and more enduring than most of the Spanish hidalgos who rode them so proudly into the far land.

Native sons saw horses, which were then entirely new to the New World, as the great secret weapon of the early 1500s. Accustomed to move only so far and so fast as their own two feet could take them, Indians looked upon these strange new beasts at first with terror, then with gradually growing appreciation. The extra number of feet, the extra speed and added height with which horses endowed their riders—these could give previously pedestrian Indians a mobility and power far, far beyond their ancestors' imaginings.

It was to be mounted Indians who, able to roam far from their safely hidden lodges, would harry California-bound emigrant trains that eventually came to camp by the pool. It was mounted Indians

who would soon be taking part in great buffalo hunts that helped
stampede the breed to the brink of extermination. It was Indians,
mounted or intended to be mounted, who would come softly into
camps in the dark of the night to steal mules and horses and, if not
killing outright those horses' owners, leaving them to die a slower
death in the trackless and waterless plains of the Southwest.

Horses were presently to become more than just a means of
transportation to the warlike Indians who coveted them. As with
automobiles in our own time, a man's prowess would be judged by
the number and quality of the horses he owned. Some Navajos, it
was said a century ago, owned as many as a thousand horses each.
Even allowing for the difficulty in counting so many and for
possible exaggeration, since no one would be able to check the
total of a single Indian's holdings, they represented considerable
skill, first in appropriating, then in breeding herds of horses.

Though conquistadors, too, placed a high value on a fine
mount, none of them could have believed that any horse could be
destined to make a mark more indelible than his own upon the land
he had helped conquer. It was, after all, not to a horse that had
come a lengthy, high-sounding, unbelievably detailed commission
from the "King of Castille, León, Aragón, the two Sicilies, Jeru-
salem, Navarre, Granada, Toledo . . ." and so on for a full page of
impressive titles. No Council of the Indies in far Seville had issued
to a horse some forty-five pages of instructions "for new discover-
ies, conquests, and pacifications." A horse, though high-priced and
essential to any conquistador, was yet only a horse.

After a long, exhausting, financially unrewarding trip that took
horses and men into modern Kansas, Coronado had finally returned
to Mexico City to face a judge of the Royal Audiencia commissioned
to investigate the conduct of the expedition. There would, of
course, have been no such investigation had Coronado been able to
bring back the wealth expected of every Spanish officer who explored new regions of the Americas.

While now impoverished Coronado faced the Audiencia, his
bands disintegrated. Reluctant to admit the total failure of their
once sanguine dreams, they would carry throughout New Spain
tales of exploration and adventure that continued to grow as
passing years dimmed the memory of sufferings and failures while
magnifying the few successes. Listeners, undeceived by the boasts,
would nod their heads sagely while assuring themselves, "Ah, I

would have brought home more riches, I would have perceived where the gold was to be found."

The boy Juan de Oñate, whose father's horse had made the memorable journey into New Mexico, growing up in a wealthy home where passing conquistadors were always assured lavish hospitality, listened openmouthed to their tales. His imagination stirred, he dreamed of following in their footsteps. He, of course, would become one of the successful explorers, not missing the treasures as others had. He would perform his task well and be rewarded with that coveted title, "Marqués." And when the king came to look upon his own Royal Fifth of the treasure which Juan de Oñate was to gather in, there might actually be no limit to the great titles and exalted positions His Most Catholic Majesty would bestow upon the successful conquistador.

By 1605, a disillusioned fifty-odd-year-old Juan de Oñate had a seven-year-old commission for the exploration, pacification, and settling of New Mexico. Seven years were a very long time for an adventurous hidalgo to spend in the frustrating routine of governing an unruly lot of settlers and an even unrulier lot of officers and soldiers.

Actually, it had taken a mere year for the glamor to dim. In 1599 he was writing to the Viceroy in Mexico City complaining of rebellious "soldiers and captains." Resentful that they found the ground of New Mexico covered with no great sheets of silver and that their governor forbade mistreatment of the native population, some forty-five (easily one quarter of the total number under Oñate's command) had nevertheless been robbing Indians of food, clothes, land, and finally of personal liberty, reducing them to slavery.

Perhaps after due and unhurried consideration, the Viceroy forwarded this letter of Oñate's to Seville. Perhaps it suggested to the king and/or his Council of the Indies that it was high time to send out to Mexico a royal snooper of the kind then called Visitador. In any case, some trusted correspondent later sent word directly to His Majesty, describing frankly the problems involved in establishing settlers in New Mexico. This letter, though undated as well as unsigned, was probably written about four years after the complaint of 1599—a reasonable period then for the mills of His Majesty to do their grinding.

The Visitador, or whoever the writer may have been, must have had unassailable social background as well as courage and understanding, for he dared be unpleasantly frank about Juan de Oñate's problems. "To me it seems certain," he wrote of New Mexico,

> that without possible profit, there would be no one willing to go thither and settle nor who, once settled, would wish to remain. With no more than just food and clothing, no one lives contented in the Indies. Moreover, with both things so limited there, it would not be easy to get men to move voluntarily from New Spain to New Mexico. Since food of itself conveys no luxuries, nor clothes a title of nobility, I believe that to continue settlement there would require either men so devoted to the spread of Christian faith that I have to doubt such exist today, or men condemned for misdemeanors and useless and impoverished because of bad consciences and bad habits. [22]

The writer further urged His Majesty to pay for recruitment and eighteen months' service of a troop of one hundred soldiers and six officers. Thus might be ensured the enlistment of men of a quality the no longer wealthy Juan de Oñate could not afford. Spanish kings, like their colleagues of other lands, rarely accepted such expensive advice.

Juan de Oñate's troop resembled Coronado's of a half century before in that it included many of the problem youth of the day—younger sons of Spanish nobles whose entailed estates must, by law, pass to the eldest son of each house. None of these young men, many of them still teenagers, really wanted to settle anywhere save back in Spain, where they could find no place to settle nor means to live unless they somehow managed to endow themselves with fortunes from the Indies.

When New Mexico yielded them none of the gold or silver or jewels expected by men who knew of the fabulous riches yielded by Mexico and Peru, they grabbed whatever else they could, including the persons of natives. Should hidalgos from the noblest houses of Spain go unrewarded and unattended? None of them, in any case, had the slightest intention of letting themselves be governed—certainly not by an oldster like Juan de Oñate, certainly not in a wild land where no one who really counted need know what was going on and where anyone who seemed to be learning too much might conveniently fall victim to the land or to disease or to marauding Indians or to who knew what.

By 1604, Adelantado Oñate wanted out, as would anyone else on
his spot. Yet as he remained committed to the governorship, for
which he had once schemed, his only legitimate out would be in
exploration that might justify absence from the seat of government
in the zealous search for greater treasure to pour into the bottomless
coffers of His Most Cathloic Majesty, Philip III of Spain. It could
have served no useful end for the adelantado to have resigned his
post. A resignation had to take its risky months-long route to the
city of Mexico. If it met with eventual acceptance there—no certain matter—that acceptance would have to take an equally slow
route back. Years of frustration could pass while the adelantado
waited and grew old.

So Juan de Oñate undertook exploration, first vainly seeking
treasure along Coronado's old route eastward into what today is
Kansas. Then he turned his efforts toward the South Sea. Should
he also fail there in the discovery of negotiable wealth, he might be
able to claim the distinction of having explored a short and direct
route thither, one that could have real value for a Spain whose
galleons already plied that sea. Having arrived there in January
1605, Juan de Oñate started back for New Mexico, on his way
making imperishable through a few gouges on the sandstone face of
a mesa a name that, through the complaints of soldiers and colo-
nists and the impatience of uninformed superiors in old and New
Spain, was already losing its lustre.

Here Juan de Oñate had set one example, at least, which even
his most active detractors would not hesitate to follow. Passing
that rock, which dominates the ancient Ácoma-Zuñi Indian trail,
would come increasing numbers of explorers, soldiers, padres. In
one way or another, all the passersby would add to the record,
though not always with inscriptions. We of today who look upon
the rock find there a record immeasurably more vivid than accounts on the yellowing pages of some book printed in far away
Spain or, even, in nearer Mexico City. We become aware of the
dim presence of men of ages past—men whose human needs
brought them to the pool's brim, while a remoter inarticulate
yearning to communicate with men who might stand there in years
to come guided their hands across the face of the rock.

Soldiers and settlers and padres, those Spaniards continued to
pass by, continued to pause at the pool, continued to add to the
lengthening record on the rock. By implication they add to another
record which would not be cut there because the people involved

had no way of making inscriptions that could convey meaning to men of European antecedents. Inevitably, against Juan de Oñate's explicit orders, those soldiers and settlers had continued to rob and enslave native populations. Inevitably the well-meaning, soul-saving padres added to the mounting misery of natives whose ancient rites the padres' missionary zeal bound them to denounce as works of Satan.

Small wonder, then, that some natives came to feel it an act of their own faith to kill the interfering padres. To this the rock bears witness in an inscription signed by one "Luján" who "passed this way in 1632 to avenge the death of Father Letrado." This, ironically, constitutes Luján's only claim to immortality. Father Letrado had died a martyr to his own faith by insisting that Indians attend Mass on a day otherwise sacred to their ancient religion.

The revenge perpetrated by Luján's expedition could only serve to feed the sadly mounting antagonism between native populations and newcomers. By 1680, Indians had become miserable enough to risk everything in following an articulate leader who urged on them the slaughter of all Spaniards. Rising, the Indians killed every Spaniard upon whom they could lay hands. The Spaniards who managed to escape fled to the south to gather strength, plan punishment, and devise ways to teach a lesson to the barbarous folk who had murdered friends and relatives.

Twelve years later, with plans complete, there stopped by the rock one Diego de Vargas, who, "at his own expense, in the year 1692, conquered all New Mexico for our Holy Faith and the Royal Crown." Typically, the Royal Crown was profiting by an eager beaver's personal expenditure.

"All New Mexico" soon proved to be too large a claim or else the boasted reconversion was too superficial to mean anything. By 1716, "There passed this way Don Feliz Martínez, Governor and Captain General . . . to the reduction and conquest of Moqui" —Moqui long being the named used for the land and people today called Hopi. The Hopis, deeply religious according to their ancient standards, would not bend to the teachings of the new "Reverend Father Friar" and paid for their intransigence by having their crops uprooted and livestock driven off by Don Feliz's orders—an edict of starvation if ever there was one.

Such are most of the records left behind on the rock by Spanish hidalgos of ages past. Each reveals a small bit of the turbulent history of that area—history that may be followed more in detail by anyone having the patience, as well as a knowledge of seven- teenth- and eighteenth-century Spanish, to pore over some of those lengthy legal documents that even in our own day, mark almost every episode from birth to death in lands of Spanish origin.

One record, surely, will not be repeated elsewhere though we could wish it might. It is a mysterious inscription that appears to inform the world that two men, one possibly a certain Vicente Synergosta *(Bysente Synergosta)*, the other name incompletely decipherable, argued about certain matters *(reñeron ciertas quys- tiones)* in the course of which argument one called the other a liar *(trolero)*. The date is lacking as also any suggestion as to what subject might have been of sufficient moment to merit a record in stone. Was the record made in fun or could an argument between proud and prickly hidalgos have reached a fatal climax? Defying interpretation, it remains more challenging than all the others, though in no way of less human interest.

By the third decade of the eighteenth century, the number of new inscriptions had declined as Spaniards came to realize they were reaping no harvest of souls or gold, but rather one of hatred. Settlers hesitated to wander far from the relative safety of their settlements. Then, during the latter half of that century, in the enlightened reign of King Carlos III (1759–88), there came a brief upsurge in travel as that king attempted to provide better living conditions for those dwelling in Spain's far-flung empire. Save for the brief upswing in recorded names of passing explorers, the limited number of inscriptions on El Morro was to grow more limited still after Carlos's passing. Imperial Spain was growing jaded, her enthusiasm for conquest and conversion waning.

2

The Making
of a Mountain Man

By the end of the eighteenth century, Imperial Spain was not only losing her preeminence as a world power but at home the stronger powers in Europe had come to look upon her as decadent and a fair spoil. Though the Treaty of Paris (February 10, 1763), which ended the Seven Years War (French and Indian War to Americans), transferred the Louisiana Territory from France to Spain, her grip on it was feeble. By the turn of the century, a world-conquering Bonaparte was forcing return of sovereignty over Louisiana to the French under the Second Treaty of Ildefonso. France, in turn, agreed that should she ever be moved to divest herself again of the Territory, it should be to no other power but Spain. Within three years of that agreement, a financially stripped and forsworn Bonaparte was selling Louisiana to the United States.

Naturally, Spaniards, those overseas even more than those at home, were infuriated by the bad faith this sale demonstrated—the fury being directed especially toward the purchasers. But what had they purchased? No one knew precisely what that Louisiana Territory included. No one had surveyed it and drawn lines on a map indicating where it ended and New Mexico Territory began.

So exploring parties went forth to find the answers. There was the U.S. government-sponsored expedition of 1804–6, directed to locate the source of the Missouri River. There was also an expedition, sent out in 1806 by General Wilkinson of dubious fame, under Lieutenant Zebulon Montgomery Pike, to search out the sources of the Red and Arkansas rivers. This latter exploration of the more southerly areas ended in Pike's running afoul of Spanish authorities in Santa Fe, New Mexico. Of course those authorities knew no better than their United States counterparts just where the line of demarcation should run. They were, in any case, growing suspicious of the motives of any U.S. explorer and, more particularly, of the sponsors of this one, who, they feared, might be scheming toward a takeover of all Mexico. Thus when forced by the bitter cold of winter in the Sangre de Cristo mountains to seek refuge in Santa Fe, Lt. Pike was immediately seized, though politely so, marched south into Mexico, then forced to abandon his expedition altogether and return to the United States. Two nations, which miles of separation had previously kept in reasonably friendly attitudes, now were looking at one another across the vague borders of the Louisiana Territory with suspicions that were not completely unjustified.

By 1821, Mexico, without the U.S. aid that authorities in Spain had long been anticipating, broke away from Spain and declared her independence, thereby assuming formal control of New Mexico, which she intended to hold inviolate from the grasp of ambitious adventurers from the east and north. So far these adventurers had, for all practical purposes, been confined to two classes—traders and mountain men. Traders were bound to be the least menacing to authorities in Santa Fe since they could not conduct much profitable trade in secret. Beside, the wares they brought at their own risk to such isolated communities must have been something of a compensation for their unwanted presence. A mountain man, on the other hand, killed fur-bearing animals, took the furs, and offered little in return save the reckless spending of wages in the night spots of towns like Santa Fe. And always there was the menace of an attempt at takeover by the government in Washington.

For twenty-five years, the Mexican government tried to enforce strict rules against the infiltration of her remote northernmost province by adventurers from the United States who, if encountered, could count upon less friendly treatment than Lt. Pike had received. So it is small wonder that for this period, El Morro shows only a single, now nearly effaced inscription—"O.R. 1836."

Who was O.R.? A trader? A mountain man? What nationality and where from? Surely, while New Mexico remained a territorial possession of old Mexico, no non-Mexican mountain man who knew what was good for him—and only a mountain man who knew

what was good for him could long survive—would have left his
name on El Morro, thereby announcing ʰo the world he was a
trespasser. The trapping and hunting on which he depended for
food, clothes, excitement, and income was strictly illegal for any
United States citizen. Even had he been one of the rare mountain
men who were literate, he must have known better than to defy
the authorities by leaving a damning confession upon a rock to
which Mexican officials had access.

This is not to suggest that mountain men did not continue to take
the thirty-fifth parallel route if they thought there might be some
profit in it for them. Having explored the unexplored western
wildernesses, they felt them to be theirs to use as they saw fit. The
spoils should come to the men who took the risks and defied death
there in any number of forms. Only an unusually intelligent,
brave, cautious, self-reliant man could hope to survive long at their
trade. Such a man cared little about restraints imposed from the
outside, whatever the government imposing them. Living from
one day to the next, mountain men concerned themselves very
little with what another month or year might bring. Immortality of
any kind, notably that to be achieved by a few scratches on soft
sandstone, would look to them as silly as it must be valueless.

Though most mountain men seem to have gotten along quite
well in their particular limited world without reading or writing
skills, their lack is our real loss. If only some of them had sent
letters to distant friends telling of their unique kind of life and if
only a few such letters might have survived! If only, like Juan de
Oñate, they had recorded their passing on Inscription Rock—
"Christopher Carson passed this way bearing dispatches from California to Washington"—but such "if only's" are of small use now.
Today we must rely upon legends or upon the comments of more
literate friends and admirers to picture the kind of life that was
theirs.

The name of that most famous of mountain men, "C. Carson
1863," was actually once seen upon the rock, though today it cannot
be found. Who put it there? Who later removed it? And when, and
why? And why that special year when Kit must have passed that
way numberless times both earlier and later, including those many
dispatch-bearing missions? Perhaps his first visit to the rock was in
1829 when the twenty-five-year-old Kit left Taos with a group of
men, mostly traders, headed for California on an expedition that

the Mexican authorities, had it been brought to their attention, would have sternly forbidden.

It might be that Kit himself made that inscription on the rock, for by 1863 he had learned to write his name at least, as it is known that he did before his death in 1868. Or perhaps his name was placed there by one of the soldiers serving under Kit during his years of army service when he finally attained the rank of brigadier general. Perhaps it was cut by a friend who thought that among the names of so many brave and adventurous men, Kit Carson's should not be lacking.

Kit had a host of such admirers that included both his illiterate one-time mountain-men companions and highly literate officers like the Lt. Beale, whose name, undated and in modest script, still survives on a protected area of the rock. In 1863, however, Lt. Beale could have cut no inscription there for at that date he was, by President Lincoln's special request, acting as surveyor-general for California and Nevada.

Always, since chance had first thrown him into Kit's company, Beale had cherished the deepest admiration and the warmest affections for this man, "who had not the advantage of an education but was wise as a beaver." It would be Ned Beale who would rise swiftly and indignantly in Kit's defense when, in 1871, with Kit no longer able to defend himself (had he been of a kind to think it worth the trouble), Joaquin Miller published a smart-alecky poem that Beale felt depicted Kit Carson as a coarse border ruffian.

"Dear old Kit," Beale wrote:

Looking back through the misty years, I see a man calm, serious, and sweet of temper; a man of very moderate stature, but broad-fronted and elastic, yet by no means robust of frame though gifted with immense endurance and nerves of steel. A head quite remarkable for its full size and very noble forehead, quiet, thoughtful blue eyes, and yellow hair, and very strong jaw. . . . This was the outward shape which enclosed a spirit as high and daring and as noble as ever tenanted the body of man . . .

Oh, Kit, my heart beats quicker even now, when I think of the time twenty-five years ago, when I lay on the burning sands of the great desert, when you had, tenderly as a woman would put her firstborn, laid me, sore from wounds and fever, on your only blanket. I see the dim lake of waterless mirage. I see waving sands ripple with the faint hot breeze around us, and break upon our scattered saddles. I see the poor mules famishing of thirst, with their tucked flanks, and dim eyes, and hear their plaintive cry go out to the wilderness for help. . . .

Without a thought of ever seeing water again, you poured upon my fevered lips the last drop in camp from your canteen . . . afterwards, on the bloody Gila, where we fought all day and travelled all night, with each man his bit of mule meat and no other food, and when worn from a hurt I could go no further, I begged you to leave me and save yourself. I see you leaning on that long Hawkins gun of yours (mine now) and looking out of those clear blue eyes at me with surprised reproach as one who takes an insult from a friend. And I remember when we lay side by side in the midst of the enemy's camp when discovery was death and you would not take a mean advantage of a sleeping foe. [16]

The "twenty-five years ago" was in 1846, during the Mexican War, when Edward Fitzgerald Beale, twenty-four-year-old alumnus of the United States Naval Institute, came to know Christopher Carson, thirty-seven-year-old graduate of innumerable hunting-trapping expeditions into remote western wilderness. In war, as well as on such expeditions, nerves of steel and inexhaustible endurance counted most and the wisdom of a beaver could far outweigh the knowledge of a genius. Gallantry, of a kind that refused to take advantage of a sleeping foe, which Ned Beale described in Kit and which Kit, though he was unable to record it, sensed in Ned—this was something extra, something upon which the friendship of a lifetime could be based.

In 1810, Christopher Carson's frontier parents had moved from Kentucky to Franklin, Missouri, half way up the Missouri River from the city of St. Louis to the very little town that was to become Independence. In Franklin, one-year-old Christopher, as well as all his brothers and sisters, would grow up without a chance to master the three R's, without even becoming more than vaguely aware of a need for learning. In any case, for such youngsters no printed tale could possibly have rivaled the excitement of word-of-mouth accounts that passing adventurers from far western mountains told to the young and old alike.

Those fur-laden trappers and hunters, fresh from expeditions to remote areas known to few but themselves, would pass a few days, maybe, in Franklin before moving on downriver to St. Louis. In that Mississippi River metropolis, they'd sell their furs and have themselves a wild and wonderful time with the proceeds. Then they'd start upriver again to head for the mountains, supplied with equipment for the new expedition, purchased, usually, against the income from the next year's furs. It was a life of adventure and freedom and danger.

Kit's father could not have failed to read in his son's eyes the lad's hero worship for these passing mountain men and, fatherlike, he must have become alarmed. No such wild risky life for a son of his! The boy should settle down and learn a steady trade that could support him, and help his family, of course. In a community dependent on horses and mules for any transport away from the river thoroughfare, saddlery was as safe a bet for the future as a filling station or garage now might be. The local saddler, David Workman, was willing to receive Kit as an apprentice, so an agreement was soon drawn up and Kit found himself bound to a trade "that did not suit me."

"Having heard tales of life in the mountains of the West," he later confessed, "I concluded to leave him. He was a good man, and I often recall to mind the kind treatment I received from his hands, but taking into consideration that if I remained with him and served my apprenticeship, I would have to pass my life in labor that was distasteful to me, and being anxious to travel for the purpose of seeing different countries, I concluded to join the first party for the Rocky Mountains." [48]

The first party for the mountains to which Kit, after reaching the decision, could attach himself left the river in early September. Kit was along, though, by the rules of the game, he was legally bound to serve out the apprenticeship in which his father had placed him. His master was equally bound to watch over and provide for the youth entrusted to his care.

The kindness that Kit so long remembered was shown in the advertisement placed by his master in an 1826 issue of *The Missouri Intelligencer:*

Notice: To whom it may concern. That Christopher Carson, a boy about sixteen years old, small of his age, but thickset, light hair, ran away from the subscriber, living in Franklin,

Howard County, Missouri, to whom he had been bound to learn the saddler's trade, on or about the first day of September last. He is supposed to have made his way toward the upper part of the State. All persons are notified not to harbor, support, or subsist said boy, under penalty of law. One cent reward will be given to any person who will bring back said boy. (Signed) David Workman, Franklin, October 6, 1826. [16]

One cent could hardly have been David Workman's estimate of Kit's worth. Nor could it have taken him six weeks to become aware that the lad had left Franklin. Least of all could he have expected that any boy bound for "the upper part of the State" had not in six weeks managed to get himself well beyond the reach of Missouri law. By thus advertising, the master was fulfilling his legal obligations and could smile his kindliest smile at the thought of the restless boy happily headed for the land of his dreams.

Three years later, in Mexican Santa Fe and after some kinds of employment that could not have been much more to his taste than saddlery, Kit managed to approach his dreamed-of goal by joining a California-bound expedition under the direction of an experienced fur trapper named Ewing Young. "In those days," Kit later recounted, "licenses were not granted to citizens of the United States to trap within the limits of Mexican territory . . . We travelled in a northerly direction for fifty miles then changed our course to the southwest." [33, 48]

This was typical strategy for the times. During the California-bound trip, which ended with the band's return to Taos in 1830, they crossed through Zuñi and Navajo country. Since Zuñi lies not many miles west of El Morro, it is a safe bet that they paused by the tank to water both horses and mules, not to mention themselves. Without a license for exploration and trapping, even the most literate member of the band would not then have dreamed of adding a damning personal inscription to the roster already on the rock.

"In April, 1830," Kit told of that trip, "we had all safely arrived at Taos. The amount due us was paid, and each of us having several hundred dollars, we passed the time gloriously, spending our money freely, never thinking that our lives were risked in gaining it." Kit was learning that it was routine for most mountain men to risk their lives in gaining money which they would spend riotously.

During the following decade, Kit, now a full-fledged mountain man, built himself a formidable reputation both as a hunter (notably to supply meat to Bent's Fort, a private establishment on the Arkansas River) and as a trader (notably for the Bents of Bent's Fort and of St. Louis, Missouri). He also managed to fall in love, twice. The first time was with a girl of a proud St. Louis French family, which sternly forbade marriage with a man who not only had taken a now deceased Indian squaw to wife, but who published his unfortunate union through a half-breed daughter he would not dream of disowning.

The second time, deeply in love with the aristocratic Mexican belle María Josefa Jaramillo, Kit was determined not to let the child stand permanently in the way of his own romance. She was not, however, to be denied loving care or the best upbringing and education available. Certainly she was not to grow up among her mother's people to become the squaw of some wild Indian. The way out would be to persuade one of his Missouri relatives to take the child into her home and keep her there until she was old enough to be received into a proper St. Louis convent school. A niece in Howard County, Missouri, agreed to this and Kit heaved a sigh of relief that his little Adaline would now have a far better chance of growing up happily than in a community like Taos that already had no real place for its too many half-breeds.

In 1842, when Kit had made that return journey to Franklin and completed the family arrangement, he decided to go on downriver to visit St. Louis, center of the fur trade and of fur traders. Ten days of that metropolis, which seemed overcrowded and too noisy, sufficed for the mountain man. He was soon again bound upriver on a boat headed for Westport Landing, just beyond the western extremity of the state.

As fate would have it, a fellow passenger on that same boat was John Charles Frémont, planning the first of his several western exploring expeditions, one of the earliest government-subsidized explorations of the country lying between the Missouri River and the Rocky Mountains. To an ambitious twenty-nine-year-old army man hoping to make a name for himself in the strange wild land ahead, the thirty-three-year-old mountain man must have seemed like the answer to a prayer. As homesick Kit spoke knowledgeably about the mountain land toward which Frémont was headed, Frémont listened delightedly. By the time the boat reached Westport, in May 1842, Kit had been persuaded to serve Frémont for $100 a month, just about three times the amount the Bents had been paying him.

Perhaps the respectable government employment helped convince María Josefa's critical parents that the now Catholic Kit Carson might not be an unacceptable husband for their daughter. Early in 1843, Kit and Josefa were married. They would establish a good home and raise eight children—but Kit's growing reputation made it difficult for him to settle down near Taos to the uninterrupted life of a family man and rancher.

3

Deeds and Dispatches

Within a month of his marriage, Kit had set out with Frémont as guide to his first expedition. The two men soon formed a friendship that, outlasting Frémont's several expeditions, would continue throughout Kit's life. It would serve to set Kit Carson apart from other mountain men, for Frémont's official report, full of admiring references to his guide, was widely read throughout the land.

A typical incident he recounted deals with Kit's response to some greenhorn's announcement that he had seen a large party of Indians skulking nearby. "Mounted on a fine horse, without a saddle," Frémont wrote, "and scouring bareheaded over the prairie, Kit was one of the finest pictures of a horseman I have ever seen. A short time enabled him to discover that the Indian war party of twenty-seven consisted of six elk, who had been gazing curiously at our caravan as it passed by." [31]

In 1847, Frémont's admiration for Kit having grown with the years, he was moved to state, "With me Carson and Truth mean the same thing. He is always gallant and disinterested." Such outspoken enthusiasm expressed by a literate man of position would build for Kit a reputation far beyond that enjoyed by other mountain men, even perhaps equally deserving ones. Kit's own special qualities of integrity, loyalty, resourcefulness, courage would enlarge the reputation thus started.

Of course everyone became eager to see the great scout in the flesh—not just the obscure hero-worshippers but men of resourcefulness and daring who would become heroes in their own right. Always the flesh and blood Kit came as a surprise. "I well remember the first Overland Mail," General William Tecumseh Sherman reminisced later. "It was brought by Kit Carson in saddlebags from New Mexico. His fame was then at its height, from the publication of Frémont's books, and I was very anxious to see a man who had achieved such feats of daring . . . I cannot express my surprise at beholding a small, stoopshouldered man, with reddish hair, freckled face, soft blue eyes, and nothing to indicate extraordinary courage and daring. He spoke but little and answered in monosyllables." [48]

Fate and politics were to combine in bringing Kit Carson and Ned Beale together. When, in 1845, the Republic of Texas joined the Union by Act of Congress, Mexico was understandably furious. During the following year came a clash of arms on Texan soil, and the Mexican War was soon in full swing. The summer of 1846 saw General Stephen Watts Kearny marching his "Army of the West" from Fort Leavenworth, Kansas. Arrived at the junction of the Arkansas River and the Santa Fe Trail, Kearny paused to issue a proclamation informing the people of New Mexico that he was there "for the purpose of seeking union with and ameliorating the conditions of its inhabitants"—by which, of course, he meant substituting the United States government for the Mexican. Hastily setting up a territorial government, he, with his 1,700 men, set off for California and what Kearny intended to be undying personal glory.

Encamped near Socorro, New Mexico, on October 6, General Kearny was haunted by a dread that he might arrive in California too late for the fighting and fame. Ahead lay that long stretch of waterless desert ending by a river whose impassable canyons were notorious. Guide Thomas Fitzpatrick, though a famous and knowledgeable mountain man, was not personally familiar with the desert route ahead. Suppose he missed the direct and shortest route! What price glory then?

It was Kit Carson's luck to turn up there, in charge of a party of fifteen that included six Delaware Indians. Kit was headed express for Washington carrying sealed dispatches from Commodore Stockton, then the ranking military officer in California. Hearing from Kit that the war seemed to be winding down, Kearny was in a fever to hurry on to glory and for this he commandeered the services of the man Frémont had described as the very best guide in all the West.

Kit promptly pointed out that he had pledged himself to deliver in Washington the dispatches that had been entrusted to him. General Kearny had an answer for that. A man bound on military business should take orders from the military. And as for the dispatches—he, Kearny, would see to it that they went forward in trustworthy hands.

Today we'd call General Kearny a "stuffed shirt"—in his day the word was "uppish." On October 6, he issued the curt order without which Kit would not move one foot toward California with him: "Mr. Carson who arrived express today from California to Washington, having engaged to return with the general, will deliver his letters, despatches, &c., into the hands of Mr. Thomas Fitzpatrick who will convey them with all despatch to the City of Washington. By order of Brigadier General S. W. Kearny." [41]

No suggestion here of the pressure he had used on Kit. About two months later he would write to the secretary of war, mentioning the encounter with Carson, saying nothing of the part he had played in the scout's rapid turnaround. Similarly, he would give an account of the grim battle that preceded his report by a week, while he failed to acknowledge his own indebtedness, once again, to guide Kit Carson as well as to Naval Lieutenant Edward Fitzgerald Beale and the Delaware Indian who accompanied them on a perilous mission. Kearny mentioned, of course, his own several wounds, that many of his own officers had died, but never a whisper of how his plea for aid had been carried to Commodore Stockton.

This all happened two months after that October day when, practically within sight of the home and family Kit had not visited for nearly a year, he "turned his face westward again," as one admiring biographer wrote of Kit, "just as he was on the eve of entering the settlements after the arduous trip. . . . It requires a brave man to give up his private feelings for the public good; Carson is one such."

It required also a general of domineering personality, determined to become the great hero of the Mexican War. Thomas Fitzpatrick, being a skilled mountain man, would have managed to see the troops safely through to California. But Fitzpatrick admittedly was not acquainted with the most direct southern route as Kit was. Speed looked very important to the general. And it may have fed his vanity to have under his command the already illustrious scout.

The consequences, in any case, were both more far-reaching and more enduring than either general or scout could have forseen. For Kit was not only on his way to California, but also to the Battle of San Pasqual and to a friendship that would outlast his life.

Lieutenant Colonel William H. Emory, serving with the advance guard of the "Army of the West," was the man who gave a detailed account of the events in which that army was involved. He recorded on December 5, 1846: "We marched to [the Ranchería] Santa María. On the way we met Captain Gillespie, Lieut. Beale, and Midshipman Dunbar of the Navy, with a party of thirty-five men, sent from San Diego with a despatch to Gen. Kearny" [28]—and to a memorable encounter between two future friends.

The friendship between Beale and Carson began almost at the moment of their meeting. What a pair they were—the handsome, highly educated, adventurous Naval lieutenant who had already carried dispatches in two continents, and the mountain man whose frontier Missouri boyhood had afforded him no chance for formal schooling. They were to be equally one another's teachers— Carson in wilderness know-how that was to him second nature, Beale in matters to be found in the books that would long remain closed to Kit.

Before their shared campfires, Kit would sit, in later years, alert to the slightest sign of hovering danger while Ned read aloud from the book he happened to have tossed into his pack before setting out. It was from such a book—*Tristram Shandy*—that Kit gleaned William the Conqueror's oath, the only one Ned ever heard him utter, border ruffian though poet Miller had depicted him.

"He drew a long, single-barrelled pistol," Ned later described the incident that brought forth the oath, "which Fremont had given me and I [to] Kit. . . . and with slow, deadly speech which carried the sense of imminent mischief in it, said to one who was in the act of committing a cowardly wrong upon a sick man, "Sergeant, drop that knife or *'by the splendor of God'* I'll blow your heart out!"

The day following Beale's arrival at Kearny's camp—December 6—saw the Battle of San Pasqual, with Beale and Carson fighting side by side. Complete disaster threatened all as the battle ended with the general's fine "Army of the West" on a waterless hilltop, completely surrounded by Mexican troops. Of the 7th, Colonel Emory wrote, "Day dawned on the most tattered and ill-fed detachment of men that ever the United States mustered under her colors." The total number had been reduced to one-third, with many of the surviving officers, including General Kearny, wounded.

By the 8th, the general was having to face the bitter truth that unless his army soon received aid, all must either die of thirst or of their wounds or give themselves up as prisoners of war. Help could not come to them, though, unless someone sent it and no one would send it unless made aware of the need.

In those prewireless days, a message must be carried by messenger. To order a reluctant man to set forth as messenger was not to be thought of since even the most willing, the general knew all too well, had less than an even chance of arriving at his destination. It would take both skill and dedication to reach Commodore Stockton's headquarters in San Diego.

General Kearny had to face his discouraged, exhausted troops and ask for volunteers. He could see the tired eyes glancing doubtfully at him, then still more doubtfully at the Mexican encampment surrounding the hill. He understood the swift glances along the line as each asked himself, "Will not some other volunteer? Must I be the one to take the risks for all these others?" Yet each, he knew, was as aware as himself that if someone did not undertake that risk, all must pay a grim price.

In that split second of awareness, the young naval lieutenant stepped forward, volunteering to carry the message to his superior officer, the Naval commandant at San Diego.

Later, when the event was past, the general would overlook his indebtedness to the young man and his companions. At the moment he felt real relief, though carefully concealing it as he spoke in businesslike tones, "You may choose your companions. Perhaps you'd like time to consider . . . ."

Though he had been associated with those particular troops so briefly, Ned Beale wanted no time to consider. Knowing the mission was bound to demand the utmost of endurance even from men who had graduated from the stern school of scouting, Ned spoke up promptly, "Kit Carson and my Delaware"—that Delaware, endowed with the skills of his race and tribe, had long served Beale as scout and hunter. Beale did not need to ask either man if he was willing to undertake the mission. All three would far rather take grave personal risks than remain inactive in camp, dependent upon the skills of others.

"At night," Colonel Emory wrote of the 8th, "Lieutenant Beale of the Navy, Mr. Carson, and an Indian volunteered to go to San Diego, 29 miles distant—an expedition of some peril, as the enemy now occupied all the passes to that town." [28]

Equipped with a blanket, a revolver, and a sharp knife apiece, but without food or water (since there was none of either in camp) the three set out in the darkness, moving noiselessly, feeling their way on hands and knees down the rough, stony hillside. Sharp spines of desert plants lodged in hands and faces and, presently, in bare feet. For when their shoes seemed to be making small but possibly disastrous noises against the stones, each took off his shoes and thrust them inside of his shirt front.

Even their almost soundless whispers were stilled as they approached the sentries—"three rows, all on horseback," as Kit later told. "We would have to pass within twenty yards of one." The dispatch bearers lay still as the hillside rocks, hearing the Mexicans' soft Spanish, seeing the face of one illuminated by a match that lit his cigarette, smelled the smoke, while waiting for the sentries to start moving again. When the gap between two was widest, each scout took his turn at slipping through, hardly believing that he would be overlooked.

Overlooked all were, partly because of their scouting know-how, partly because no sentry really believed any gringo could be so reckless as to attempt to pass the rough hillside and the closely guarded line. Even the famous Kit Carson, whom they knew to be with General Kearny, would have sense enough not to get involved in a venture like this that was doomed to failure.

Outside the sentry line there followed about two miles of relatively level ground before they could attain the protection of woods. Finally daring to stand up, they discovered they no longer had shoes to stand in. These had disappeared from the now tattered shirt fronts, so that the three must continue on bare and bleeding feet until they found refuge in a mountain gorge, there to await the protection of another night.

Twelve miles from San Diego, the messengers took counsel and decided to separate, hoping that of three separate routes, one at least might bring success. All arrived—the Indian first. Ned came in second, collapsing so that he had to be carried into his commodore's presence. Carson arrived last. All were completely exhausted, all needed food and water and rest as well as medical care for their blood-streaked faces, hands, and feet.

Back on the hilltop, "There was little expectation that Carson and Lieutenant Beale would succeed in reaching San Diego." Colonel Emory told of the night of December 10 with the discouraged troops: "We were all reposing quietly, but not sleeping when . . . one of the men . . . reported he heard a man speaking English. In a few minutes we heard the tramp of a column followed by the hail of a sentinel. It was a detachment of 100 tars and 80 marines under Lieutenant Gay . . . from whom we learned that Lieutenant Beale, Mr. 'Carson, and the Indian had arrived safely in San Diego. The detachment left San Diego on the night of the 9th, cached themselves during the day of the 10th, and joined us on the night of the of that day. These gallant fellows busied themselves till day by distributing their provisions and clothes to our naked and hungry people." [28]

"Got to San Diego the next night," was Kit's laconic account of their mission as dictated years later. "I remained at San Diego, Lt. Beale was sent aboard the frigate, *Congress;* he had become deranged from fatigue and service performed, did not entirely recover for two years." [33]

Ned's "derangement" was most likely due either to aggravated malaria or to the kind of high fever now recognized to accompany acute infections. Blood poisoning it might then have been called, and in those preantibiotic days, it could make even a slight scratch dangerous if dirt was rubbed into it (as must have been the case with Ned Beale's wounds). Certainly the derangement must have been more physical than mental. Within a few weeks a fully recovered Kit Carson was busily selecting ten expert marksmen to accompany him on yet another mission to deliver Army dispatches to Army Headquarters in Washington, D.C. Ned Beale was then still convalescing aboard the frigate when he received a letter no commodore would have dreamed of sending to a mentally incapacitated junior officer.

Sir,

I have selected you to be the bearer of the accompanying despatches to the Navy Department in consequence of your heroic conduct in volunteering to leave General Kearny's camp (then surrounded by the enemy) and go to the garrison of San Diego for assistance and because of the perils and hardships you underwent during that perilous journey, to procure aid for your suffering fellow soldiers.

You will proceed without delay with Mr. Carson's party by
the most direct route overland . . .

Faithfully, your obt. servt. R. I. Stockton. [16]

It was a high honor thus to be selected, even though a risky one
under the circumstances. A young adventure-minded lieutenant
like Ned Beale, however, would hardly call his commodore's
attention to the fact that he was still so weak that he would need
help in the simple acts of mounting and dismounting a horse. No
such young man would willingly pass up an opportunity to spend
weeks in the company of a nationally famous scout while crossing a
continent still rarely crossed in its entirety and then only successfully
crossed by men of the experience and skill of Kit Carson. Perhaps,
even, he himself might acquire the skill to join that small but
distinguished band of solo continent crossers.

Fortunately Kit raised no objections to having a sick youth join a
dispatch-bearing expedition risky enough to require the enlistment
of ten expert marksmen. Though Ned's presence could add both a
handicap and a risk, Kit realized the handicap would be just as
temporary as Ned could make it, while recovery would be speeded
up rather than retarded by the challenge of the so-desired adventure. Cheerfully assuming the added risk, Kit won himself thereby a
lifelong friend.

"Beale, during the first twenty days," Kit said, "I had to lift on
and off his horse." "Tenderly as a woman would put her firstborn,"
was the way Ned would recall it twenty-five years later.

"I did not think he could live," Kit remembered, "but I took
good care and paid to him as much attention as could be given to
anyone in the same circumstances and he had, before our arrival,
got so far recovered that he could assist himself." [33]

The Gila River route was the one Kit selected as the most
direct—the "bloody Gila," Ned remembered, "where we fought all
day and travelled all night" and when "without a thought of ever
seeing water again," Kit poured upon the lips of his feverish
comrade his last drops of water.

Ned, despite his sufferings, was having the chance he wanted to
observe at first hand the practice of Indian lore that was second
nature to Carson. From Kit he learned to recognize the barely
visible signs that bespoke hovering Indians. Though visible Indians
might be friendly, invisible Indians dogging their trail were an

almost certain threat that at nightfall the camp would be invaded, its two-legged occupants scalped, its four-legged ones driven off laden with the party's belongings.

No one could fight a pitched battle with invisible shadows, but a knowledgeable mountain man could play the game—as Kit would demonstrate—skillfully enough to win. When you became aware of those hovering shadows, you concealed your awareness, showing not the least outward concern, going about the usual camp routine in precisely the usual way. The shadows would think nothing of it if weary travelers settled into camp a trifle early, built cooking fires, prepared the evening meal without obvious hurry. With just the right show of weariness, you'd quench the fires while each party member threw himself upon the ground, drawing his blanket about him for the obviously much desired sleep.

No one, of course, would really go to sleep for all were too painfully aware that it was intended none should wake. When darkness fell and there was nothing to reveal to watching eyes exactly what was going on, all sleepers would rise and silently move camp to about a mile's distance. The Indians would have no way of knowing exactly where the new camp was, their attack would fail and the attackers withdraw to await better odds.

It was a kind of lesson no newcomer to the Southwest could ever forget. Years later Ned Beale, commanding a surveying party of his own, would employ similar strategy to win against similar odds. Even on that first trip, though, he soon demonstrated that he'd need no review lesson.

"Things was whirring like birds on the flight wing over us," Kit Carson later told of his young friend, "and I was trying to sleep by the campfire and Ned was sleeping, or leastwise, was snoring. Then, suddenly, he sits up and says, 'What's that, Don Kit?' and I says, 'Them's arrows!' and they was and could you believe it, before I could hold him down Ned was wrapping his buffalo robe around him and standing in the fire kicking out the embers. 'Now,' says he as them arrows came whirring along, 'Don Kit, they won't be able to get our direction any more and you know they don't dare rush us.' And then he tumbled down on the ground and went on with his sleeping." [33]

It must have been very cold for them to risk keeping even a small fire going all night. No one, however, kept a journal of that trip. Ned undoubtedly had no energy to spare for one. Kit didn't

know how to write—so all that remains for us are the few episodes
he recalled years later.

Somewhere after they left the Gila River, the route turned north
to connect at Santa Fe with the trail on into Kansas and Missouri.
Thus they could have passed El Morro where there was known to
be water aplenty for the men and their beasts. In any case, Kit
already knew the place well though he may not before have had a
companion able and willing to read off the inscriptions. Would Kit
have thought them silly? Was it then Ned who was moved to cut
the modest "Lieut Beale" into the sandstone? If so, why did he not
add "Kit Carson"?

From Santa Fe, Kit and Ned could take the already famous Santa
Fe Trail northeastward. It was in reality a road already well worn by
the mules and wheels of hundreds of traders' heavy wagons, bound
out of Westport Landing, Kansas, with trade goods for the Mexi-
cos, old and new. From Westport, the dispatch bearers could
embark comfortably on a riverboat bound for St. Louis, where
they arrived in early June.

St. Louis was delighted to meet and entertain the famous scout
so praised by Missouri Senator Benton's son-in-law, John Charles
Frémont. Senator Benton was hospitably delighted to receive
both—Kit because of Frémont's praises, Ned Beale because he
could not have failed to meet, in Washington, Ned's charming
mother.

Ambitious for her son and determined to help him rise in a
highly competitive service, Mrs. Emily Beale—as Secretary of
State James Buchanan (presently to become United States president)
pointed out—was the daughter of Commodore Truxton and the
widow of a gallant Naval Officer (decorated for gallantry shown
during the Battle of Lake Champlain). "What is better," Buchanan
added, "she is in all respects worthy of both." She had, moreover,
learned from both that to succeed in the Navy, a new "Passed
Midshipman," fresh out of the Naval Academy as was her son,
could use all the influence her associations and her charm might
elicit. She would not fail to bring Ned to the attention of the
influential senator from Missouri.

As Benton's guest, Ned knew well how to face formal society
such as they encountered in St. Louis. The wilderness scout, on
the other hand, being aware of no need to shine in society, was less
than delighted to be so entertained. He bore it with an outward

patience such as the most serious of Indian attacks might have elicited. He found, though, as he had five years earlier, that he had no taste for the noise and tumult and excitement of that kind of life. Soon he reminded his host that it was his duty to be off to Washington to deliver the dispatches entrusted to him.

Though less strenuous than the trip from California, a trip to Washington was then no simple matter of jumping on a train. Still, four years later—in November 1851—Senator Benton and his wife were anxious to get out of Washington and well started on their journey home "before ice fills the river." Having finally arrived safely in St. Louis, Benton wrote young Beale a letter dated November 24: "We had a pleasant travel and, for the season, a short one, reaching this place on Sunday week after leaving Washington. . . . The cars were comfortable and we had fine boats on the Ohio and Mississippi." [1] The cars must have delivered the Bentons to some Ohio River port, possibly Pittsburgh.

In Washington, Mrs. Emily Beale was even more eager than the St. Louisans to welcome her son as well as to entertain his kind and famous friend. The senator's Washington home was equally at Kit's disposal.

Sometime during his Washington stay, Kit was introduced to an army lieutenant named George D. Brewerton, who would presently add his bit to the Carson legend by writing and publishing (in Harper's Magazine, 1853) an article entitled "A Ride With Kit Carson."

> The Kit Carson of my imagination was over six feet high—a sort of modern Hercules in build—with enormous beard and a voice like a roused lion. . . . The *real* Kit Carson I found to be a plain, simple unostentatious man, rather below medium height, with brown, curling hair, little or no beard, and a voice as soft and gentle as a woman's . . . During this journey, I often watched with great curiosity Carson's preparations for the night. A braver man than Kit Carson never lived, in fact I doubt if he ever knew what fear was, but with all this he exercised great caution. . . . Except now and then to light a pipe, you never caught Kit exposing himself to the full glare of the camp fire. . . . "No, No, boys," Kit would say, "Hang around the fire if you like it, but I don't want to have a Digger slip an arrow into me when I can't see him."

Caution of this kind was second nature to Carson, as it was to all mountain men who knew they could not survive long at their trade without it. Because of it, Christopher Carson would live to become a brigadier general in the United States Army, to bring peace to warring Indian tribes, and then to serve as government agent among Indians who accepted him because they could respect his courage and daring and, most of all, his absolute integrity. They, like Frémont, felt Truth and Carson meant the same thing. So in Indian country, Indian fighter Kit would live to end his days happily and peacefully, surrounded by his large family, on a ranch not far from Taos.

4

Messenger from
El Dorado

Already on that 1847 visit, Kit Carson was mounting the first rung of the military ladder.

"I remained in Washington some time," Kit said, "received the appointment of Lieutenant of Rifles, U.S. Army, from President Polk, and was then ordered back to California as bearer of dispatches. Lieutenant Beale went with me but, on account of his illness, was compelled to return to St. Louis." [33]

Return from where? How far along the road west had he been able to get? Certainly, such a return must have spelled bitter frustration for the ambitious young naval officer. Soon he was back in Washington where family and friends were only too eager to look after his health and his interests. He spent considerable time with relatives in Chester, Pennsylvania, where there was also a charming young lady named Mary Edwards from whom he soon had a promise of marriage. Marriage itself, unfortunately, would have to wait, for the young man was all too conscious that he yet had his way to make in a highly competitive service in a highly competitive world.

Within a few months, Ned was setting wheels in motion through the agency of Senator Benton—"Old Bullion," as he was called because of his support of a gold and silver currency. The senator wrote to the secretary of the Navy: "Sir: Passed Midshipman Beale, now ill at Phil[a], has written to me to desire the Department to charge him with despatches for the North Pacific—I do so with pleasure. . . . Having a high opinion of the young man for

33

honor, courage, truth, modesty, enterprize and perseverance, I should be happy to see him noticed and countenanced by the Department. . . ." [1]

Honorable Mr. Mason, Secretary of the Navy, was happy to make prestigious Senator Benton happy even though Mason could then probably not have cared less about any young midshipman. By December 1847, a newspaper *(The Mobile Register)* published that "Lt. Beale" had set out from Fort Leavenworth, Kansas, the previous month, "with a command of 17 mounted men, all raw recruits, and a few adventurers." The adventurers—whatever the term may have meant—as well as those raw recruits were to find adventure more than they had bargained for. In early December Ned was writing to his future brother-in-law, Harry Edwards, from Big Timbers, on the Arkansas River, in what is now southeastern Colorado.

"I get from the traders here the most discouraging accounts of the Raton Mountains," he wrote, "which I am now just about to cross. It is said they are impassable but I have passed *impassable* places before. They tell me to tie my hair on before starting, as every party ahead of me has been attacked and defeated by the Apaches." [1] He ended on a less chilling note with, "Love to all those who love me."

The newspaper account, possibly because there was no loving reader to be distressed by it, was more detailed about the crossing.

In crossing the Taos or Ratón Mountains, they encountered all the severities of winter in those difficult and gigantic passes covered with the snows of an unusually cold and inclement season. Many of their mules perished from the rigors of the weather and march, and a number of the men were frostbitten and disabled for further service. Upon arriving at Santa Fé, which he reached the 25th of December, Lt. Beale gave permission to such of his men as were unwilling to proceed to return, and seven did so. He was unwilling to be accompanied in the dangers and trials before him by any upon which he could not rely with implicit confidence.

What a merry Christmas for a man himself not completely recovered from the illness that had prevented his making the crossing in Kit Carson's company!

With eight new volunteers added to his company, Ned set out from Santa Fe on January 11, 1848, taking a more southerly route, possibly in the hopes of encountering there less bitter weather. They must have followed the Rio Grande south for perhaps two hundred miles before turning west. The newspaper account places him in January in the wild mountains that may be seen to the west of today's north-south Highway 25. "The Sierra de los Mimbres," it continued, "a vast range of lofty mountains, was enveloped in snowstorms and the route was most hazardous and oppressive. So intense was the cold that several mules were frozen to death at night, even under tents and covered with blankets. Here the fortitude of a number of men failed and a sergeant and six men (privates) deserted. They no doubt perished under the violence of the weather or were assassinated by the Indians who infest these regions." In other words, those deserters were never heard of again.

Beyond those mountains lay the headwaters of the Gila River, which Beale had come to know during his trip of the previous year. They went on through the all but impassable Mogollon Mountains where deep snow filled the vast gorges and a mule that lost its footing on the icy path rolled down, to end with every bone broken and its saddle damaged beyond repair. The river, beset with whirlpools and cascades, offered no means of transportation even had they canoes. Somehow all the men and some of the mules survived to get through. All, however, were convinced that a better route must be found if the newly acquired Pacific lands were to be successfully joined to those east of the Mississippi. That better route—the western extension of the Santa Fe Trail—would presently take a less rugged but more northerly way over the almost imperceptible height of the Continental Divide a few miles east of El Morro.

However chilled the men may have been on their way west, once in California they were soon heated to fever pitch. It was in January 1848, at about the time Beale's party had set out from Santa Fe, that a Swiss miller named Sutter had decided his mill-race needed widening. In the glittering sands dug there were grains of pure gold—gold which, ironically enough, might have assured fame and fortune to Juan de Oñate had he found it on his expedition to the South Sea. In 1848, the fame went immediately to the western land, California—as soon as the news got into the papers there, that is. In March, at about the time Beale's weary party arrived, the whole state went mad.

By June 1, a newspaper correspondent was writing that they

had there "only one serious apprehension, that we are in danger of having more gold than food; for he that can wield a spade and shake a dish, can fill his pockets *a su gusto.*"

A month later:

> You can hardly hire a laborer here for $10 a day, and on the gold river he charges $50. Mechanics, lawyers, and doctors have all left for the gold region. Soldiers run from their camps, sailors from their decks, and women from their nurseries; their cradles answer for machines to wash out gold.
>
> San Francisco, Sonoma, Santa Cruz, and San José are deserted of their inhabitants. . . . I shall soon be in the position of a colonel with his regiment disbanded. . . . It is supposed that ten thousand persons might work for years and not exhaust it [the gold]. As yet they have worked only the margin of the streams, on account of its convenience to the water; but gold has been found leagues distant. . . . Bowls and basins have been in great demand among the gold washers. Tin pans have found a ready sale at $8 each; shovels at $10, a trough scooped out of a log, with a willow sieve in it, $100. . . . The price of board on the gold stream is $3 a day. For this the boarder gets coarse bread, beef, and beans, a tree to sleep under, and an owl to hoot in his ear at night. The gold is sold here for $14 an ounce and is worth $18 at any mint. I know a little boy only twelve years of age who washes out his ounce of gold a day, while his mother makes root beer and sells it at a dollar a bottle. [16]

Root beer sellers, as it turned out, would end up richer than most gold diggers.

In ports, sailors abandoned their ships. Churches lost their congregations. San Francisco homes gaped empty while their owners rushed off by the hundreds to dig fortunes from river sands. Soldiers to whom $1,000 owed in back pay had recently seemed like a fortune deserted both the army and that pay to run in pursuit of the golden will-of-the-wisp. Naval ships would have been similarly deserted had not their commanders kept them cruising offshore, permitting no direct communication with ports. Commodore Jones reported frankly to the Naval Department in Washington that "to send troops out here would be needless as they would immediately desert."

The gold fever was as contagious as it was virulent. People who thought to remain immune presently found themselves succumbing to the temptation to have a try at winning themselves fortunes. Few who succumbed would easily be cured, no matter how discouraging their own luck. Always the next day would bring them that bright fortune. If not the next, then the next but one.

There is no record as to how many of the men who arrived in California with Lt. Beale ran off to the gold fields. Probably most of them did. Ned Beale himself, however, had too level a head not to perceive the dangers to his companions—dangers of bankruptcy and of ruined lives. For young Beale, the gold fever was of personal concern largely in the light of news that authorities in Washington were bound to find interesting. Whispers of the find had already reached those authorities' ears but the news was being shrugged off as a wild exaggeration—probably due to nothing better than iron pyrites, the "fool's gold" that had in the past deluded so many. A sample of California gold would be needed to persuade official Washington, through an official assay, that the find was indeed gold beyond the possible shadow of a doubt.

Ambitious Ned, aware of the value of focussing attention upon himself, wanted to be the first man to bring to Washington both the news and the samples of gold to prove it. He did not mine those samples in the usual way. He did not have cash to pay for the purchase of gold or nuggets. But he had with him something his own personal experience had taught him might be more precious than gold—the quinine that in those days offered the only means of controlling attacks of ague, as malaria then usually was called. Ned had contracted malaria himself, probably during one or another visit to South or Central America, and understood that a man shaking miserably with chills and fever could mine little gold. In the California of 1848, quinine was bound to sell higher, weight for weight, than gold itself. It was some of the quinine that Ned forehandedly carried with him that went to purchase the little store of gold he'd carry back to Washington by the quickest route.

The quickest route, of course, would not be by retracing his steps overland. In 1848, it would be by shipping south, making a land crossing somewhere between California and the Isthmus of Panama, then taking ship again to a North American port. The shortest land crossing was at the isthmus but it involved two relatively long sea routes. If a man, knowing Spanish and his way around Spanish-speaking lands (as Ned did), took ship to San Blas on Mexico's Pacific coast, then managed a rapid and safe land crossing (as Ned felt he could), he might pick up a northbound ship at a Mexican Caribbean port to reach Washington ahead of all competitors.

In late August 1848, a reporter in Mexico City sent a dispatch to the *Daily Picayune* of New Orleans to the effect that Lt. Beale of the United States Navy was in that city (Mexico City) on his way to Washington with dispatches from Commodore Jones, commander of the squadron in the Pacific. A dispatch bearer would be supplied the fleetest of horses and bandits probably couldn't care less about relieving him of scraps of paper. Best of all for Ned and for the gold he carried, he was deeply tanned enough by recent desert crossings and fluent enough in Spanish acquired during dispatch-bearing missions throughout the Americas to pass as a Mexican and thereby to escape the attentions of the gringo haters.

"We have had the pleasure of seeing Passed Midshipman Beale, who arrived last evening in a southern boat," a newspaper of the south stated. "He brings despatches from Commodore Jones. . . . He left La-Paz on the first of August and travelled from the Pacific to Vera Cruz in the unprecedented short period of ten days—from Mexico [City] to Vera Cruz (275 miles) in forty-eight hours."

Thus he attained his aim of becoming the first man to arrive in Washington with the means of convincing authorities there that real gold was being washed out of river sands in newly acquired California. Folk who had been pooh-poohing the earlier whispers gave way to excitement. Everybody now wanted a sight of the gold young Beale had carried to Washington. Ever sensitive to public enthusiasm of this kind, P. T. Barnum sought some of Beale's gold to exhibit in his Philadelphia museum of curiosities. Unsuccessful in purchasing a sample, he tried to persuade the young man to permit some to be exhibited as a loan.

Ned Beale may well have smiled at all the to-do. In California he'd had an object lesson in the price paid for quinine that it was not gold itself that mattered, but the things it could buy. In California he had seen gold buying less and less of the truly valuable things of life for which men vied with one another for the privilege of paying more and more.

Though gold may have put him there dramatically, it would not

taught him would not be well invested in mining property. In any case, what he wanted was acreage in the mountains he'd come to know on his cross-country treks. His problem was not that it was not for sale but that the owners who should sell it had no idea that the acres were theirs. He had to begin by persuading the absentee owners, Spanish or Mexican, who'd never set foot there, that they really held title to the lands that had been deeded long ago to ancestors of theirs. To the owners, the cash Beale offered seemed an absolute and unexpected windfall.

Years later when the gold fever had subsided and Beale's long public career had run its course, an impressed visitor would write enthusiastically of the property young Beale had been forehanded enough to purchase with his then limited earnings: "The Rancho from which I write, the Tejon as it is called, the home of General Beale, contains nearly 200,000 acres and lies at the junction of the Sierra Nevada with the coast range . . . The Tejon pass, a narrow defile, separates them and gives egress from the Valley into Los Angeles County." [16]

At an altitude of some five hundred feet above Bakersfield, the ranch had, as Beale later wrote a friend, "a refreshing atmosphere of perpetual spring which never becomes close summer." It was a place to remember and to anticipate during those strenuous years when Beale was passing back and forth from California through a land where spring meant high winds laden with sand and summer was always hot and close.

It was in that very land, however, that the purchaser of Tejón had made another investment of which he could scarcely have been aware at the time. The gold epidemic, having spread across the continent, was bringing numberless men hurrying westward to grasp their share of the inexhaustible wealth. At first leaving their families behind, they'd take their lonely way on horseback to join up with Oregon-bound wagon trains until they reached the parting of the ways where they'd turn south toward California.

Horseback, of course, would not provide adequate transportation when later the emigrants, having returned east, would take their families and possessions to California. For these, wagons would be needed, and for wagons there must be some kind of wagon road, however crude it might seem by today's standards. The wagon route, it was hoped, should not have to detour via the

Oregon Trail. It should be considerably smoother, so that the wagons would not fall apart before arriving at their destination.

Such a road should, if possible, take its way through country warm enough—that is, southerly enough—to allow hope of avoiding the bitter winters faced by folk delayed along the more northern route. A southerly route through New Mexico Territory (which included much of today's Arizona as well as the state of New Mexico) could be the answer. This would be the better route for which Ned had expressed hopes. And this, as it turned out, would recall Inscription Rock from the oblivion that had enshrouded it during the decades of Mexican dominion.

5

Half Acre
of Inscriptions

In 1849, newly acquired New Mexico Territory was under the rule and command of a military governor. It had to be, for it was a wide, little populated land where no civilian governor could have had effective control even without the aggravated problem of rarely controlled marauding Indians. The new sovereign power, the United States, was committed to protect not only the interests of settlers, but also of peaceful Pueblo Indians and of the older New Mexicans. Moreover Mexicans residing south of the border were to be reimbursed for depredations made by warlike Indians from north of the treaty line.

Colonel John Marshall Washington—the same who had acknowledged dispatches brought by Mr. Beale—was the man then assigned to the task of governing the new territory along with all the other tasks involved in making such governing effective. Naturally, one of the most important of these was to pacify the warlike raiding Navajos and to persuade their chiefs to place crosses of assent on a treaty of eternal peace.

Colonel Washington achieved this in a meeting he held with the tribes in the Canyon de Chelly. What he could not achieve was to change the Indians, who, like later and better educated diplomats, found a treaty just another scrap of paper. Cynics would soon be claiming that before Colonel Washington and his accompanying troops, on their return trip to Santa Fe, were able to reach the Rio Grande, Navajo raiding parties were already there at work.

However limited the military success of Colonel Washington's expedition turned out to be, there was one aspect of the trip whose value no one has ever questioned. "Lieutenant Simpson, Topographical Engineers," instructions read, "will accompany the expedition, making such a survey as the movement of the troops will permit." The Topographical Engineers were then a highly skilled, mentally alert group of surveyors and mappers of the wide and unknown areas of our land. Of this corps, Lieutenant Simpson was an outstanding member—the kind of man to see to it that the movement of Colonel Washington's troops should permit him great latitude in pursuing both topographical and archaeological investigations. Among the surveys thus achieved was the rediscovery of El Morro and the resurrecting of Inscription Rock from the oblivion of decades.

Thirty-six-year-old Lt. Simpson had graduated in 1832 from the United States Military Academy at the rather young age of nineteen. Six years after graduation he joined the Topographical Engineers, where he happily performed the kind of work which, with or without a military commission, he would be performing brilliantly until his retirement in 1880 (at his own request).

Simpson's western career began in early 1849. He was to accompany Captain Marcy from Fort Smith, Arkansas, "as engineer officer of the expedition to be fitted out at that place" destined for "Santa Fé, New Mexico, for the purpose of affording protection to our citizens emigrating to our newly acquired territories" and, incidentally, of surveying for a road. Wherever possible, the surface of the road was to be improved so as to make easier the passage of future expeditions, and he was specifically instructed to keep transcontinental railroad routes in mind.

Lt. Simpson, only too well aware of this trend, remained a staunch wagon-road man, seeing expansion as beginning with local roads, then progressing to postal routes and settlement along these. A railroad, he believed, would become practicable only when it had scattered settlements along the right of way to serve it, support it, and use it. A railroad, planners in the East believed, would possibly enrich them, and certainly would help bring unity to a great nation, whose parts seemed increasingly unaware of the interests of the whole.

Simpson found the Southwest "an unmitigated desert," which may have helped to sharpen his interest in the folk who had managed to survive there long enough and successfully enough to build the once great pueblos whose many ruins he visited with ever growing fascination. His report on the long deserted ruins in Chaco Canyon (which the lieutenant was the first white man to investigate) remains a classic of American archaeology to this day.

For us his report on El Morro seems still more important since he has left pictures in both words and lines to show how the rock appeared in 1848 when all the legible inscriptions were in Spanish. Today some of those are no longer legible. At the summit of the great rock, he expressed a wonder which all non-Indians must share: "What could have possessed the occupants of these villages to perch themselves so high up, and in such inaccessible localities, I cannot conceive, unless it were, as it probably was, from motives of security and defence." Certainly, he reflected in further wonder, it was not because there was any easily accessible water supply for those dwellers atop the hard stone that caps the softer sandstone. Water was to be had there only from the very occasional rains or from that pool far below at the Rock's base, as still testified by the precarious footholds cut by an ancient race into sheer rock walls. Could they possibly have carried water up that way and, if so, how?

Originally instructed to return east after accompanying Captain Marcy all the way to Santa Fe, Simpson found awaiting him at the army post there instructions to continue west in Colonel Washington's company. This new assignment forced him to scurry around "ransacking every store in the place"—a place of very limited supplies like most frontier posts—in search of materials to last out the expedition.

Particularly needed was paper of a kind required by the artist who, in those prephotography days, would accompany every such expedition. Simpson's walking camera was artist Richard H. Kern who would, during the few years left him before he became victim of an Indian massacre, make an outstanding pictorial record of the Southwest he saw during the 1840s and early 1850s.

Topographical engineer and artist and supplies were very much on hand when, on the return trip from the Canyon de Chelly, Colonel Washington decided to detour through the Pueblo of Zuñi, whence had come reports of raiding Apaches. Apaches, as it turned out, were not this time raiding the "hardy, well fed and well clothed" Zuñis, sympathetically described by the newly arrived Indian Agent, James S. Calhoun, who was taking advantage of the troops' escort to make a personal visit to Indians of his agency. His heart was moved by those Pueblo Indians who were constantly being victimized by warlike Navajos and Apaches.

"But what is shockingly discreditable to the American name," Calhoun wrote frankly, "emigrants commit the grossest wrongs against these excellent Indians by taking, in the name of the United States, such horses, mules, and sheep, and grain as they desire, carefully concealing their true name, but assuming official authority and bearing. A wrong of this kind had been perpetrated a few days prior to our arrival there." [6]

A less depressing incident of the visit of Colonel Washington's troops to Zuñi was Lt. Simpson's encounter there with a man who was long familiar with the country. On September 17, the lieutenant was recording in his carefully kept journal: "The incidents of today have been particularly interesting," a masterpiece of understatement. "Meeting in the road Mr. Lewis, who was waiting for me to offer his services as guide to a rock upon the face of which were, according to his repeated assertions, half an acre of inscriptions, many of them very beautiful, and upon the summit some ruins of very extraordinary character, I at once fell in with the project." [54]

Mr. Lewis, as trader among the Navajos, must have passed that way many times, with or without the consent of Mexican officials in Santa Fe. Simpson does not state whether he had been able to read the inscriptions or simply sensed their value to more literate men. Certainly Mr. Lewis left there no inscription of his own.

"There were many in the command," Simpson wrote of Lewis's promises, "who were inclined to the belief that Lewis' representations were all gammon . . . as respects the fact of there being some tolerable basis for so grandiloquent a description, I could not, reasoning upon general principles of human nature, reject it . . . my faith was rewarded by the result."

Having obtained from Colonel Washington the necessary permission and

taking with me one of my assistants, Mr. R. H. Kern, ever zealous in an enterprise of this kind; and the faithful Bird, an *employé* who had been with me ever since I left Fort Smith —Mr. Lewis being the guide—and a single pack animal loaded with a few articles of bedding, a few cooking utensils, and some provisions, we diverged from the command . . .

Bearing off slightly to the right from the route of the troops, we traversed for eight miles a country varied, in places, by low *mesas,* blackened along their crests by outcrops of basalt, and on our left by fantastic white and red sandstone rocks, some of them looking like steamboats, and others presenting very much the appearance of heavy Egyptian architecture. This distance traversed, we came to a quadrangular mass of sandstone rocks, of pearly whitish aspect, from two hundred to two hundred and fifty feet in height, and strikingly peculiar on account of its massive character and the Egyptian style of its natural buttresses and domes.

Skirting this stupendous mass of rock, on its left or north side, for about a mile, the guide, just as we reached its eastern terminus, was noticed to leave us, and ascend a low mound or ramp at its base, the better, as it appeared, to scan the face of the rock, which he had scarcely reached before he cried out to us to come up. We immediately went up, and sure enough, here were inscriptions, and some of them very beautiful. . . . The fact then being certain that here were indeed inscriptions of interest, if not of value, one of them dating as far back as 1606, all of them very ancient, and several of them very deeply as well as beautifully engraven, I gave directions for a halt—Bird at once proceeding to get a meal, and Mr. Kern and myself to the work of making *fac similes* of the inscriptions . . . The greater portion of the inscriptions are in Spanish, with some little sprinkling of what appeared to be an attempt at Latin, and the remainder in hyeroglyphics, doubtless of Indian origin. [54]

Archaic seventeenth-century Spanish would have seemed to him somewhat closer to "Latin." Up to the time of Simpson's visit in 1849, there were no inscriptions that could be identified as belonging to anyone of English-speaking antecedents. Simpson went on to describe the face of the rock as

of a fair, plain surface, and vertical in position. The inscriptions, in most instances, have been engraved by persons standing at the base of the rock, and are, therefore, generally not higher than a man's head.

The labor of copying the inscriptions having employed us from about noon till near sunset, and there yet being more

> than enough to keep us at work for the balance of the day, we
> suspended copying the remainder until tomorrow, in order
> that before dark we might visit the "wonderful ruins" Lewis
> had assured us we would find on the summit of the rock. So,
> taking him as our guide, we went around to the south face of
> the wall, along which we continued until we came to an angle
> . . . where, canopied by some magnificent rocks, and shaded
> by a few pine trees, the whole forming an exquisite picture,
> we found a cool and capacious spring—an accessory not more
> grateful to the lover of the beautiful than refreshing to the
> way-worn traveller. Continuing along the east face of the rear
> projection or spur of the rock a few yards further, we came to
> an accessible escarpment, up which we commenced our as-
> cent, the guide taking off his shoes to enable him to accom-
> plish it safely. After slipping several times, and with some
> little apprehension of a slide off, and a pause to take breath,
> we at last reached the summit, to be regaled with a most
> extensive and pleasing prospect. [54]

Clearly Lt. Simpson's feet, if not his dignity, were too sensitive
for him to follow the guide's example. With or without shoes, the
ascent is still difficult and when the wind blows, as it so frequently
does there, the possibility of a slide off remains to worry a climber.

Arrived at the summit when the late afternoon sun was casting
long shadows, the newcomers found what must indeed have been a
pleasing prospect:

> On the north and east lay stretching from northwest to south-
> east the *Sierra de Zuñi*, richly covered with pine and cedar; to
> the south could be seen gracefully swelling mounds and dis-
> tant peaks, beautifully blue on account of remoteness; to the
> west appeared the horizontal outline of mesa heights, with
> here and there a break, denoting an intervening cañon or
> valley; and lying between all these objects and my point of
> view was a circuit of prairie, beautifully tasty on account of
> solitary and clustered trees, or sombrously dark on account of
> low mesas and oblong ridges covered with cedars.
>   This extensive scene sufficiently scanned, we proceeded to
> examine the ruins which the guide, true to his word, pointed
> out immediately before us . . . To the north and west, about
> three hundred yards distant, a deep cañon intervening . . . on
> the summit of the same massive rock upon which the inscrip-
> tions are found, we could see another ruined pueblo . . . [54]

For nearly a page, Lt. Simpson gave expression to his puzzlement as to how the mesa top dwellers had secured enough water to keep alive. Then his account returns to his immediate environment: "But to continue my journal: the shades of evening falling upon us in our labors, we were constrained to retrace our way down to the plain; and it was not long before we were at the base of the rock, hovering over a bivouac fire, eating our suppers and talking over the events of the day—the grim visage of the stupendous mass behind us occasionally fastening our attention by the sublimity of its appearance in the dim twilight."

The nineteenth-century discoverer of those records left by men long gone found his imagination profoundly stirred. On the following day, he admitted in his journal: "The excitement of yesterday's discovery, together with a rather hard pallet, and the howling of wolves, prevented my having as comfortable a night's rest as I would have wished . . . The dawn of day at three o'clock appearing, we got up for the purpose of hastening breakfast, in order that by daylight we might be ready to continue our labors upon the inscriptions." [54]

Those labors, fortunately, involved the carefully detailed copying of every inscription then to be seen there, even including the ancient petroglyphs. Some of the inscriptions have, in the intervening years, been dimmed by weathering or removed by unappreciative latecomers desiring to replace the old, to them unintelligible records, with their own names and dates. We are fortunate, then, that though Simpson was pressed for time through his need to rejoin Colonel Washington's column, he stopped there long enough both to complete the copying of previous inscriptions and to add the first ones in English: "Mr. Kern having engraved on the rock," Simpson wrote, "'Lt. J. H. Simpson, U.S.A. and R. H. Kern, artist, visited and copied these inscriptions, September 17th, 1849,' we found ourselves ready by 8 o'clock to commence our journey to overtake the command." Actually Simpson's and Kern's names were inscribed in two separate places, both really dated September 17 and 18. Above one of those inscriptions appears the name of the "faithful employé"—"W. Bird, 1849." The carving is not like Kern's, so it appears Bird did his own cutting. Mr. Lewis, if he was literate, must have placed small value on that kind of immortality.

As for the fearfully early hour of rising, it hardly seems likely that dawn could have appeared at three o'clock in the morning in any latitude at a date so close to the equinox. How was the exact hour decided upon in that place and year? Were they relying upon some timepiece set months earlier, before leaving the eastern seaboard? If so, extremes of temperature and the roughness of the journey could well have affected the timepiece's accuracy. Mountain Standard Time, checked by radio signals, was then something of the far future. Simpson's three o'clock dawn, like the hours mentioned by other travelers of those days, conveys little conviction to readers of our day.

With artist Kern's inscriptions of his own and Simpson's names, the rock was again taking its proper place in history. Thenceforth, many people would be camping by the rock, adding names and inscriptions in the new language of the land. In this, Lt. Simpson was continuing to play a part, for, with the 1850 publication of his journal, more and more eyes began turning westward. People found a special fascination in the land he described, giving both careful details of the route he followed all the way from the western limits of Arkansas, adding delightful descriptions of the country passed through and of the people there encountered.

It is Lt. Simpson's obviously warm response to people of all kinds that raises his journal to heights far above that of many another topographical engineer. Through his writings shines his interest in all men, living or dead, wild or civilized, emigrants, Mexicans, or Indians. Two days after leaving Inscription Rock, he caught up with Colonel Washington's company at Laguna Pueblo whose Indians, "like the Zuñis, regard us with considerable reserve; but how could it be otherwise when they have been so shamefully treated as they have been recently by persons bearing the name of Americans, like ourselves." [54] He went on to note happily that the antagonism gradually gave way before the warm friendship of most of the men in the troop and before the encouragement given them by Colonel Washington, who assured the Indians that they would not be censured for defending themselves against such depredations, even to the point of taking life if it turned out so.

By March 1853, Simpson had risen to a captaincy and by the outset of the Civil War he was a major. For the first few months of that war, he served as chief topographical engineer of the Department of the Shenandoah. Then, perhaps feeling he should be serving the Union in active combat, he accepted a colonelcy in the

Volunteers organized in his native state, New Jersey. This active military career soon ended with his capture by the Confederates at Gaines Mill.

Exchanged in August 1862, Simpson resigned his commission in the Volunteers, undoubtedly because such an arrangement involved withdrawal from active service for men so exchanged. Apparently, it did not imply that he should not serve in a nonfighting capacity. He promptly became chief engineer and chief topographical engineer in the Department of Ohio, in 1863 transferring his engineering and mapping activities to Kentucky, where he continued in service until the end of the war. In 1865, he was cited for "faithful and meritorious" service and breveted colonel and brigadier general—"breveting" implying that the appointment was to become a reality for Simpson when the position became vacant through the death or promotion of the man already occupying it, a promise it cost the Army nothing to make.

With the war ended, Simpson was charged with the general direction and inspection of the Union Pacific Railroad, then under construction, as well as of United States wagon roads. This was highly appropriate employment for the former lieutenant of the former corps of Topographical Engineers, legislated into oblivion in 1863. Until his retirement in 1880, Simpson continued in civil engineering projects—road construction, harbor improvements, lighthouse supervision—largely in the South and Middle West.

On retirement, James Hervey Simpson took up residence in St. Paul, Minnesota, far from those unmitigated deserts he'd deplored, as well as explored, thirty years before. Ironically, he paid for that preference by contracting pneumonia and dying therefrom three years later, within a week of his seventieth birthday.

Though with his published journal of 1849 Simpson's personal involvement with New Mexico explorations came to an end, his concluding advice to the War Department was destined to continue influencing the region of Inscription Rock. He wrote:

> I think it proper to bring to the notice of the department the expediency of having the country examined west of the Pueblo of Zuñi, for the ascertainment of a wagon-route from the former point to the Pueblo of Los Angeles or, failing in this, to San Diego . . .

Mr. Richard Campbell [trader and fur trapper] of Santa Fé
. . . has informed me that, in 1827, with a party of thirty-five
men and a number of pack animals, he travelled from New
Mexico to San Diego by way of Zuñi . . .

The Colorado, when he crossed it near the mouth of the Rio
de Zuñi, was fordable; but he is of the opinion that it might
not always be found so. [54]

We know today that the Zuñi River does not enter the main
Colorado. Moreover it is—and always has been within recorded
time—a poor apology for a river, ranging in a southwesterly direction from the Pueblo after which it is named, at times disappearing
into the sands to reappear only after heavy rains. In the end, it
merges itself not in the main Colorado but in the Little Colorado,
or Coloradito, which runs northward to join the main Colorado just
before that river enters its Grand Canyon.

At the time Simpson was writing, no one knew much about
either Colorado. Simpson himself was rather inclined to question
statements made by other trappers who insisted that "the Colorado
is so deeply cañoned from its mouth upwards as to make a wagon
road in that direction impracticable." When he'd closely questioned
such trappers, they'd had to admit they really knew nothing about
those reputed canyons from firsthand experience.

6

Search for
a Better Route

The general route Lt. Simpson suggested would turn out to be that better route Lt. Beale had dreamed of two years before when passing through the rough country of the Sierra de los Mimbres and the Mogollon Mountains. Dreams, of course, brought fewer positive results than the steadily increasing numbers of pleas from voting citizens. Only too conscious of the need for such a road to make the movement of troops and supplies to and from remote outposts easier, men in the War Department were more than inclined to listen. Passing emigrants, whom troops were being assigned to protect, needed a road for their wagons, as did those men determined to settle in isolated areas. All such men—military commanders, settlers, passing emigrants in a hurry to get somewhere else—were adding their voices to the clamor for a wagon road west to California.

To cap it all, railroad planners and investors with an eye on connecting East and West Coast lands, some of these latter looking still further toward the Orient, put the weight of their influence on the side of a railroad survey. Politicians, already painfully aware of the increasingly divisive forces at work in their own land, felt the urgency of this link to join newly acquired California firmly to one or the other side, according to the special interests of each man. Southerly New Mexico Territory might, all hoped, offer a route free from the deepest snows of winter, but only if there were no great natural barriers like uncrossable rivers and unspannable canyons to make this route impracticable.

This dreamed of route, therefore, had to avoid the northern mountain passes and take its way to a negotiable Colorado River crossing, if such could be found, somewhere above the point where that river debouched into the Gulf of California. This turned out to be the "35th parallel route," approximately today's Highway 66 (or Interstate 40). The question long remained—could the Colorado River be crossed as hoped? If crossable, where and how? Certainly there could be no possible crossing if those tales of fearful canyons extending the full length of the river were true. To answer these questions, another exploring expedition was in the books—an expedition to make a thorough survey.

In 1851, the chief of the U.S. Topographical Engineers, Col. Abert, was instructing Captain Lorenzo Sitgreaves to find the answers: "The River Zuñi is represented on good authority"— Simpson's, of course—"to empty into the Colorado, and it has been partially explored by Lt. Simpson to the Pueblo of Zuñi. You will therefore go to that place, which will be, in fact, the commencing point of your exploring labors. From the pueblo of Zuñi you will pursue the Zuñi [River] to its junction with the Colorado. . . . You will then pursue the Colorado to its junction with the Gulf of California." [54]

Just like that—with no "ifs" and "ands." Had Capt. Sitgreaves been the kind of man who blindly followed instructions to the letter, believing it not his to reason why, then surely it must have been his to do and to die. For that little River Zuñi, so deceptively negligible near the town whose name it bears, flows only briefly in a southwesterly direction: when it flows, that is, for in times of drouth it can disappear into the sands. Merging with the Coloradito, its waters reach the main Colorado just above the beginning of the Grand Canyon. Only in 1869 would anyone, and that an incredibly courageous and determined one-armed Civil War veteran, successfully "pursue the Colorado" thence toward the Gulf of California by taking a small party down the whole fearful length of the Grand Canyon. This he would do by boat in the tumultous waters of the river that flows a mile below those deceptively flat, bleak plains by the canyon's brink. It was a feat rarely to be duplicated during the following century.

In Santa Fe, during the summer of 1851, the Sitgreaves party assembled. In addition to the over fifty essential mules with their fifteen essential mule drivers and packers, there was a second topographical engineer, Lieutenant James G. Parke, assigned to assist Capt. Sitgreaves, a Dr. S. G. Woodhouse doubling, as seemed then to be the custom, as physician and naturalist, and the same Richard H. Kern who had already traveled much of the proposed route as far as Zuñi with Lt. Simpson. These last three would, with Sitgreaves, leave their names, dated August 31, 1851, on the rock—Kern's twice, according to the pattern he had established two years earlier.

Even more important to the expedition was the man who would never leave his name on the rock though he must have stopped there many times. Possibly, like Kit Carson, he could not write. More likely, since he had had an opportunity of learning the three R's in his native city, St. Louis, he held such writing in small esteem. This was Antoine Leroux, experienced mountain man and highly reliable guide who knew the country ahead as few others had had a chance of doing.

Already in 1846, Leroux was serving the army well during the Mexican War and while accompanying Doniphan's battalion of volunteers south. The officer commanding that battalion acknowledged Leroux's excellence with: "Of the guides sent me by the General [Kearny], only Leroux joined me this afternoon; the others have come up tonight, more or less drunk." [23] This appears to have been expected of the average guide. What the officer needed was an above average guide such as Leroux: "Mr. Leroux left me this morning, with four other guides, to descend the river to the point where it is practicable to leave it with the wagons to explore beyond. After advancing several miles, I met one of the party that he had sent back ostensibly to settle upon signals by smoke, but really, I believe, because he had no use for him. This fellow . . . has been drunk for a week or two; his gun is broken past use." [23] Such were the majority of men who then offered themselves as guides.

Such, however, was not Antoine Leroux. Like Kit Carson, Antoine Leroux was an expert mountain man. Taste, experience, and the times had made him one. All mountain men, fortunately for the surveyors of the West, did not fit the pattern of drunken brawlers set by some of the more notorious of the breed. It was the essence of belonging to that individualistic group that no two should be quite alike. Fate, assisted by John Charles Frémont, had selected Kit Carson as the typical legendary mountain man. Fate and John Charles Frémont might equally well have settled the laurels upon Antoine Leroux's head.

Antoine Leroux had even better reasons than Kit Carson for traveling the kind of Missouri River boat that had brought Carson and Fremont together. Leroux, St. Louis born, had family to visit in that city. It had been conspicuous advertisements in St. Louis newspapers of February and March 1822, that started the then twenty-one-year-old Antoine on his hunting-trapping career. Designed to catch the eye and stir the interest of "enterprising young men," the notice stated that there were needed "one hundred men to ascend the Missouri River, there to be employed for one, two, or three years." The object, as anyone then must have realized, was furs in general, beaver furs in particular.

Nothing if not enterprising, young Leroux signed up for period that ended in 1823. With a fine physique and a spirit to match, he, like the younger Kit Carson a hundred miles or so upriver, had had his ears filled with hair-raising tales of the mountains. The trappers who had stopped in Franklin usually ended their travels in St. Louis, where they sold their furs and blew their profits on metropolitan excitements. Then, having outfitted themselves for the next year's trip, usually against expected profits, they'd start back for the mountains and the kind of life they really enjoyed. Naturally the eager lads like Kit Carson and Antoine Leroux, whose ears had been filled with their tales, were ready to grasp at any chance of ascending the Missouri River to the mountains or to any other place where similar adventure might be had.

By 1824, Leroux's travels had taken him southwest to Taos, New Mexico. Taos was in his blood. His grandmother, born near there of a prominent family, was his passport to acceptance in Taos society. Josiah Gregg, a Missourian who traveled the Santa Fe Trail to write and publish in 1844 his famous *Commerce of the Prairies*, told the touching tale of that almost legendary young woman and of how she finally came to live in St. Louis. [34]

"The first settler of the charming valley of Taos, since the country was reconquered from the Indians"—this would have been thanks to Diego de Vargas's expedition of 1692—"is said to have been a Spaniard named Pando, about the middle of the eighteenth century. This pioneer of the north, finding himself greatly exposed to the depredations of the Comanches, succeeded in gaining the friendship of that tribe by promising his infant daughter, then a beautiful child, in marriage." Pando did not seem to think his womenfolk needed to be consulted in the matter. No Indian chief would have considered their consent of the slightest importance. That it was highly important became evident years later when the chief came to claim his now teen-age bride.

The naturally unwilling maiden "having subsequently refused to ratify the contract, the settlement was immediately attacked by the savages, and all were slain except the betrothed damsel who was led into captivity. After living some years with the Comanches on the great prairies, she was bartered away to the Pawnees, of whom she was eventually purchased by a Frenchman of St. Louis. Some very respectable families of that city are descended from her; and there are many people yet living who remember with what affecting pathos the old lady was wont to tell her tale of woe. She died a few years ago."[34]

Nine years of servitude had passed between the time María Rosalia Villalpando (as the Pando had presently become) was captured by the Comanche chief and when he, undoubtedly tiring of her, sold her to the Pawnees. From them she was ransomed by that French-born trader who, having fallen in love with her, took her to St. Louis, where he officially married her in July 1770, when she became "Marie Rose." This man of the imposing name Jean Baptiste Sale dit Lajoie had come to St. Louis in the party with Pierre Laclede and young Auguste Chouteau when they established the first fur trading post there in 1764. To him, deprived of society of his own kind, a purchasable young woman of pure Spanish antecedents must have seemed a highly acceptable bride. But when he decided to return to France, he cheerfully deserted her and their twin daughters—to receive, we may hope, his just deserts during the French Revolution.

Brought up in the ingrown social environment of the St. Louis French, Marie Rose's daughters were bound to marry French men. The husband of Helene Joseph was the French emigré trader named William Leroux. The fourth and youngest son of this union, born in 1801, was Joaquin Antoine Leroux, more generally known simply as Antoine Leroux.

Antoine grew up and had some schooling in St. Louis. By the time he arrived in Taos in 1824, he showed he was not the typically rough frontier type but a man whom Villalpando relatives need not blush to acknowledge. For him, the prominent family connections gave entrée into New Mexican drawing rooms otherwise closed to most men of his calling. Perhaps, too, they made it easier for him to pursue that calling without too open opposition of Mexican authorities.

Always, Antoine Leroux remained a mountain man at heart. His special section of the mountains was the great "San Luis Park" of the upper Rio Grande where he came to know every stream and every pass within four days' horseback ride of Taos. It would be as mountain man, but not as relative of the Villalpandos or as husband of a New Mexico belle of equally prominent family, that Antoine Leroux's fame would eventually rest.

In 1833, Antoine married Juana Caterina Valdez de Vigil and therby became the principal owner of the huge Los Luceros Ranch, a Spanish land grant of nearly 500,000 acres along the Rio de Los Luceros. Up to 1840, though, he passed nine months of each year in exploring all over the West, where he must have noted with growing sadness the approaching extinction of the beaver. Even before the silk hat edged the fur hat out to give the beaver a fighting chance, men like Leroux could see their own way of life coming to an end. For him, as well as for Kit Carson, this meant turning first to life on his ranch as hacendado, then becoming guide to government expeditions sparked by the annexation of California and the need for a direct route of communications with the far land.

How and why General Kearny selected Antoine Leroux to act as guide to Philip St. George Cooke and his Mormon Battalion is not stated either by Cooke or by the general. It's a safe bet that when Kit Carson was drafted to guide Kearny back across the desert, he suggested that fellow mountain man Leroux was one to be trusted to find his way along any route he might undertake. Col. Cooke would presently say, "Amen!" to this as also and later would Capt. Sitgreaves.

The Sitgreaves party arrived in Zuñi on September 1, expecting to be joined promptly there by a military escort assigned to protect the surveying party from attacks of hostile Indians. The military escort thus assigned seemed to have no great appetite for the risky trip. It would be over three weeks before they turned up—weeks during which the waiting expedition was forced to consume supplies needed for the exploration part of the trip, supplies that could be replaced only in some distant military post that itself might well be on short rations.

Mules, already in poor condition, gained little on the scanty forage to be had in pastures already overgrazed by the animals of Pueblo Indians. The Zuñis themselves became increasingly irritated as they saw thus consumed the grass their own animals might need to survive the lean winter months ahead. It was fortunate for the explorers that these were no Plains Indians, ready to fight to the death at the merest suggestion of encroachment upon their own lands and rights.

This was not the first time, as surely it was not the last, that the military kept waiting an expedition they were assigned to protect. Seven years later a member of another similarly delayed expedition would record in exasperation: "The life of no citizen is protected by the Army and the death of none has been avenged."

By September 24, with the escort at last on hand, the completed party set forth from the pueblo to follow the Zuñi River, which Capt. Sitgreaves soon reported to be "a mere rivulet, not entitled to the name of river." Since this was the "river" Sitgreaves had been directed to follow, he kept along it in its southwesterly direction until, on September 27, he arrived at the Little Colorado. This, to the commander's expressed disappointment, he also found "an insignificant stream."

Three days later, however, the party was having second thoughts as to the stream's insignificance. Today, as you drive through the same country, you may top a slight rise to see what at first appears to be unbroken and infertile flat desert land. Second glance reveals the course of the Little Colorado stretching like a great somnolent black snake across the surface of the plain. No water may be seen—only a break in the continuity of the plain—but you may guess the river is somewhere there below. Travelers of a century ago were to find just how far below that "below" was.

"The river here," Sitgreaves recorded in his journal, "runs through a deep and rocky cañon, which we skirted and crossed below it to the south bank, finding the ground much broken by ravines, which were only visible when we came directly upon them. The surrounding scenery resembled that of the northwestern prairies, the country being bare of trees and the horizon unbroken, except in one direction, where a high conical peak, that had served us several days as a landmark, varied the uniformity of the outline."[55]

"You will then pursue the Colorado to its junction with the Gulf of California," Sitgreaves's instructions had read.

The man who composed those instructions, of course, knew nothing of the frequency of canyons such as those Sitgreaves was encountering and which increased in number and depth as the Little Colorado rushed on to join the larger Colorado. No one not on the spot could quite believe in those abrupt drops, almost without warning, into increasingly forbidding depths. On the spot, Capt. Sitgreaves was now quite ready to accept the information given by "my guide and other experienced trappers that this cañon extends down the river to its junction with the Colorado, and the great cañon through which the latter flows." So he took the wise step "by the advice of my guide, [and] turned off towards the mountains, with the purpose of striking the Colorado just below the great cañon." [55]

Those mountains were the San Francisco group near today's Flagstaff, Arizona, which travelers still find refreshingly green after the drab monotony of desert plains. It was their height and ruggedness that left the most enduring impression upon Sitgreaves and his company.

Meanwhile the party's supplies, depleted by that disastrous delay in Zuñi while the escort dallied on its way, were running alarmingly short. Increasingly aggressive Indians could not fail to note the men's declining strength and to harass them with greater and greater frequency. Fatigue and hunger were the Indians' allies.

On October 13, the expedition added a handicap of another kind when, because of the roughness of the last day's journey, the chronometer stopped though it had been tenderly "carried in a pannier, packed in wool, and placed on the steadiest mule . . . which was always led by a halter." For a topographical engineer, losing the chronometer was serious. Precise longitude determinations, hence the drawing of maps, required an accurate chronometer for which pocket watches could be no real substitute. Thus, for all practical purposes, a stopped chronometer was a disaster for such an expedition.

To add to the party's discomforts, daily temperatures ranged widely—from a below-freezing 10°F to a springlike 65°F. The constantly growing fatigue of the men, aggravated by incipient scurvy, now encouraged the "Cojnino" Indians to open hostilities. On November 3, while passing a cluster of rocks, Antoine Leroux "received the discharge of a flight of arrows from a concealed party of Indians. Three of the arrows took effect, inflicting severe wounds in the head and wrist, which caused much suffering as well as disabling him for the remainder of the journey." [54] Had Leroux's fatigue led him to exercise just a bit less than his usual caution?

Dr. Woodhouse set to work at once to help the guide. The doctor's published report states that Leroux's head wound was from a stone-headed arrow which, "striking him on the left side of the head, behind the ear, after cutting a groove in the . . . bone, broke in numerous pieces, all of which I removed with difficulty. The wound healed without any bad effects." [54] A score for the doctor's surgery! The wrist wound, however, had the arrow so deeply embedded that Dr. Woodhouse had to use a dentist's forceps to remove it. That wound was the most painful and healed the most slowly, though durable Antoine Leroux would survive to guide many another party.

Only two days after Leroux received these wounds, the party was cheered to find itself on the banks of the Colorado River, which there, below its canyons, ran "two hundred and sixty-six yards wide, with six feet of water in the deepest part; the banks bluff and sandy, about twelve feet high, the current rapid."

Apparently unaware that their leader had been instructed to continue all the way to the Pacific Coast, the men saw the river, winding through a broad, if desert, valley, as the end of their trials and tribulations. To them, "the smoke of numerous fires in the valley gave evidence of a large Indian population, and the sight brought a spontaneous cheer from the men." These Indians, they persuaded themselves, must be friendly and eager to trade for trinkets the vegetables they cultivated in the bottoms close to the river. Desperately in need of fresh vegetables and fruit, the men believed what they had to.

The Indians were proud and warlike Mojaves, who would be friendly only if and when they chose to be. They could also be forbiddingly hostile, as would be proved in due time. Even as they bartered with Sitgreaves's party, they must have had some mental reservations for within a day members of the party found "hieroglyphics" scratched in the dirt of the pathway. Leroux interpreted these signs as a warning to turn back.

Sitgreaves was not now going to turn back. True to his instructions, he headed south along the river through a landscape he found "presenting a most perfect picture of desolation I have ever beheld, as if some sirocco had passed over the land withering and scorching everything to crispness."

One by one the surviving mules died, some from sheer exhaustion, others killed, all to supply food for the otherwise starving party. Scurvy—that centuries-old grim companion of explorers and travelers as well as of sailors and of settlers in remote areas—was now more than just a threat. Providentially, on November 24, the party received, according to Dr. Woodhouse's report, "antiscorbutics" sent from Fort Yuma on the river.

By then, Leroux was already out of action and the doctor nearly so, the result both of an arrow wound, received sixteen days earlier while he was resting by the camp fire, and of a later rattlesnake bite for which his treatment—a half-pint of whiskey followed by one quart brandy—must have been effective. With the supplies arriving in the nick of time came also the encouragement of knowing that help was no longer out of reach. But they still had the discouraging fact to face that their leader was bound to continue to the Pacific Coast, even though he did reject the part of his instructions that required him to go via the mouth of the Colorado River. Perhaps he'd learned that such a route would take him not to the Pacific but to the Gulf of California.

Though Sitgreaves had done his best against odds, he had not found a good route for emigrant wagons to follow to California. Yet with each passing year it was becoming increasingly urgent that California be joined irrevocably to the states of the East Coast and thereby to the Union. The hunger for California gold was becoming more and more overshadowed, in the minds of northern politicians, by the need to make certain that California and her gold should not become attached to the southern states if and when they should decide to secede from the Union. The bright dream of a great nation stretching uninterrupted from ocean to ocean was already darkened by the grim threat of a nation shattered by internal strife.

Clearly, the 35th parallel route would have to be reexplored. Yet surely this need was not excuse enough to consign Lorenzo Sitgreaves to obscurity. Of all the men who explored that route, he was the only one of captain's rank. Moreover, his whole party endured greater hardships than the ones that followed, thanks largely to faulty instructions and dilatory escort. Though other explorers of the route have found places in the Dictionary of American Biography, for Sitgreaves we have only the files of the Topographical Engineers, a corps that was disbanded before the end of the Civil War. Only his name on Inscription Rock remains to remind us that he was an explorer to whom we owe real homage.

7

Self-Made Guide

Senator Benton, for all the reasons already given, believed in the need for a road to California. He also saw it as the beginning of a "North American road to India" and to all the incalculable riches of the Orient. Of course, too, he wanted that road to contribute to the greatness of his native state, Missouri. A transcontinental railroad should, by carrying cargoes from coast to coast, materially shorten the long routes from European markets to the Orient while adding materially to the prosperity of the United States and of one state in particular—Missouri. He would have liked such a railroad to take a 38th parallel route, but a 35th parallel route would be far more acceptable than none.

Naturally, Old Bullion was also seeing the road in terms of a surveyor of his own backing. This was the young Beale whom he'd liked from the very first encounter and to whom he'd soon be addressing letters with the familiar salutation "Dear Edward" instead of the more formal "Dear Mr. Beale" or "Dear Lieutenant Beale" he'd been using previously. By then, anyway, Beale was no longer a lieutenant, having resigned a naval commission in the expectation of being appointed superintendent of Indian Affairs in California.

Beale's appointment to that post received Senate approval in early November 1852. Perhaps assured of the certainty of the appointment by influential friends, perhaps just eager to revisit his own property in California, he was already there, having left Washington some months earlier to arrive in California on September 18 on board the steamer *Oregon*. A few months later continent-hopper Beale was again back in Washington.

Perhaps he was drawn back by a warning from good friend Senator Benton that in the appropriation bill for March 1853 were provisions for surveys of possible railroad routes from the Mississippi River to the Pacific Ocean. Perhaps Benton and/or Beale felt that his physical presence in the capital was needed to help him win the post he so coveted—that of conducting one of the planned explorations that should take the middle route Benton so believed in.

On March 16, the senator sent a formal letter of recommendation to Secretary of War Jefferson Davis, to which he added the less formal postscript: "P.S. I add in my own name, in relation to Mr. Beale, that seven years' acquaintance with California and the west—three overland journeys from Missouri to California, one of them in the dead of winter . . . besides ten trips through Mexico and Panama—his acquaintance with mountain men, Indians and wilderness travel—his experience and resources in every kind of danger—his eighteen years training in the use of compass and astronomical instruments at sea—render him, in my opinion, eminently fit and proper to be employed in this exploration."

It could have been no mere chance that this commendatory letter was printed in full on April 22, 1853, in the *Liberty Weekly Tribune* of Missouri. Nevertheless, though Senator Benton's opinion was always important and frequently decisive, it failed in 1853 to win the coveted appointment for his protégé. Col. Abert, chief officer of the U.S. Topographical Engineers, was also influential, and in this particular jockeying for power, he came out ahead. His officers had been specially trained, had unquestioned experience, had been surveying the wilds from the far Northeast to the far Southwest, and he could justly argue that it was to one of them that the new commands should go.

The year 1853 saw Lieutenant John W. Gunnison, one of Abert's men, surveying a route along the 38th parallel of latitude. By the time, in that same year, Sitgreaves's report on his more southerly route was printed among government documents, Col. Abert had already dispatched another expedition under another topographical engineer, Lieutenant Amiel Weeks Whipple [61], to improve the 35th parallel route. This time the colonel's instructions were both more realistic and more explicit than the ones he'd issued Sitgreaves—to survey the line of a wagon road (and hoped-for railroad) from Fort Smith, Arkansas, by way of Albuquerque and Zuñi, along the 35th parallel of latitude or as close to it as feasible.

The rejected commander, Beale, was already heading west again on his own, determined to demonstrate that, though he had been passed over, he was inarguably the man to whom such exploration should have been entrusted. Beale arrived in St. Louis on May 2, as the *St. Louis Democrat* noted: "Lt. Beale left for his Super-intendency on Saturday and will proceed on the route indicated by Fremont and Leroux"—both with St. Louis connections. "He goes unencumbered with provisions and baggage, and has no useless company"—which sounds very much like a dig at overen-cumbered government-sponsored expeditions.

"Two trained Frenchmen," continued the account, obviously aimed at a readership that included many people of French extrac-tion, "who know how to live without a commissariat either in plain or mountain, and Mr. Harris Heap, who has had some experience in wild travelling both in California and Asia Minor, will be . . . his . . . companions. They carry no cooking utensils and rely upon pinole (powdered corn to be mixed with water and drank raw), pemmican (pulverized dried meat), and beef dodgers (called meat biscuit), to supply the difference when rifles do not supply game. A blanket apiece will be their sleeping establishment, the earth for bedstead, and the skies for canopy."

Fremont's route would be Old Bullion's favored route—along the 38th parallel. It could serve as well as any other to demonstrate that Edward Beale had the skill and know-how to take charge of exploration. It would also, Old Bullion hoped, serve his own special interests and those of his own state. Inevitably, an account of the trip was published. Ostensibly written by Beale's cousin companion, Gwinn Harris Heap, the book bears the title, *Central Route to the Pacific from the Valley of the Mississippi to Cali-fornia*.

"Mr. Beale," Heap wrote, "had selected only such men as were inured by long habit to the privations and hardships which we expected to encounter. One, the Delaware"—possibly the Indian who had been with Beale at the Battle of San Pasqual, certainly one of a tribe long famous for its scouts—"was an experienced hunter and to his unerring rifle we owed, during the journey, many abundant repasts, when otherwise we should have been on short allowance." [37]

When they had reached 189 miles beyond Westport, Kansas, they met Antoine Leroux and enlisted his assistance, considering them-selves "fortunate in securing the services of so experienced a guide." A few days later, however, brought a heavy rain which "to Mr. Leroux, who was taken suddenly ill . . . was particularly distressing. He was attacked with pleurisy, and his sufferings were so great that he felt convinced that this place would be his grave." So Mr. Leroux had to be left behind in the care of a post surgeon —to end up as guide to one of the parties Beale had vainly wanted to command.

Commanding that official 1853 expedition past El Morro was topographical engineer Lieutenant Amiel Whipple, Massachusetts born (1818) and Massachusetts educated (Amherst) until receiving, in 1837, a cadetship at the U.S. Military Academy. In 1844, he was one of a party detailed to make a boundary survey between Vermont and Canada. A few years later he had spanned the land to serve similarly on the United States–Mexican Boundary Survey that was needed after the signing of the Treaty of Guadalupe Hidalgo.

Whipple's 1853 exploring party was impressively supplied with scientists, among them Swiss geologist Jules Marcou, protégé of Professor Louis Agassiz of Harvard University. There was, too, the German artist-topographer, Heinrich Baldwin Möllhausen, sponsored by no less a personage than the great Baron von Humboldt. Mexicans, French, and Americans in various capacities completed the amazing roster with young Lieutenant David Sloane Stanley, fresh out of the military academy, officially taking charge of supplies and unofficially keeping a journal, which would be part of his published memoirs many years later. [58] The possible handicap of burgeoning rivalries in a group so constituted, confined so long to each other's company, seems to have been avoided.

Not possible to avoid, however, was the handicap of too limited numbers of scientific instruments. That was a year when many U.S. government-sponsored exploring expeditions were clamoring for their shares of the same too limited equipment. Commodore Perry was making that first historic visit to as yet uncharted Japanese waters. Ringgold was exploring the north Pacific. Elisha Kent Kane was headed for the Arctic in response to Lady Franklin's impassioned plea to President Zachary Taylor that the United States sponsor a new search for her explorer husband, Sir John Franklin, long lost in the far north. These and other explorations would require many instruments which no sum of money, however great, could purchase if there were none on hand to be purchased.

Informing Whipple that the sum of $40,000 had been set aside to cover the expenses of his expedition, Secretary of War Davis added the instructions: "Great attention will be given to those collateral branches of science which more or less affect the solution of the question of location for the proposed railway; the nature of the rocks and soils; . . . the products of the country, mineral and vegetable; its population and resources . . . the location, character, habits, traditions, and language of the Indian tribes." [61]

A "proposed railway" demanded that everything imaginable that might possibly throw light upon the new lands to be traversed must be studied and reported upon. Perhaps the most amazing part of Whipple's instructions, issued on May 14, was that the whole business was to be completed and reported upon "on or before the first Monday of February next"—February 7, 1854. Actually, members of Whipple's party would be extraordinarily lucky if they were able to arrive back in Washington by that date. As it turned out, they had not by then even reached their destination, let alone had their collections meticulously studied and their journals edited.

For the very young Lt. Stanley in charge of supplies, the experience would, from the start, be both trying and educational. "The spring of 1853," he wrote much later in his memoirs,

> was noted for the passage of the law providing for the survey of four great routes for a Pacific railroad [32nd, 35th, 38th, and 42nd parallels]. I applied for and went to Washington to procure a detail on one of the surveying parties, and in this I succeeded, joining Lieutenant A. W. Whipple, Topographical Engineer, at Cincinnati. Here we made purchases of . . . stores for our long survey of the country lying between Fort Smith, Arkansas, and San Diego, California. These were shipped by steamboat and I went in charge, down the beautiful Ohio [Stanley was a native of Ohio], the muddy but mighty Mississippi, to the mouth of the Arkansas.
>
> We were delayed several days at Napoleon, a little place of a dozen houses at the mouth of the Arkansas River. One of these was called a hotel . . .
>
> A good-natured merchant, the only one in the place, invited us to a good natured game of poker, considerately saying, "You boys are going on a long trip on the plains and won't have any use for money and I can help you spend it now." He got his game but no money.

Most of Lieutenant Whipple's party got together at Napoleon and embarked on the same boat for Fort Smith, where we arrived the first of July. [57]

Whipple planned on taking the route followed by Capt. Marcy and Lt. Simpson four years earlier, hoping to improve both grades and roadbed wherever possible. The new young lieutenant found it all a time of trial and training.

Finally, on the twenty-fourth day of July, after endless worry, we were ferried across the little river Poteau at Fort Smith, and we started on our work and our journey. Anyone who has served as a quartermaster can appreciate the miseries of my first day's start—raw drivers, raw mules, wagons overloaded, one wagon breaking down, another upset; eight miles of muddy road leading through a canebrake with the cane twenty feet high and cutting off all breezes; the day intensely hot—all loaded upon poor me. How I wished I had never started. Lieutenant Whipple was a pious man and why he should start on Sunday I could not imagine. The first day ended in sleep and the next morning our two derelict wagons came up and we moved on.

This day's worry was a forerunner of the days to come. The days for the next two weeks were varied with mules getting away at night, terrible roads, deep creeks to cross with bottomless muddy fords. Vexations fell thick and fast and I fear I did some swearing, for in my diary I turn now and see my lamentation of my wickedness and hard words at the day's closing and pray God's help that I may spend the next day more like a Christian. [57]

What he actually recorded on August 1, 1853, is a sample of this kind of lamenting entry: "Oh! That God may forgive me the wickedness I have and am constantly guilty of on this expedition, oweing to the constant crosses and consequent fits of bad temper I fall into." [58]

God may have forgiven him, but certainly did not see fit to relieve him immediately of his fits of bad temper, for the next day young Stanley was noting it again as the result of "the young gentlemen putting up their tents according to their own inclinations" without, of course, giving thought to the convenience of anyone else. In addition to all his quartermaster's worries, Stanley was constantly suffering from recurring attacks of the malaria he had contracted some years earlier before leaving his native Ohio.

Probably as they emerged from the low, hot riverbottoms, malaria, too, receded. In any case, Stanley's diary shows that his spirits gradually rose and he dwelt less insistently on those moments of bad humor. Mule drivers and mules, undoubtedly, were either learning their duties or accepting their fate. The young quartermaster was finding eyes for the beauty of the country they were passing through and the excitingly wide vistas of sky and limitless prairie, a new experience to a man whose childhood had been passed in the still heavily forested Ohio.

"We were starting over a country . . . inhabited by wild Indians," Stanley wrote in retrospect, "but so few Indians roamed over the vast prairie country that the chances were we should not meet with any of them"—a disappointment, undoubtedly, to the young soldier.

> As to hiring a guide, the fates were against us. We had hoped to get Black Beaver, a Delaware chieftain, but he was sick of the ague . . . . Jesse Chisholm, a half-breed Creek, was solicited to go with us but he could not leave his business. He was a man of force and had been many times among the Kiowas and Comanches as a trader . . . . Chisholm was of Scotch and Creek [Cherokee] Indian descent and was a man of fine presence and dignified manners.
>
> Finally we started with no guide but a little negro boy who was loaned by Chisholm because he spoke Comanche and would be useful as an interpreter. [57]

Hunting big game was another experience the young man had long anticipated. His first success was when he shot an old buffalo bull "with my English rifle, thus killing my first buffalo and getting well kicked by the gun. José and I managed to secure the tongue and boiled it all night, serving it at breakfast. . . . only after six hours more boiling was it sufficiently cooked for consumption."

The party finally reached Albuquerque, where it would remain from October 4 to November 10. This meant they were heading into a winter crossing of the high plains and mountains which certainly would be colder but, one hoped, less dry than a summer's crossing. Whipple had already served on the Mexican boundary

survey close to the 32nd parallel of latitude. He was now journey-
ing 3° farther north, following that 35th parallel insofar as might
prove practicable. Like anyone heading west along new and
incompletely explored routes, he felt the need of engaging competent guides.

Only a few weeks earlier, Lt. Gunnison's expedition had set out
from Santa Fe to explore a route along the 38th parallel. By the
time Whipple's party was ready to start again on the road west,
many of Gunnison's party, including the leader, were dead, massacred by Ute Indians. Lt. Beckwith, whose duty it became to
assume command of the remnants of Gunnison's party, wrote of
the need of guides in the report it then became his duty to make:
"Our recent experience in exploring wild mountainous country
without guides, was such as to show the necessity of profiting by
the practical lessons in geography gained in the school of trapper
and hunter." [10]

Trappers and hunters were known to congregate in Taos, nearly
seventy miles north of Santa Fe, which itself is sixty-odd miles
north of Albuquerque. Thither some of Gunnison's party had gone
"procuring what information we could of the country westward
over which we were to pass, and the services of a guide, we
returned in thirty hours to our camp, arriving at noon the 19th of
August. On the following day we were joined by the experienced
and well-known guide, Antoine Leroux." [35]

Leroux, they knew, had many practical lessons in geography to
share with the explorers. Lt. Beckwith did not mention, if indeed
he had been informed, that Leroux had then barely recovered from
that serious illness which had recently removed him from Beale's
employ and which, at his age, could well have been permanently
disabling. When that bad case of "pleurisy" developed, Beale
consigned his guide to the care of the post surgeon at Fort
Atkinson. He wrote Senator Benton: "I shall miss Leroux very
much, but I shall not fail for want of him." Ned Beale was determined not to let himself fail for want of others though he, like other
explorers, would never scorn to seek the help of guides when he
could find it.

Within four months of that consignment at Fort Atkinson on the
Arkansas River, Leroux was back in Santa Fe, sufficiently recovered
to undertake service with Lt. Gunnison. For Gunnison, this acqui-
sition was a splendid piece of luck. Of more doubtful luck was the

withdrawal of some half dozen men who asked for their discharges, "refusing to perform further duty." Lazy or timorous men, of course, could be less than useless during the trials ahead. Yet had the six not chosen to desert, their presence might just have tipped the balance of survival for the party members who were slaughtered.

Having secured in Leroux a man worth all six deserters put together, Lt. Gunnison let them go. On August 22, he sat down to write a letter to the secretary of war: "We are to start early tomorrow . . . I have secured the services of A. Leroux to the Spanish Trail, when he will return to guide Lieutenant Whipple."

It must have taken exactly a month to reach the Spanish Trail, for on September 22, "Leroux with three companions left us at the camp to return to New Mexico, having completed his engagement as guide. He expects to travel much at night and trusts to his tact and knowledge of the country for passing safely through the Indian bands along his route." [35]

Leroux's tact and knowledge of the country always served him well, as it would serve all explorers lucky enough to secure his services. A month later, without such wisdom to lean on, Gunnison, together with seven members of his party, was slaughtered by Ute Indians. Among the massacred was the artist R. H. Kern, who in 1849 had drawn those beautiful records of Inscription Rock for Lt. James Harvey Simpson and who had left his name with Simpson's on the rock. Perhaps Kern might have survived to add more of his skillful records of the early West, had not Antoine Leroux had to return to Albuquerque to keep that prior engagement with Lt. Whipple.

"After a busy day of packing, hustling and discomfort," Lt. Stanley confided to his diary on November 10, "we started at a late hour in the afternoon on our march over the unknown, but dreaded country we are to explore this winter. Night overtook us before we passed the Río Grande and, after marching ten miles, we encamped for the night. Our transportation consists of thirteen waggons and near one hundred mules. We have Mexican packers and start out with provisions for four months' journey. We have for guides Antoine Leroux, one of the most celebrated mountain-men in America, and Don Manuel Savedra, a Mexican from Cabilleta, a man who is said to be perfectly acquainted with the country between the Rio Grande and the Colorado." [58] Said by whom? By Don Manuel Saavedra, who had prefixed the respectful *Don* to his name to give himself stature above the humble Mexican mule packers.

Möllhausen described for German readers details of the trip soon to be published in that language and shortly thereafter in an English translation:

> Leroux was a man who had grown grey in his journeyings over mountains and deserts . . . . One part of the country through which we proposed to pass he was certainly acquainted with, for he had two years before accompanied the Expedition to the Colorado, commanded by Captain Sitgreaves, and gone down the river to the Gila; but as we could not depart very widely from the prescribed line of 35° North latitude, and it could not be the intention of the government of the United States to have the same route explored twice, Leroux would probably have to pass through some regions unknown to him.
>
> Lieutenant Whipple, however, did not the less urge his acceptance of the engagement, knowing that the old trapper's experience would soon enable him to find his way, even through hitherto unknown regions; and that in any meeting with the natives, he would make himself more easily understood than we should. The bargain was at length concluded, and Leroux agreed to accompany the Expedition to California for the consideration of 2400 dollars; and the confidence which he inspired—a confidence that had been earned by thirty years' toil in primeval wildernesses—made us all rejoice not a little at having secured his services. [45]

For some four pages Möllhausen (who would presently earn himself the title of "German James Fenimore Cooper") went on to describe in loving detail the lives and exploits of "the three oldest backwoodsmen in existence"—Thomas Fitzpatrick (the same who had carried Carson's dispatches to Washington at the behest of General Kearny), Kit Carson himself, and Antoine Leroux. "As a second guide," Möllhausen, returning to his main theme, recounted, "Lieutenant Whipple engaged a Mexican, who stated he had already visited the Colorado . . . as the experience and knowledge of the country he had gained. . . might prove of some value to us. The worthy Don Antonio Survedro [Saavedra] (as he was called by the Americans of our party) was engaged and undertook to go with us to California for the sum of 1200 dollars." [45]

Lt. Whipple's journal entry for November 8 is more cautious: "We have conversed with José Manuel Savedra, who professes to have accompanied the Moqui Indians upon an expedition against the Mojaves and also with the guide Antoine Leroux. . . . as no one has yet traversed the entire route designated in our instructions, in order to omit nothing that may contribute to success, we have secured the services of both Leroux and Savedra for the journey." [61]

Was that word "professes" entirely accidental? An old hand at commanding men, Whipple must have sensed something a trifle phony about the boastful Mexican. It is unlikely, though, that he'd found out that Saavedra had accompanied the Moquis for the purpose of stealing children of other Indian tribes to sell into slavery, or to use as slaves themselves. The warlike Yampais had put an end to it all by attacking the raiding party and forcing the men to flee. They would not have forgotten. A man with such a past, whether he knew the country well or not, could hardly be an asset to any expedition.

Antoine Leroux, on the other hand, was an immeasurably valuable asset. Well recovered both from those wounds received while on Capt. Sitgreaves's expedition and from his recent pleurisy, he could be of help to Whipple just by recalling Sitgreaves's route, knowing where that route should be followed, and, equally important, where it should be avoided. Surely a man like Leroux could not, as Möllhausen's account suggests, have personally enlisted the services of a man like Saavedra. Nevertheless, with Whipple already commited to Saavedra, mountain man Leroux was bound to accept his employer's decision, bound to withhold carping comment. Let time and experience tell.

Time and experience told by January 7, when Whipple wrote in his diary that Saavedra "returned from three days reconnaissance to the northwest, upon a trail he thinks he followed when he accompanied the Moqui Indians some years ago. He reports that he has now travelled thirty miles in that direction without finding any indication of water." [61] Lt. Whipple, obviously, was a kind and patient man who did not expect too much of an aging former traveler in a land where creeks—washes they were called—can disappear into the sands to reappear as floods after a downpour. Nevertheless, only a week after he made the above entry, his patience must have been tried to the limit: "Savedra thought he recognized a route he pursued with the Moquis twelve years since, and a few of us followed him to the top of a high hill to reconnoitre. He was entirely lost. . . ." [61] A guide, of course, should never be lost. This statement, from the man who employed him, was testimony enough to Saavedra's incompetence.

The young lieutenant expressed it frankly when, years later, as Major General David Sloane Stanley, he wrote his memoirs: "We started to explore northern Arizona by way of the Zuñi villages. Guides were hard to find. . . . After a great deal of negotiations, Leroux's services were procured, and also the services of an old humbug of a Mexican named Sanadio." Though Stanley had forgotten the name, he remembered the man all too well.

This man, now sixty-four years of age, had engaged at one time in catching women and children of the Tonto Indians for slaves—of course exterminating the men.

He pretended to know the country we were to explore, but he knew nothing and Lieutenant Whipple, to utilize him, put him to work with the pack train.

Leroux was a man of another sort. He pretended to nothing he did not know. His knowledge and experience were wonderful, and yet part of the route he had never seen. [57]

So young Stanley had to add the two-legged mule, Saavedra, to his responsibility for the four-legged ones. When, in early November, the party camped across the Rio Grande from Albuquerque, it included mules, wagons, and nearly one hundred men. It would be a point of honor for these explorers of a future wagon road to get those wagons through intact. Yet before they arrived at the banks of the Colorado, all wagons had been abandoned and that "first Monday of February next" was well past.

The romantic young quartermaster lieutenant was feeling more cheerful than when he'd set out from Fort Smith. Eight days after taking leave of "our hospitable friends at Albuquerque," he found himself

finally on the dividing ridge of the Rocky Mountains. On one side the water ran to the Atlantic; a few feet distant a neighboring drop of water set out on its long tour to the Pacific. My mind could not but indulge in a few strange musings, as I thought that I stood upon the summit of a mighty chain of mountains, that used in my boyhood days to be the enchanted region of everything dreadful and wild. The grizzly bear, the sheep that threw itself down from cliff to cliff safely, by falling on its horns, all the little tales of the story books which I perused as a child and which fancy had dwelt upon were recalled to my thoughts and I reflected, "Can I now be on the summit of these monstrous hills where I have imagined so much wonderful, frightful and wild?" [57]

On November 18, they were "encamped at the foot of Inscription Rock." The rock, of course, stirred the imaginations of the party, most of whom were viewing it for the first time. Yet of all that hundred men, only the name of one engineer, "N. H. Hutton," is identifiable there today. Whipple's name belongs on that great roster. So does Jules Marcou's and Baldwin Möllhausen's. So, especially, does young Stanley's. So does the name of Stanley's classmate at the military academy, Whipple's second in command, topographical engineer Lieutenant Joseph Christmas Ives, whom, strangely, Stanley's diary never mentions.

Five years later, Lt. Ives would be in charge of an expedition instructed to explore the Colorado River from its mouth upward. He made an outstandingly minute hydrographic survey, much of the way carried in an iron steamer he'd had constructed in Philadelphia, then shipped west in sections, via Panama and San Francisco, to the river's mouth! Though that boat could not steam all the way upriver into the Grand Canyon (then called the Big Canyon), it enabled Lt. Ives to become the first man of European antecedents to set foot on the floor of that canyon.

Surely this feat was as worthy of a record on the great rock as had been Juan de Oñate's expedition to the South Sea. But Joseph Christmas Ives, taking the easier sea route, did not choose to pass that way on his return trip.

Like Juan de Oñate's feat, that Colorado exploration was the man's crowning achievement, as his delightfully written and meticulously documented account, published among government papers in 1861, demonstrates. By that year, New York City–born and –educated Ives was throwing in his lot with the Confederacy, having refused a captain's commission with Union forces. For the Confederates, Ives first became a captain of engineers, then chief engineer of the department that included the coasts of South

Carolina, Georgia, and eastern Florida, finally aide-de-camp to Confederate President, former Secretary of War Jefferson Davis. At the war's end, Ives retired without commission or status (like Juan de Oñate of two and a half centuries before). He died in his native New York in 1868 when only forty years of age. Such fluid and ill-starred loyalty belongs to the times and mentalities of those Spanish conquistadors.

Even the 1853 expedition's commander, Lt. Whipple, seemed to see no reason to add his own name to the distinguished list on the rock. Nor did his report try to enlarge upon the detailed description Lt. Simpson made four years earlier. Möllhausen would sketch the impressive pile for openmouthed German readers. Both he and Whipple climbed it to gaze with wonder across the wild land and to ask yet again how any people could have managed to build there the fortress town whose ruins they visited or to dwell there with no water source closer than the pool far below at the rock's base.

Three days later they were visiting the Zuñis in their town. Young Stanley, perhaps expecting a wild, untutored savage, was inpressed by the talent of the Indian governor of the place. At the same time he was "disagreeably struck by the frightful state in which the smallpox had left some of its surviving victims" with no clothes to keep mercifully hidden any part of their horribly scarred bodies. Smallpox, along with other foreign diseases, was one of the grimmest gifts of white men to natives of many lands, none of whom could have developed any slightest resistance to the inroads of such infections.

That same night was "killing cold" and the next day was passed in camp with the young quartermaster "resorting to any and every expedient to kill time"—except, perhaps, fraternizing with his classmate Ives. November 30 saw the party at Mud Springs where Navajos approached, but firmly, in view of possible smallpox, rejected an invitation to visit the camp. Their wisdom was demonstrated the next day when one of the exploring party (apparently unprotected by vaccination) developed that disease.

Within four days, they were realizing that the disease was still widespread among the Indians. Some men, returning from a visit to the Moquis, "report that the smallpox has been awful in that place. Only six persons are left living in a place that lately contained four or five hundred. The dead are left unburied to the ravages of wolf and vulture." Everyone felt depressed and Leroux, sensing this, outdid himself to entertain the whole company with tales of his many past adventures and hairbreadth escapes.

December 13 saw the party within sight of the San Francisco Mountains where they came upon "a chasm probably one hundred feet in depth," as Whipple estimated, "the sides precipitous, and about three hundred feet across at the top. A threadlike rill could be seen below but descent was impossible. There was not the slightest indication of a stream till we stood on the brink and looked down into the cañon. . . . Beyond, upon the course we wished to explore, the country looked like a nearly level prairie." [61]

This was Canyon Diablo—Devil's Canyon—still to be located upon today's roadmaps whence so many names familiar of old have disappeared. Now it is spanned by a highway bridge, and it's the rare passerby that pauses to give it more than a quick glance or to gaze into its depths and reflect upon the kind of barrier that made the early exploring expeditions so risky.

Nearly twenty years after Whipple had passed that way, Major John Wesley Powell—that first man to navigate in a frail boat the full length of the Grand Canyon—would describe the whole region in dramatic terms: "Every river . . . has cut another canyon; every brook runs in a canyon; every rill born of a shower and born again of a shower and living only during these showers has cut itself a canyon; so that the whole upper portion of the basin of the Colorado is traversed by a labyrinth of these deep gorges." [49]

Unaware of such an approaching drop until they had stampeded to its rim, runaway mules plunged headlong into the canyon while men pursuing these animals narrowly escaped breaking their necks. In such an area, Capt. Sitgreaves had finally become convinced that there could be no percentage in continuing his northward course toward the main Colorado. No wagon road was to be built and maintained there.

Young Stanley was finding the canyons gloomily uninviting, yet admitted a debt of gratitude to the Little Colorado for the many "hearty draughts I have taken of its pure wholesome waters," which compensated for the difficult descent with water free from the alkali contamination of many springs and washes.

There turned out to be enough snow to make a white, if intensely cold Christmas, which they "were not behind our friends in the States in celebrating." Beginning on Christmas Eve, a huge eggnog was enjoyed by all (did they have hencoops on their wagons?) in a hilarity that "made the solitary mountains resound." Whipple recorded,

> Christmas Eve had been celebrated with considerable éclat. The fireworks were decidedly magnificent. Tall, isolated pines surrounding the camp were set on fire. The flames leaped to the tree tops and then, dying away, sent up innumerable brilliant sparks. An Indian dance by *ci-devant* Návaho prisoners, was succeeded by songs from the teamsters, and a pastoral enacted by the Mexicans, after their usual custom at this season. Leroux's servant, a tamed Crow Indian, and a herder then performed a duet improvisatore, in which they took the liberty of saying what they pleased of the company present. [61]

While raucous laughter at certainly obscene topical comments filled the air and eggnog compounded the atmosphere, unrelaxed Leroux—as Möllhausen tells it—sat "with a face considerably redder than the fire alone could have made it, smoked his pipe and, as he looked on complacently, observed, 'What a splendid opportunity for Indians to surprise us tonight!'" [45]

Clearly, Lt. Whipple's number had not yet come up. He would survive all the hazards of his expedition—smallpox, venomous snakes, icy winds, yawning chasms, as well as that most reckless of Christmas Eve celebrations—to receive, as a Union officer ten years later, a mortal wound at the Battle of Chancellorsville. Ironically, this would come at almost the precise moment the battle ended.

For their uncontested passage through the same land Sitgreaves had found so inhospitable, the explorers might have thanked the gruesome smallpox epidemic that Whipple, as well as young Stanley, described. "Smallpox has been making terrible ravages among the people," he had noted of Zuñi. Moqui he found still worse, with the whole population practically wiped out where, as Leroux told him, Sitgreaves had found "the hills covered with savages." At that point, Whipple had not yet come upon the fresh track of a single Indian.

Such epidemics were to remain a constant menace to native populations until widespread vaccination became available and was practiced. As late as 1898–99, another terrible epidemic would be raging in Zuñi, but this time ministered to by a European (by ancestry, at least) missionary. Andrew VanderWagen and his wife remained with their charges, nursing them to the best of their abilities. Nevertheless the toll was large—289 out of a total population of about 1,800. "A.v.d.W.—Zuñi—1898" carved on the rock insures that the minister be not entirely forgotten.

By February 7, 1854, Whipple's expedition arrived at the Colorado at a point, as they had hoped, well below its forbidding canyons. Even without the wagons, all of which had been left by the wayside, crossing presented many problems. "Crossed the river today," wrote the lieutenant in charge of the operation, "crossing our goods over on a pontoon boat, sustaining various upsets—and swimming our mules. The Indians, who swim in the water like so many beavers, put our sheep across"—one hundred out of the five hundred that had set out from Albuquerque—"not without drowning some, owing to their becoming entangled in the rope by which we drew the boat across the stream. . . . Perhaps a thousand naked savages—men, women and children—surrounded us all day and some of the scenes of the day were highly picturesque and interesting."

For years to come this crossing would remain picturesque and interesting and a very serious problem, military as well as technical. Here was always a time and a place where the river crossers were perfectly at the mercy of Indians whose mercy was ever doubtful, and whose motives—to keep their land inviolable—increasingly certain.

At the time of Whipple's crossing in one of their friendlier moods, those Mojave Indians came in to trade, as well as to look the newcomers over: "They examined Leroux pretty closely," Whipple noted, "and then pointing towards the northwest, indicated that they had seen him before in that direction. The accused blushed but stoutly denied the fact, at the same time pulling his hat over one side of his head to conceal the wound they had given him there two years ago." [61] This time, apparently, the Mojaves were not on the warpath.

The way to the coast now presented relatively few problems so that Whipple could arrive in San Diego almost exactly a month after the Colorado River crossing. More of a problem would be compliance with Secretary of War Jefferson Davis's request, expressed in a letter dated four days before that crossing, that Whipple should "with as little delay as possible furnish the department with a report of your operations." [24] With the original deadline long passed, perhaps the secretary of war hoped for a promit preliminary report. The final report, with all its impressive scientific data and beautifully hand-colored illustrations, would not be published until 1857.

As a compensation, Davis and his fellow Southerners must have been delighted to be told by an impartial Northerner like Whipple that no insurmountabie barrier stood in the way of joining their section of the States to California. Whipple assured them that he saw no doubt remaining "that, for the construction of a railway, the route we have passed over is not only practicable but in many respects advantageous."

While the armchair railroad planners in Washington kept on planning, something practicable must be started toward the realization of their hopes. A still more precise survey, combined with actual roadbuilding, should now be undertaken. The expense of all this might be justified in that it would serve the need for better cross-country roads for the constantly increasing numbers of emigrants to the far West. The surveyor should be instructed to keep in mind, too, the projected railroad—to seek out not-too-steep grades through negotiable mountain passes, wood for burning in locomotives, water for steam power. Grass for emigrant cattle would, of course, be found conveniently near the water.

The man finally chosen to take charge of this survey-plus-roadbuilding venture would be no topographical engineer but that former naval lieutenant whose scientific education at the Naval Institute had supplied the needed technical know-how. His post-graduate training under Kit Carson had added both familiarity with the route to be traversed and with the techniques needed for wilderness survival (which, perhaps Lt. Gunnison had lacked). Even so, it would be the summer of 1857—four years after Whipple had set out—before the new party was prepared to make its start from Albuquerque.

8

Westward Drifters

California-bound emigrants were supplying a happy excuse for the investment in time and money being expended upon a wagon road thither. Actually, though, many of those California-bound emigrants would have headed west with their families, wagon road or not, with or without the protection of military escorts. Those men, neither reckless nor quite indifferent to their families' needs, were just incurably restless and temperamentally unequipped to settle anywhere for long.

Had they really wished to settle, such emigrants could have found plenty of land and space for their families well to the east of New Mexico Territory. What they lacked was a capacity to put down roots anywhere. Always beyond the setting sun, they persuaded themselves, were richer lands, an easier life, wider opportunities, better living conditions. Always they kept on moving westward, eyes still on the setting sun, until, learning of the gold strike in California, they took the last wide leap to a land whence they could trek no farther west and where the bright metal, no matter what its assay, would always prove to be just another kind of fool's gold.

In a sense, these restless men formed a transition between the hunter-trapper-mountain men, whose way of life was inevitably passing, and the determined settler, ready to die if need be in defense of his landholdings. A few exceptional mountain men, like Carson and Leroux, were bridging the gap by accepting employment as expedition guides or in government service. Marriage to a charming Mexican lady who could preside graciously over a real home, completed the transformation of each of these outstanding mountain men. And there were some settlers like Ned Beale, who so valued his Tejón property, yet shared enough of the mountain-man, wilderness-loving temperament to keep open lines of communication with those mountain men and help interpret their lives and points of view for ages yet to come.

It was the in-between men, belonging to neither extreme, equipped with neither's special skills, who would restlessly fumble and grope their way into disaster. Typical of these in most ways was the "John Udell" who in July 1858 left his name in Inscription Rock as "first emigrant" along Lt. Beale's newly scouted road but who, less than a year later, would be relying upon Beale's steadiness and wilderness know-how to see his emigration through to its destination.

Fortunately, the one way in which John Udell was not typical of his kind was in his systematic keeping of a journal. John—lay preacher, ex-farmer, peddler, and what-would-you—concerned himself little with types, whether hunter-trapper, settler, or in-between. Pious, hardworking, and literate, he has bequeathed us a picture not only of his own life, but of the kind of background that produced so many of those westward drifters who rode the trails to the Pacific.

Through that record, we can see that John was an almost predictable product of a long line of hard-luck Udells. It was Lionel Udell, who arrived in Connecticut in the late 1600s, at the time of the rebellion against King James II, who set a pattern of mobility, bad judgment, and bad luck for his American descendants to follow. A pill pusher and innkeeper of Exeter, England, Lionel departed thence on the run a few paces ahead of arresting officers who had discovered he had been guilty of the capital crime of entertaining in his inn a party of rebels.

Knowing it could do little good to risk his neck by insisting he had been unaware of the true character of his guests, Lionel hastily conferred with his wife, instructing her to dispose of their property and then follow him to America with Lionel, Jr. After this, Lionel, Sr. "escaped through the back window with his pillbags on his arm, and went on board a ship owned by him, then lying in the harbor, and set sail for America." Overtaken by a storm, both ship and cargo were lost. The passengers were picked up by another vessel bound for Stonington, Connecticut, and it was there, John later wrote, that "my grandfather settled and resumed the practice of medicine."

English wife and child never made it to America. They died in England, according to husband Lionel, though of what and in precisely what year his grandson seemed uninformed; the plague, perhaps, for it was raging at about that time. Presently, the "physician" of Stonington married a local girl by whom he would have eleven children.

Lionel's tenth child, grandfather of our John, followed the Udell pattern of bad luck by taking to the sea as a ship's master. In some port he contracted yellow fever and died, leaving his family a large legacy of debts to clear. The shipmaster's son also went to sea in a sailing vessel, also met with bad luck, being twice captured by the English, twice by the French, and finally losing his ship by fire. Exactly what, one wonders, was he doing at sea that he should have been captured so many times. Freebooting, perhaps?

By 1807, the career of independent shipmaster began to lose its glamor and the family moved to Schodak on the Hudson River so that the erstwhile shipmaster "might rig and run a sloop on that river in the employ of the Schermahorns. I was employed as cook and cabin boy, and here we remained two years." During those years, "some inventions of great utility and improvement were presented to the public." One of these, Robert Fulton's application of steam power to propel a vessel, may have suggested that the handwriting was on the wall for the profession of sailing master.

In any case, it was all the excuse a restless Udell needed for turning his back upon both sea and river. In 1810 he moved to western Pennsylvania, while 1816 saw him progressing to Ohio, whither he had been preceded by his twenty-one-year-old son, New York City–born John. Over four decades later, John, not having deviated from the family pattern of keeping on the move, would have spanned the continent several times, on the last trip leaving his name upon Inscription Rock in far New Mexico.

In Ohio, John soon made a gesture toward settling down with schoolteaching Emily Merrill, a year older than himself, who thus became bound to keep on the move with her restless husband, eventually accompanying him in the wagon train that camped by the rock in 1858. "She appeared," John wrote in his autobiography, "to possess quite an amiable, modest disposition, was somewhat intelligent, with unblemished character, and had been taught the principles of piety and religion by strictly pious Presbyterian parents. . . . This lady possessed a degree of beauty, with her other qualities, but I was more enamored with her accomplishments and engaging manners, and concluded to make suit for her hand in marriage. . . . We were married on the third of the following December." [60]

Just the faintest whiff of romantic impulsivemess is suggested in John's admission that "perhaps this [marriage] was premature, as we had neither house nor home prepared. . . . My wife had a bed and a few articles wherewith to commence housekeeping." As it turned out, John would never have any house or home fully prepared.

He would acquire land, erect a log cabin thereon, put together some crude furniture. After that, with enthusiasm for settling down gradually cooling, John "made some improvements on my land, but the greater part of the time, worked by day at sundry small jobs; often walking five or six miles through the wilderness to the scene of my labors, which were of the heaviest kind. . . . I carried home all my provisions on my shoulders for two years, not being able to buy a horse." [60]

Soon he was absenting himself from home for weeks, peddling herb distillates of his own brewing. When he could borrow or hire a horse and wagon, he carried things to sell on commission, adding, further, some kind of religious tract of his own composition. When no wagon was to be had, John walked like any old-fashioned pack peddler. Later, in 1856, he made the amazing estimate that he had by then, covered some 76,075 miles on foot. Physical effort, even of the most strenuous kind, he could accept. It was the act of settling down irrevocably, even though comfortably, that was completely alien to his temperament. His wife's reaction to all this never seemed important enough to be mentioned.

Soon leaving that first cabin home for "a house I built on the road," John erected a barn and planted apple trees (which no farmer could possibly expect to yield any kind of fruit in fewer than ten years). When, long before the ten years had passed, his house burned down, he deserted those tender shoots and "having walked fifteen miles to Jefferson [Ohio], bought my three acres of land, chopped house logs and rolled up my house." No reason suggested, save the obvious one of keeping on the move, as to why he did not "roll up" a house on the site of his burned one. Later he added more land to those three acres, and again planted fruit trees whose fruit, of course, he would never remain to harvest. In 1828, he built a "fine, comfortable framed house," which he improved two years later, and inevitably sold in 1831, together with the surrounding sixteen acres.

Almost at once thereafter, John had "contracted for sixty acres of land in Madison, Geauga County," but 1832 saw him back in Jefferson, 1834 in Windsor, Ohio. In 1837, he was acquiring eighty acres of land in Zanesville. Always on the move, he would, within the space of thirty years, make fifteen "permanent" moves that involved building at least seven log cabins and two framed houses on plots of land ranging in size from small city lots to one hundred and sixty acres. Fire, flood, foreclosure took one house each, the remainder he sold or traded.

Meanwhile the family was growing, a matter John seemed to take so much for granted as not to find it worthy of mention. Though none of this could have been easy for his wife, she perhaps accepted it as woman's unavoidable lot. Since in those days it was a rare family whose every child survived the hazards of childhood to reach maturity, we can only guess at the agonies of bearing a child in the wilderness, as Emily Udell did, only to see it die in some mortal illness. In 1856, when all surviving children must have been grown, John listed eight by name. Beyond that, he gives no slightest inkling as to their personalities, though it is reasonable to guess that some, at least, took after their parents in restlessness, vigor, and narrowmindedness.

In 1841, John was moving his family from Ohio to Missouri, the reason given being that "my family were no longer satisfied to remain in the rough, broken country where we were living. A number of German families had settled around us, whose language, customs, and manners differed unpleasantly from our own." Missouri, of which one of John's brothers had given "a most flattering description," seemed to beckon irresistably.

Making the journey alone and entirely on foot—this must have been one of those many times when he could afford no horse— John purchased land on the Missouri River. By his forty-seventh birthday, June 22, 1842, he was back in Ohio, busily disposing of property there and arranging for the move to his Missouri land. The whole Udell family arrived there in May 1843.

John "immediately raised a log cabin . . . and bought provisions to last us through the summer, having to go twenty-five miles to get my grain ground." With inevitable Udell bad judgment, he erected his cabin too close to the river, which, unlike the short, relatively tame rivers he'd known in northern Ohio, drained the melting snows and rainfall of a huge and distant mountain basin.

This mistake in judgment was almost immediately brought disastrously home to him. "I had just got my provisions, and cows and calves, and two yoke of oxen all home, and had moved into my cabin, when it commenced raining. For twenty-four hours, the rain fell in torrents. . . . The river rose with alarming rapidity."

When, during the night, a makeshift dam upriver gave way, "the floodgates of destruction seemed thrown open. We perceived that our cabin was filling, and we had no chance of escaping. We had only a temporary door; this gave way and our provisions, furniture, and clothes were carried off in the flood . . . I was obliged to get my family on the roof for safety. Here we spent the night." [60]

An awful night of thunder, lighting, and flood it must have been. Calmer morning light revealed that though all the calves had been drowned, oxen and cows had found their way to higher ground where they were just able to keep their heads above the flood. Fortunately, the very green cabin logs had been too heavy to float off, so John could hitch his oxen to the logs and draw them to the hillock where a man of better judgment would have erected his cabin at the start.

Were the Udells, now at a safe distance from those so-distasteful German neighbors, at last contented? Not for long, of course. Especially when they came to realize, as they soon did, that they were bound to perform tasks regarded in Missouri as fit only for slaves. "Not satisfied to live in a slave state without owning slaves," John's family talked John into returning to the Ohio they'd left so hopefully less than three years before. "In this move," John, now fifty, wrote, "I sacrificed nearly all that I had left."

Life resumed the old pattern. Taking another book agency, John kept on the move—to Missouri again, to Iowa, to Ohio, back to Missouri. Inevitably, with the excitement engendered by the little sack of gold Ned Beale carried to Washington, John must set out for the far West. Three times he crossed to California via the northern plains. Three times, neither richer nor wiser, John returned to Missouri via the Central American route, which entailed crossing the Isthmus at some point farther south than Ned Beale had taken with his gold.

"At the time of my first visit to California in 1850," John tells us,

the only miner's tools in use were pick, shovel, pan, and rocker,
or cradle—an apparatus about the size of a common cradle, with
a sieve in the head, into which we poured the dirt containing the
gold. Then, with one hand rocking the cradle, we poured water
upon the dirt with a tin dipper in the other, thus washing all the
earth which contained the gold into the box underneath, while
the water carried away the dirt. By this means, one man could
dig and wash from fifty to two hundred buckets-full of dirt a day.
A yield of five cents to each bucket was considered profitable,
less than that not.[60]

Longer and longer troughs were eventually to replace the cradle, the one absolute essential being a reliable supply of water:
"some very good mines could not be worked at all because there
was no water."

Good mines, water or not, would never be for a luckless Udell.
Even the five-cent minimum escaped him. In 1853, he reported,
he "mined steadily and made little over $2 a day." He did better
peddling a wagonload of melons in Sacramento or cutting and
selling hay at $40 a ton for mules of luckier miners. Nevertheless,
though he returned to the East later in 1853, he'd be back working
in the goldfields in 1854 and again in 1855, always without
conspicuous success.

After the third trip, it occurred to John that there yet remained
one untapped source of profit from those otherwise unprofitable
trips. The book agent in him perceived that many of the dedicated
stay-at-homes who'd been asking about the plains and the Indians
would readily pay for a book by a traveler who obviously knew his
way west. Would-be travelers could be sold such a book, too. The
hand that had rocked the cradle with limited success should now
do a lot better wielding the pen.

Having spent a summer assembling and copying his material,
John set out "to solicit subscribers for the narrative of my life and
travels . . . walking hither and thither, east and west, north and
south. . . . My success is good, but the fatigue . . . tells upon my
time-worn constitution." That narrative, *Incidents of Travel to
California Across the Great Plains. . .*, issued in 1856, is most
interesting for the detailed and explicit account of life in a series of

frontier settlements and, by implication, of the type of person inhabiting those settlements.

"Every two persons," John advises would-be travelers in an appendix, "should have two good yoke of well broken . . . oxen, and one yoke of young cows or . . . steers—all well shod; a good strong, light wagon, covered with Osnaburg cloth . . .

"Two men are enough to travel peaceably and comfortably with one wagon. Let them take such a team, with the necessary provisions, and follow the instructions of my book, and unless some act of Divine Providence prevent, they will go through safely." [61]

John was to challenge that Divine Providence once too often by emigrating, in 1858, "to California, across the Plains, with my aged wife—she being in her sixty-fifth year and I in my sixty-fourth year of age." The old folks had decided to join their grown children residing in California "to have the care of, and to be sustained . . . in our feeble old age." [61]

Feeble, indeed! Fourteen years later, after adventures that should have exhausted far younger men, Udell would still be alive in California.

April 8, 1858, saw the Udells setting forth from Missouri, with two young men "to drive and take care of my team and to do all the necessary labor to be done while on the journey." He took with him sufficient livestock, a good riding horse, and "everything necessary to make travellers to California as comfortable as they could be made. . . . Travel today, 10 miles." With that extra-sticky, deep, spring mud Missouri residents know so well, ten miles would not be a very short day's trip.

A bit over two weeks later, they crossed the Misssouri River on a "steam ferryboat," to join forces nine miles beyond, on the border of Kansas Territory, with a wagon train that included about twenty men, a "number of women and children" as well as about thirty-five horses and mules and nearly ten times that number of cattle. The train's proprietor was prosperous L. J. Rose, who ten years earlier, at the age of twenty-two, had arrived in Iowa from Illinois. Superintendent of Rose's train was Alpha Brown, aged forty-six, of a character sufficiently high to win even critical John Udell's approval, with the additional qualification of having already once crossed the Plains to California.

"I made arrangements," recorded Udell, "to travel with this

company. . . . We all agreed to travel the Santa Fe route, through
New Mexico." Though he did not elaborate, this choice was the
result of "the Mormon troubles in Utah," as one of the former
cattle hands reminisced years later. [61]

It needed the incurable optimism of westward drifters, thus
encumbered with families and livestock, to undertake to travel a
little traveled desert route where pasturage must be scanty, water
even scantier, and the terrain so rough as to damage the feet of the
livestock that had to walk every weary mile. They were bound to
meet not only settled and civilized Indians like the Zuñis, but
Mojaves, who would cut out whatever cattle they might covet for
food.

Though attacking Indians could possibly be held off, the emigrants could do little about the cattle stampedes that usually
followed upon Indian attacks. At the Missouri River, such problems could have little urgency. Thereafter, for the two months it
took for the train to arrive in Albuquerque, things seemed to go
smoothly and happily, through all we learn from unimaginative
John's diary is a catalogue of water availability, weather, pasturage,
road conditions, miles traveled—all-important details to a would-
be traveler of those days but monotonous to a reader of today. Too
rarely does he offer us a glimpse of some truly interesting episode
of wagon train life, though he does favor us with an occasional
interesting sketch of places visited.

June 22 shows a typically pious entry: "This is my sixty-third
birthday. My three score years and ten are almost spent; may I so
appreciate it that I may be prepared to leave this earthly house
sooner than that, if my Lord should call me." (Though he might
have prepared himself, he had not, as it would presently turn out,
resigned himself to leaving his earthly house.) "We came three
miles and camped two miles from Albuquerque, making it 826
miles from the Missouri River according to my calculation by time
and gait." Time and gait had brought his calculation of the distance
amazingly close to that we may now compute from road maps.

On the following day: "Took my effects into town to have some
repairing done on my wagon." A few days later, still camped in the
same spot, he was explaining, "The Rio Grande River is about one
mile wide here, from bank to bank; it rises in the Rocky Mountains
and enters into the Gulf of Mexico; it runs with great velocity," but

only in June floods, he might have added, had he remained there long enough to see the summer's rainlessness shrink it to a trickle.

Udell went on to give a brief description of the early town near what residents of the large modern city call Old Town.

> Albuquerque is situated on the east bank [of the Rio Grande] at the crossing of Mr. Beale's route; it is a large Mexican village; the houses are built of adobe, like all other Mexican villages, in a rude manner; it has several mercantile houses, a Catholic church, and several blacksmith and carpenter shops; there are one hundred and eighty-nine soldiers stationed here, under the command of Colonel C. H. Bonneville. There are several intelligent American families living here; they treated us with great attention and respect. [61]

"Mr. Beale's route" would have been on many tongues, for town gossip had to be full of the successful 1857 wagon road survey and of the new one now about to set out from Fort Smith, Arkansas. That road just might turn frontier Albuquerque into an important stopping place for California-bound wagon trains in need of fresh supplies and equipment repairs.

Beale's former guide Saavedra was certainly there, making sure that wagon train leaders knew how much experience he had had, letting the timorous and inexperienced guess what dangers lay ahead, and, acknowledging that he, Saavedra, was just the man a wagon train needed to guide it safely through to the Colorado River crossing. With Beale's official report yet to be published and Beale himself safely occupied hundreds of miles to the east, the too-persuasive guide could give his tongue free rein.

Strangely, Udell does not whisper of the other talk that must have been raging in Albuquerque; about the weird new kind of animal Beale had been testing for service in dry desert land where mules and horses, often without water to drink or forage plants to eat, might drop in their tracks. The very fact that those new animals, imported at considerable government expense, were being put to such a test, should have warned the emigrants of the grave water and forage problems bound to harass a train encumbered with great herds of cattle. Had the would-be guide been knowledgeable enough to use that argument, John Udell could hardly have failed to note it.

9

The Great
Camel Experiment

Were watching ghosts of those Indians who once dwelt atop
Inscription Rock to cast votes as to the strangest sight passing
centuries had brought to their view, to a ghost they must vote for
those incredible animals Lt. Beale brought to their pool in August
1857. Stranger and less believable than horses once had been,
these ungainly, shaggy, long-legged, humped beasts seemed to
regard the dry, infertile land with fiercely supercilious eyes.
Deserts were nothing new to them.

In part it was this quality that had brought them there. In part,
though the Indians could not realize it, it was thanks to the horses
earlier generations of Europeans had brought to the land. Taking
to horses with the avidity of a resourceful, transportationless race,
mounted Plains Indians soon had become the scourge of Pueblo
Indians, of settlers, of the bands of soldiers who, stationed in
widely separated frontier forts, often found it hard to hold their
own against highly mobile bands of marauding Indians. Wagon
trains were bound to be less successful in dealing with marauders.

Though limited in numbers, the soldiers could have done better
had their animals—horses and mules—been secure from the twin
threats of Indian thefts and of death by starvation and thirst during
long desert treks. Because of the first of these threats, oxen were
often the emigrants' draft animals of choice since Indians valued
slow-moving oxen only as possible food. Yet oxen were equally
likely to fall prey to that grim second threat.

What the Southwest had come to need was an all-but-impossible animal: one that few Indians would covet, but that could pack heavy loads, walk endless miles, feed upon the unappetizing plants native to desert regions, and survive days, if need be, without fresh water. What the Southwest needed, in short, was the camels that August 23, 1857, brought to Inscription Rock.

Not, of course, that most of the Southwest was aware of its needs for camels or ready to welcome them with open arms. Indians were frankly terrified of them (which should have been a score in the camels' favor). Mule skinners detested them from the start. Not only did camels frighten mules and horses out of their wits, but they posed an active threat—as would, much later equally unfamiliar horseless carriages—to the old accepted mode of transportation over which the mule skinners presided. It did not help that the newly arrived animals ignored commands in good English, responding only to the outlandish tongues of professional camel drivers—Arabs, Armenians, and Greeks—who had been imported along with their charges.

So the camels gathered near the rock on that memorable day in 1857 were, quite unawares, facing all the problems always belonging to an alien minority. They had their active and enthusiastic sponsors and their violently unreasoning antagonists, and probably cared equally little about either. Far from home and the comfortingly familiar sights and smells of Near East camel caravans, they must have had twinges of homesickness for the life they'd left behind. Certainly they could not have cared less that they were part of a new experiment that might, so their sponsors dreamed, revolutionize all frontier transportation.

Their sponsors, caring a great deal about them, watched over them with yearning eyes and a determination to make the experiment succeed. How heavy a load could a camel carry? How much was it right or wise to ask one to carry? How were they to be loaded? Could their unshod feet withstand the sharp bits of lava that strewed so much of the rough terrain? How many miles per day might be expected of them? Would they take to plants growing native in southwestern deserts or must grain and forage be packed for them as it was for mules? And what about water? Was it really true, as legend had long asserted, that camels could go for days without a fresh supply? None of these questions, as applied to the American Southwest, could be answered by reading books about Oriental camel caravans.

It was highly appropriate that the first man to undertake there a full-fledged test of navigation with these newly acquired ships of the desert should be the naval Lieutenant Edward Fitzgerald Beale. Instructed to chart and lay out a road from Fort Defiance in New Mexico Territory (today just across the Arizona State line), to a Colorado River crossing into California, Ned found the assignment doubly welcome. Not only was he finally receiving the appointment of his dreams, but having played an active part in urging the trial of camels and in getting the project started, he was far more eager to undertake this trial run with camels than would a man who was secretly convinced that it was all a harebrained scheme.

The plan itself had been in Ned's mind for some years. A highly literate as well as exploration-minded young man in an exploration-minded century, Ned had been among the first to purchase the Abbé Huc's *Travels in Tartary, Thibet, and China* when, in 1851, a year after it appeared in France, it was published in English translation. It was a copy of this book, he later told friends, that he had tossed into his pack the time he and Kit Carson set out together to explore Death Valley on the California-Nevada border, probably the first white men so to do. Of course it was from this book Ned read aloud, as was his custom, while the two friends sat in camp in the midst of one of the bleakest desert areas of the continent.

The sandy wastes of Mongolia which the Abbé so effectively described had their counterpart in the surrounding Death Valley, as plaintive sounds from thirsty mules reminded reader and listener alike. "The absence of rich pasturage and fresh water," Ned Beale read, "is very adverse to the growth of cattle." One can see Kit yawning at this all too obvious fact, then listening more attentively as Ned continued, "but the camel, whose robust and hardy temperament adapts itself to the most sterile regions, affords compensations to the Tartars. . . . This animal, a perfect treasure to the dwellers in the desert, can remain a fortnight, or even a month without eating or drinking." [38]

Shaking his head in disbelief, Kit nevertheless continued to listen politely. "However wretched the land upon which it is put to feed," Ned continued reading, "it can always find wherewithal to satisfy its hunger, especially if the soil be impregnated with salt or nitre. Things that no other animal will touch, to it are welcome; briars, thorns, dry wood itself, supply it with efficient food." [38]

At this point the campers would take long looks at their unhappy mules and decide, "Huh! We could do with a couple of camels right here and now."

Ned, who had already been told of the remarkable beasts by relatives who had served in consular posts in the Near East, read on in growing excitement, "Though it costs so little to keep the camel, it is of a utility inconceivable to those not acquainted with the countries in which Providence has placed it. Its ordinary load is from 700 to 800 pounds, and it can carry this load ten leagues a day. Those, indeed, which are employed to carry despatches, are expected to travel eighteen leagues per diem, but then they only carry a despatch bearer." [38]

Eighteen leagues! Fifty-four miles, possibly more! No horse or mule, loaded or not, did that, especially not in the desert. It was enough to make both men gasp, though Kit still hesitated to accept the tale as truth. To Ned it seemed that if Providence had failed to place the camel in the American Southwest, it should be no sacrilege to assist Providence in the task. Looking about at the unmitigated bleakness of Death Valley, his enthusiasm for giving camels a try in such areas grew momentarily.

Within two years after the publication of the English edition of the Abbé's book, Beale and cousin Gwinn Harris Heap (fresh from the Orient), were taking that "central route to the Pacific." Heap could not have missed the basic similarity between the dry lands of the Southwest and those near Tunis, in North Africa where, as an American consul's son, he had grown up. Certainly the cousins talked it all over of an evening before dousing their campfire. And perhaps ghosts of camel caravans haunted them through the nights.

When the book about their travels was published, Heap added an appendix entitled *Camels as a Substitute for Horses and Mules, etc.*:

During our journey across the continent, I took particular note of the country, with reference to its adaptation to the use of camels and dromedaries, and to ascertain whether these animals might be introduced with advantage on our extensive plains.

Having by residence of some years in Asia and Africa, become well acquainted with their qualities and powers of endurance, I am now convinced they would be of inestimable value in traversing the dry and barren regions between the Colorado and the Sierra Nevada; and I am glad the Secretary of War has asked for an appropriation for the purpose of importing a certain number, in order to test their usefulness. [37]

To the camels' credit, Heap went on to list "their power to endure hunger and thirst," with quotes from the Abbé in support of this; "their strength, speed, and endurance," again citing the Abbé; and the "longevity of the camel" which, estimated to be from forty to fifty years, should make the purchase of camels a good long-term investment. There would, he suggested, accrue an extra economic advantage in the milk to be obtained from female camels, though how and by whom the temperamental animals were to be milked, he forbore to suggest. There was, further, wool to be had from camels of both sexes. Some years later, when a camel camp had actually been set up in Texas, a lady there sent President Pierce a pair of camel's hair socks for which she had carded, spun, and knit the wool obtained as a part of the animal's annual shedding of hair.

Without a gift of this kind to prod him, Secretary of War Jefferson Davis had already asked Congress, as Heap mentioned, to make an appropriation sufficient to pay for an experimental camel herd. Congress was under pressure from other sources to provide for a U.S. Camel Corps, camels being a too obvious answer to many of the problems of desert transportation not to have suggested themselves to military minds faced with the urgent need of getting supplies to remote outposts. For about twenty years, a Major Crossman had been urging the establishment of a camel corps. More recently Major Henry Wayne of the Quartermaster Corps was particularly interested in making the trial since it was directly involved with the problems of keeping military supplies moving to wherever the military might need them.

None of the distant southwestern outposts could be self-sufficient. With luck, guns of soldiers and officers, supplemented by hired Indian hunters, might keep an outpost supplied with sufficient meat. In a good season mules might find sufficient grass to keep them alive. Practically everything else must be brought in from far away, if it could be brought in at all.

Today, if you are interested enough, you may visit crumbling ruins of once remote outposts, located primarily with the strategic importance of the site in mind—Fort Selden or Fort Cummings or others named for now long forgotten heroes. Others boasted more evocative names like Fort Union or Fort Defiance.

In all these places soldiers lived on limited supplies, fighting wind and sand and scurvy and loneliness as much as the Indians they had been sent to hold in check. Some of their forts were built of adobe—large compacted bricks of sun-dried mud—for building timber is a rare and costly commodity in areas where trees are, when encountered, small and few. Today the drab adobe ruins have mostly weathered back into shapeless piles of dirt. Other forts were built of stone, so that remains of quarters and stables and storehouses still stand forth in impotent menace against the stark landscape and wide, wide sky.

Except for the all-too-rare times when rain falls, the wind that sweeps down unchecked from great mountain heights still picks up masses of sand, still mercilessly drives the stinging grit into skin and eyes. The only escape from these blows of indifferent nature is behind walls. The only compensation for the soldiers in their crowded quarters would be in such creature comforts as supply trains might manage to bring in. The Sahara or the deserts of Arabia could not, it seemed, be more hostile to both men and animals. In such a land, only an animal born and bred to desert life could be truly at home.

Perceiving this, those officers of the Quartermaster Corps were actively lobbying for the introduction of animals which could, reputedly, carry within themselves several days' water supply and could pasture on desert plants. Admittedly, there might be unforseen problems in the use of camels in the American Southwest, yet problems could only be pinpointed and dealt with when and if a trial of camels under field conditions might be made.

The biggest problem of all was that no trial of camels could be made until camels were on hand to try. And there could be no camels to try until camels were purchased in the only markets where they were for sale—North Africa or the East, Near, Middle, or Far. Camels, furthermore, could not be purchased anywhere until money was made available with which to make the purchase and to provide the means of bringing the purchases home. None of this could be brought about until a majority of congressmen were so persuaded that the trial was worth making that they would vote the funds needed to make it possible.

In 1851, Jefferson Davis, still a senator from Mississippi, was chairman of the Senate Committee on Military Affairs. When he proposed that the War Department's annual budget carry an extra appropriation to be used for the purpose of having camels imported, he was turned down promptly by a vote of 24 to 19. Thereafter camel sponsors must have worked upon some of the bill's opponents, for at least one of them had a public change of heart. This was Senator Shields of Illinois, who actually proposed an amendment to the next year's appropriation bill for the purpose of having camels purchased. This time the Senate voted in favor of the bill by a vote of 26-12. Members of the House thought it very funny, cracked a few jokes, had a good laugh, and dropped the amendment.

Today no one seems quite certain just how the persuasion was finally accomplished. The inevitable aging of the idea through time and repetition may have helped. Meanwhile Jefferson Davis moved on and up to become secretary of war. Coming from such a vantage point, the suggestion that camels be tried was bound to look less funny. Encouraged by Davis, both Ned Beale and Maj. Wayne must have worked upon the congressmen each of them knew. Old Bullion would, as always, have been working behind the scenes. Finally it could have been no handicap to the scheme that just then a civilian, Vermont-born George Marsh, who had been filling diplomatic posts in the Near East, gave an enthusiastic lecture in praise of camels at the Smithsonian Institution in Washington where congressmen could so conveniently attend. Some of these must have been impressed with what they were told.

In any case, on March 3, 1855, they finally voted the appropriation—$30,000—"to be expended under the direction of the War Department for the purchase and importation of camels and dromedaries to be employed for military purposes." "Camels" meant beasts of burden, "dromedaries" were select riding animals. The laugh might now be turned upon the men who had to solve the problem of purchasing animals and of bringing them back home from the markets.

Assigned to that task by a cooperative secretary of the navy was the sailing ship *Supply*—wooden, with two decks, three masts, and a "billethead." Her complement of officers and men numbered forty. Naval officers, however, could not be expected to show enthusiasm for accepting command of a vessel ingloriously destined to be no more than a stable for camels. Knowing it was important to have the ship commanded by an intelligent officer interested in the unusual scheme, Ned Beale persuaded his relative, Naval Lieutenant David Dixon Porter, to apply for the command of the *Supply*. Lt. Porter had an additional qualification of being already somewhat familiar with the camel's native haunts, his father once having served as a U.S. Consul in Constantinople (today's Istanbul).

Assisting in this camel purchasing venture would be the Major Henry Wayne who had been so active in urging its adoption. Now he must really learn something about camels before he had to deal with them directly, so he took passage in a ship that crossed ahead of the *Supply*, to visit England and the camel keepers in the London Zoo who, he hoped, would share with him all they had learned about the "feeding, care, and hygeian" of their charges. However strenuous this may have been for the major, it was pure delight for his young son Henry, whom he took along.

Having gathered all the information available in London, Wayne took his son on to Paris, there to talk with officers of the French Army, which, he knew, used camels in North Africa. Gen. Daumas, Directeur des Affaires de l'Algérie, listened politely while the American major explained his hopes for the future use of camels in America: "The experiment possesses much of scientific interest, as well as commercial and political importance. Its object being to introduce the camel into the heart of our continent, where there are neither navigable rivers nor practicable roads, and by means of it to hold in check the wandering tribes of Indians that are constantly warring upon civilization, to carry on commerce and facilitate communication." The general graciously responded by sending the inquisitive American a pamphlet on the camel isssued for the benefit of officers of the French Army.

Meanwhile Lt. Porter, with his ship *Supply*, was approaching the Italian rendezvous agreed upon with Wayne. While waiting near Spezia, he made a special effort to learn what he could about the camels that, he understood, had been used in Tuscany for the previous two hundred years. The cholera epidemic then raging in Italy, however, made it unwise for visitors to linger there.

Painfully aware that he would soon have a shipload of camels to stable, feed, and transport in a ship never designed for such a purpose, Porter's concern increased daily. Camels were not designed for passage on any ship, especially not one that would be crossing the Atlantic in the winter when storms could rage furiously, and his ship might be expected to pitch and roll mercilessly. Definitely, he had many problems to solve before he could start on that trip.

To begin with, how was he to get the great gawky beasts aboard, from shore to lighter and from lighter to the *Supply?* How should he stable them once he had them on board? How were the animals to be tied so that even violent storms need result in no physical injury to them? Since all these questions must be answered before he had a full load on board headed out into the Atlantic, he decided the only way to answer them was by having an experimental camel or so on board immediately. Though they were to purchase the beasts at the eastern end of the Mediterranean, Porter decided to acquire an experimental camel in a Tunisian port.

Under the diplomatic guidance of the American consul-general stationed there, they paid the Bey a formal visit,

at the end of which, the consul-general requested from the minister of state, Count Rafo, a teskorah (permit) for us to bring off to the ship some livestock for the vessel and the camel I had bought. The Bey, hearing the request, inquired what I wanted with a camel, and if it was a fine one. Upon being informed of the purpose of the purchases, and that I was not yet sufficiently versed in camel knowledge to say whether or not he was a fine one, he promptly desired the interpreter to say to me that he would send me a fine one —from his own herds. The gift I accepted in the name of the President and people of the United States, and yesterday we received on board . . . two camels (instead of one) presented to our country by the Bey. We have, then, on board three camels, and they have already demonstrated the admirable fitness of Lieutenant Porter's arrangements for hoisting them on board and for their transportation . . . . The animals presented by the Bey . . . are apparently of fine blood. They have been much admired by the resident Americans and Europeans who have seen them. [24]

August 13 saw the ship in Malta, there to secure the cash they would need for camel purchases. The next day they sailed "for

Salonika, Smyrna, &c., &c," where they had to spend the money to the best advantage. Here, fortunately, they were joined by another Beale cousin, Gwinn Harris Heap, who, after accompanying Beale the year before, had gone out of his way to recommend the use of camels in country such as they had passed through. Heap had other assets. He was a skilled artist, able to draw the various types of animals as he had done for his book scenes along the trail he and Beale had followed. Best of all, he knew the Near East and was serving there in a consular capacity.

A consul was in a good position to see to it that only good camels were purchased and the purchase price not too inflated. Yet how were amateur camel buyers to know a good camel when they met one? What might be a good price for a good camel? Inferior ones, even at bargain prices, must not be considered, for an inferior camel would occupy shipboard space that should be reserved for a better beast. How did one bargain with a wily Oriental camel seller without making a fool of oneself as an easy mark or, on the other hand, becoming downright obnoxious when obnoxiousness could wreck the success of the expedition? An unforseeable problem arose when the Egyptian ruler offered a gift of camels which, when delivered, turned out to be definitely inferior. They could not be allotted space, yet the ruler must not be insulted. It took special tact to inform him that an underling must have disobeyed his instructions and that, of course, a ruler of his standing could not convey such shabby gifts.

Already in Alexandria, it was becoming obvious that would-be camel sellers were determined to exploit the buyers from America. Realizing this, Wayne decided to send to Smyrna, "Mr. Heap, in advance of us, to make arrangements for procuring camels, as I find the presence of the vessel, or of Lt. Porter or myself, who are now well known to be connected with the enterprise, materially interferes with our selection and purchases, by exciting speculation among a certain class of men resident in all the towns of the East." [25] This was a delicate way of saying that they were expecting to be cheated.

Here, as in Tunis, export permits were necessary and another delicate diplomatic problem confronted the officers. How were they to manage to persuade government officials to issue permits for exporting animals they might well be reluctant to see leaving their own land? And was it or was it not wise to grease their palms? If right or wise, then to what extent?

In Constantinople, the camel purchasers realized they had on hand an unexcelled opportunity to observe camels in military service. War was then being actively waged in the not very distant Crimea, a war, incidentally, whose wounded were being nursed by Florence Nightingale in the Scutari hospital just across the Straits from Constantinople. An observation trip to the Crimea was soon arranged.

There Heap, Porter, and Wayne not only watched but asked questions, carefully recording the answers. On October 17, Wayne remarked,"Colonel McMurdo informed me that in the expedition against Sinde, he had in service twenty-five hundred camels, and that from his experience he esteemed them highly; so much so that he had at Sinope three thousand of them, in addition to the few now in use in the Crimea, in readiness for the campaign next spring." So impressed had the general been that "he procured five or six for his personal use." [25]

Turks listened with amazement to the visitors whose queries revealed their utter ignorance of basic camel lore. "But have you no camels in America?" one asked incredulously. When told none were yet to be had in that land, he exclaimed pityingly, "My, but you must be years behind the times there!"

Behind the times or not, the visitors were doing their best to narrow the gap, finally securing the thirty-two camels and drome-daries Lt. Porter regarded as a full load. Some were the one-humped African variety, some two-humped Bactrians, with a few crosses between the two called "camel mules" by the purchaser from the Quartermaster Corps.

Also secured were three Arabs and two Turks to accompany the cargo to America and "to serve with the camels for one year," apparently with a promise of repatriation at the end of that time. In charge of these camel drivers was "Wagon and Forage Master, Albert Ray, who . . . enlisted with Lt. Porter for that purpose." A veteran of the Mexican War and a man of much experience in caring for animals, Ray was by this appointment "thus well able to learn about camels and care for them."

Tied down on their knees, as Lt. Porter had arranged, the camels now faced a winter's ocean crossing so exceptionally rough that Lt. Porter would not take his clothes off nor sleep in his bunk for over three weeks. The camels accepted the frightening novelty of the trip with truly Oriental resignation, remaining throughout "enduring, patient, uncomplaining." Two died during the crossing, though not from the rough weather. One was lost in camel-birth, the other through what Lt. Porter was convinced was callous mistreatment. Even so, births on board more than balanced the deaths, so that by the time the animals reached Texas, the original thirty-two had become thirty-four.

The Arabs and Turks all too often regretted they had let them-selves be persuaded, even at generous wages of $10 per month, to abandon the familiar hardships of desert camel caravans for those of a kind their wildest imaginings could not have forseen. To a man, they would have fled from this new hardship, had they seen any possible way to escape the misery they dreaded might go on forever. Inevitably, Lt. Porter found them perfectly helpless in heavy weather and in good weather not of much use. As they saw it, undoubtedly, their business was to pack and drive camels on very dry land, not to minister to them in the midst of an infinite waste of water.

Even the man who had managed to convince Lt. Porter that he was a skilled "Camel M.D." turned out to be worse than useless. He did nothing to care for the newborn or their mothers. Some of the young died during the voyage, Lt. Porter believed for want of attention altogether. For a cold this M.D.'s remedy was a piece of cheese. For swelled legs, he administered a mixture of tea and gunpowder. Finally, his ministrations were interdicted in favor of Lt. Porter's or Ray's common-sense treatments.

Like everyone else in any way associated with the venture, Lt. Porter had studied Abbé Huc's book carefully. The Abbé Huc saw camels as highly useful animals doomed to lives of drearily un-relieved servitude, as perhaps they were in the Orient. A newborn camel, he wrote, was "impressed from its birth with a sense of the yoke it is destined to bear throughout life. It is always grave, melancholy, and slow in its movements." None of this applied to the young, not born into such servitude, that survived birth during the *Supply*'s winter crossing, one of which was appropriately christened "Uncle Sam." Not having studied the good Abbé's book, they were unaware of their foreordained yoke. Playful and frolicsome even during storms, they cheered everyone on board with their frisky precocity and obvious high spirits. Happily undismayed by rolling and pitching that forced even seasoned sailors to hang on for dear life, they moved about freely as if running no risks at all.

For all the camels, nevertheless, there were other risks that would only increase as time passed. These would not be from storms or even from the callousness of camel hands, but from active partisans of other modes of transportation who saw camels as a threat. Meanwhile the camels had explicit partisans of their own, notably ones eager to encourage any competition with a transportation monopoly they were finding galling.

During the previous year, before receiving news of the appropriation Congress had tardily made, the *Los Angeles Star* predicted happily

> that, in a few years, these extraordinary and useful animals will be browsing upon hills and valleys, and numerous caravans will be arriving and departing daily. Let us have the incomparable dromedary, with Adams & Co's express men arriving here tri-weekly with letters and packages in five or six days from Salt Lake and fifteen or eighteen from Missouri. Then the present grinding steamship monopoly might be made to realize the fact that the hardworking miner, the farmer and the mechanic were no longer in their grasping power as at present. We might have an overland dromedary express that would bring us the New York news in fifteen to eighteen days. We hope some enterprising capitalists or stock traders will take this speculation in hand, for we have not much faith that Congress will do anything in the matter. [16]

The Dromedary Express was a lovely dream on the point of becoming a possibility. Congress had already done the unexpected and on May 14, 1856, those thirty-four camels were landed from the *Supply* at Indianola, Texas, "in better condition," Lt. Porter asserted, "than when taken from the sandy wastes of their native deserts."

The camel experiment, therefore, was now ready to begin in dead earnest and the camels were going to need all the partisans they could get even though they posed no real threat to the grasping power of the grinding steamship monopoly. Fortunately, some of their partisans were highly placed, perhaps the most highly placed being the secretary of war, who was at last seeing his hoped-for plans coming to fruition.

In his annual report for the year 1856, Secretary Davis would write,

The cargo of camels . . . have been landed on the coast of Texas and taken into the interior of the country . . . On one occasion, it is reported, that a train consisting of wagons and camels was sent out from Camp Valverde to San Antonio, a distance of sixty miles . . . and the result as given is, that the quantity brought back by six camels (3,648 pounds) was equal to the loads of two wagons drawn by six mules each, and the time occupied by the camels was two days and six hours; that by the wagons four days and thirty minutes . . .

When it is remembered that this is the year of their acclimation, in a climate subject to sudden and violent changes, and of the use by them of herbage very different from that of the countries from which they have been imported, there is every reason to believe that as little difficulty will be encountered in the acclimation of the camel as that of the horse or ox.

The very intelligent officer [Maj. Wayne, of course] who was sent abroad to procure them . . . expresses entire confidence . . . of their great value. [25]

Secretary of War Davis ended this report on the camels by saying Lt. Porter had again taken his ship to the Near East whence he was bringing forty more camels to be landed "during the present winter." With all this, no more than two-thirds of the original appropriation would be used up. Those amateur camel purchasers seem to have become worthy matches for the wily camel sellers.

Convinced of his charges' great value, the intelligent officer was taking a long look into their future: "The animals, I think, should have a permanent home where breeding can be carefully attended to . . ." he wrote Davis on June 28, 1856. "In this way, and with the addition of more breeding cows, the climate proving favorable, I have little doubt but that in ten years the race can be well spread through Texas, whence it can be carried to any part of the continent." [24]

Ten years, the secretary of war was all too sadly aware, were not to be allowed his administration for the carrying out of such a long-term experiment. This conviction must have influenced him when he wrote the far from enthusiastic endorsement to Wayne's letter before forwarding it to Quartermaster General Jessup: "The establishment of a breeding farm did not enter into the plans of the department. The object at present is to ascertain whether the animal is adapted to military service, and can be usefully and economically employed therein. When this is satisfactorily established, arrangements can be made for importing or breeding camels to any extent that may be deemed desirable."

Two weeks later, conservative, unimaginative Gen. Jessup thought it well to underline his inflexible determination to keep first things first—as if, with a decision finally arrived at, needed camels could be bred, raised, and trained on a rush military schedule: "The first and most important point to be determined is their fitness for our military service, and until this be established, it is needless to inquire whether they may be bred in the United States."

A highly competent organizer who had managed to bring order to the previously chaotic Quartermaster Corps, Jessup was not going to let himself be swept off his feet by new and untried methods of transportation or by a junior officer's enthusiasm for any particular method. Trying the camels at the august order of Congress was one thing, while long-distance planning of a camel corps through the immediate establishment of a breeding farm was quite another.

Poor old Jessup, obviously, would have preferred to be spared involvement with this radical new kind of transportation. He was the image of a correct public servant who lived strictly by the rules, but time would run out for him in 1860. Unfortunately, time would soon thereafter run out for other officers, removing some of the camels' strongest partisans to the Confederacy. More fatal still to the camels' future, the events causing that remove would be filling all men's minds with matters of greater urgency than a decision as to whether to maintain a camel corps in the deserts of the contested Southwest.

In addition to Beale, Wayne, Davis, and a handful of other officers, the camels had—it should not be forgotten—civilian partisans, none of them particularly objective. "Let us have the incomparable dromedary," the *Los Angeles Star* had said with an eye to humiliating the "present grinding steamship monopoly" but not to improving communications with southwestern territories. "Without much faith that Congress [would] do anything in the matter," they were trying to prod local entrepreneurs into underwriting camel importation.

Congress, finally having done something, was leaving the rest to the War Department which, in turn, was leaving a great deal to Maj. Wayne at Camp Valverde in Texas. Like the congressmen of five years before, the men in the camp were finding the whole camel idea very funny, perhaps because camels were such funny-looking beasts to the eyes of occidentals. Those ignorant jesters, Wayne decided, would profit by being given an object lesson in camel lore. Before the gathered jokesters he ordered one of the finest camels brought out. It knelt obediently on command though its ungainliness earned it loud laughs. Paying no attention to those, Wayne ordered two bales of hay, each weighing 314 pounds, placed upon the animal. The bystanders, certain no animal could rise under such a load, were shocked into sobriety when Wayne calmly ordered two more bales added to the load, to make a total of 1,256 pounds. The noisy onlookers were, at last, shocked into speechlessness when, at the Major's command, the camel rose and walked off unconcernedly.

Amazement was one thing, acceptance another. Those huge, solemn beasts towered frighteningly over men and other animals. Who but a fool would plan to make useful burden carriers of camels, which, if they knew their own strength, could easily destroy their owners! Accepting heavy loads was not enough. Mules and horses were patently terrorstricken when they first encountered the camels. Mule skinners wanted no part of animals that they sensed were posing a twin threat to their own way of life.

Should mules survive their fright only to see camels taking over their duties (if those damned aliens really could do so on a long-term basis), then the mules might just as well have died of fright and mule skinners would have to turn camel handlers (perish the thought!) or retire from business. But, of course, the whole business was bound to turn out a huge joke.

Those shambling newcomers would make a hit in circuses—come to think of it, that was just where they belonged—but not in serious undertakings. What did that smart newcomer, the major, know of the real work of desert transportation? He'd learn, when he took those fool pets of his out on a real trail, that it was one thing to give adoring little girls camel rides, quite another to tackle the desert. Good for a big laugh, it still was.

The little girl would remember when she was an old, old woman how the weird animals had stalked into camp near her home, covered with red blankets, bells jangling. Of course they'd frightened her at first, but not after the major—the most handsome major you could ever imagine—had invited her to take a camel ride. So high she sat, and the motion made her a wee bit seasick, but the ride was something she'd always remembered, couldn't possibly forget, that and the time two of the camels got into a most ferocious fight. In Valverde, though, the noisy men never stopped making fun of that nice major and of his animals. [27]

To serious camel fans it soon became obvious that a real, long-term test of the animals must be made under field conditions. How else were conservative regimental officers to be convinced it could be worth their while to have their men master the exotic new art of packing and managing camels? Thus, when he was put in charge of the Fort Defiance–Colorado River road survey, camel fan Beale was more than willing to include twenty-five camels in his train—camels to pack, camels to ride, camels to make transportation history in the Southwest of the United States.

10

Boys and Beasts

Perhaps Ned Beale's eagerness to test the camels helped secure for him the appointment he had so long dreamed of. This meant edging out the topographical engineers. Perhaps Col. Abert, Chief Topographical Engineer, willingly concurred, knowing as he must that the new survey must include long halts for roadbuilding with the inevitably increased risks thereby of Indian attacks. Such an appointment should best go to a man who had practical experience in meeting such attacks. Lt. Gunnison's death may have been lingering in Abert's mind and on his conscience. Perhaps, too, he saw that the many anticipated delays along the route might too long absorb the time and energies of a small corps whose topographical engineering officers never boasted a total of more than thirty-six.

On the other hand, Abert's feelings may not have been consulted in the matter. Beale may have been given the command as the result of accumulated political pressures managed by that expert in such matters, Senator Thomas Hart Benton. The appointment, of course, was just the beginning and Beale was only too well aware that his whole future might hang on the outcome of the controversial expedition he was undertaking.

On August 27, 1857, as he was making ready to start out from Fort Defiance, he wrote sombrely,

This morning . . . we take leave of our kind and hospitable friends to start our journey into the wilderness. No one who has not commanded an expedition of this kind, where everything ahead is dim, uncertain, and unknown, except the dangers, can imagine the anxiety with which I start upon this journey. Not only responsible for the lives of my men, but my reputation and the highest wrought expectations of my friends, and the still more highly wrought expectations of my enemies [Did he mean by these the topographical engineers or the political rivals of Old Bullion?], all these dependent upon the next sixty days' good or evil fortune. Today commences it. Let us see what I shall say in this journal, if I live to say anything, on the day of my return here. [9]

At his home in Chester, Pennsylvania, Mrs. Beale—the former Mary Edwards to whom he'd become affianced after his first cross-country trip and whom he'd married in June 1849—had watched with both concern and pride as he made preparations for the trip. Young men, most of them knowing nothing at all about the vast lands to the west of the Mississippi, had been practically lining up for the privilege of learning at first hand. Three youths— sons of friends—volunteered and finally persuaded Beale to take them along. He would, throughout the trip, refer to them in his diary with the fatherly, "My boys, May, Ham, and Joe." In more formal terms, they were May Humphreys Stacey, romantically confiding to his own journal his feelings about the strange places visited; Hampden Porter, who, a relative of the chief officer of the *Supply*, was to become a driver of the *Supply*'s cargo; and Joseph M. Bell, whose name alone of the three boys' has survived a century's weathering (plus vandalism!) on the face of the rock.

Young Stacey joined Beale in Texas, having taken a train as far as Cairo, Illinois, where the Ohio River empties into the Mississippi. Railroads had been busily extending themselves during the past four years since young Stanley had made the trip to join Whipple in Fort Smith. From Cairo, Stacey took a riverboat to New Orleans, where he transshipped to a sidewheeler bound for Galveston.

By mid-June, his romantic young eyes were gazing entranced upon a new land: "It was the first time I had seen the Prairies and my impressions were like those of a man who beheld, for the first time, the ocean. A feeling of insignificance and worthlessness I felt when I gazed over the wide expanse of land—and my eyes were opened to the magnificence of Almighty God." [56]

Officially, the expedition started from Fort Defiance, situated on the edge of today's Arizona, somewhat over fifty miles and a two days' trip northwest from Zuñi village or El Morro. The real start had to be made from the camel camp far to the south in Valverde, Texas. At the outset, the commander was almost as highly wrought as those expectations of friends and enemies put together, for it was his future that depended upon how successfully they all got through. He was determined not to lose a man or even a mule or camel or one of the government-owned wagons, it being a point of honor with him to demonstrate that the route he laid out could be safely passed over by loaded emigrant wagons.

During the very early days of the expedition especially, damage to any of the wagons would seem disproportionately serious, with the man who had let such damage occur disproportionately blamed. That this man happened to be cousin Gwinn Harris Heap and that the anger of quick-tempered Ned Beale fell upon him goes to show that, though being a relative might win a man a place under Beale, that place could be kept only by the most rigorous attention to duty. During a later expedition, he would write to his wife about two "useful men" who, having gotten into a row, were summarily fired. He consented to rehire them only after being "implored by the whole party." "I think you will laugh at the military discipline I keep in my camp," he added later, "but you may rest assured it is necessary to the highest degree."

Such discipline, he felt deeply, was doubly necessary on this expedition for which his command had been contested. So he lost his temper at his cousin though he may very soon have regretted it, for not a whisper of that row comes through in his own journal. It was young Stacey, who had undertaken service with the expedition's master of stores, "Old Alex" Smith, who kept a record of the incident. It clearly upset him considerably.

On June 13, he confided to his journal:

We tonight had an occurrence in camp which filled us with regret. When we started this morning, Mr. Heap took charge of the train in the absence of Mr. Beale, who was hunting strayed mules, and Mr. Smith, who was busily engaged attending to some imperative duty in the rear. After going about eighteen miles, we came to a steep hill or rather a deep valley, through which passed a stream of water. The first wagons (eight in number) passed safely over, and Mr. Heap, thinking the rest would go over the same way, gave orders to resume the march. [56]

Mr. Heap, bred near the deserts of North Africa and without experience in western wagon transportation, had made an unwarranted assumption. Each wagon that negotiated the downhill grade and stream and far bank was bound to add to the difficulties of the one that followed, wearing down both banks, splashing water, making the whole slipperier and steeper. Inevitably, almost, the crossing was climaxed by the last two wagons having the greatest difficulty in passing over, finally being brought through only "after immense labor."

When that night the whole party had settled into camp and geologist Williams said, not too tactfully, to the commander, "Mr. Beale, you look tired," Beale exploded, according to young Stacey, with "I am not tired but most damnably disgusted." The few who heard this speech at once knew a storm was brewing somewhere and got out of the way. Very soon he walked over to Mr. Heap and commenced speaking in a very harsh and ungentlemanly manner, telling him he had not performed his duty as wagon master. Mr. Heap said that he "was not wagon master, and did not come on the expedition with any such intention." Mr. Beale continued speaking very harshly, and Mr. Heap finally said, "Sir, I will not submit to this. I resign my post tomorrow." Wrote Stacey, "We are about to lose a man who is invaluable as an officer, and the assistant to Mr. Beale. . . . I regret this occurrence more . . . than anything else I can remember. Everything seems to be going wrong, and it is my opinion, founded on the remarks of others, that the party will never get through." [56]

Such forebodings were commonplace in the early shakedown days of any such expedition. Beale, who understood quite well how people felt on the eve of setting out into the unknown, was aware of this eroding criticism and was showing his boys what in the way of loyalty and service he expected of them, sons of friends or relatives though they might be. No Sunday School picnic this and it was for the boys' protection that he should bring it home to them before they came face to face with those dimly threatening uncertainties on the far side of Fort Defiance.

Shortly after the row that so upset young Stacey, the leader was confiding to his journal that "many of the party have seen Indians, but for me, 'Ah! Sinner that I am I was not permitted to see so glorious a sight.' I encourage the young men, however, in the belief that deer, bushes, &c., which they have mistaken for Indians, are all veritable Comanches, as it makes them more watchful at night." [8]

Thanks to thus keeping everyone on his toes, and despite all gloomy forebodings of those prophets of doom, the party would get safely through. Whether the two cousins amicably composed their differences is not easy to guess, for young Stacey made no more mention of the row and, from the tone of his journal, seemed to settle happily into camp routine. That, after reaching the Coast, he should choose not to accompany Lt. Beale on his return winter trip, was certainly less due to Beale's quick temper and rigid discipline than to the fact that the young man saw a chance to know more of the world by taking ship bound for the East Coast through the Straits of Magellan, with stops at South American ports on the way. Steamer or clipper ship—one wonders which—it was offering an opportunity no imaginative and adventure-minded youth would willingly pass up.

Within a week of the flare-up that so filled him with gloomy forebodings, Stacey was writing calmly of the quick-tempered leader. On June 21:

> Mr. Beale returned from Camp Verde today. He was accompanied part of the way by the camels and being anxious to push ahead, he left them in charge of Messrs Bell and Porter . . . The first intimation we had of their approach was the jingling of the large bells suspended from their necks. Presently . . . the whole twenty-five had come within range in the dim twilight. And thus they came, those huge ungainly beasts of the desert, accompanied by their attendants, Turks, Greeks, and Armenians . . . Our mules and horses were very much frightened at the approach of the camels. They dashed around the corral, with heads erect and snorting in wild alarm. They were so much excited that the whole camp was aroused and put on watch. However, in a few hours they became more quiet. [56]

Mr. Beale was staking not only his judgment but the finances of the trip on the performance of those great beasts. Just before leaving Chester, Pennsylvania, in May, he'd received a letter from some acquaintance in the War Department telling him that "the governor," unable to place more than $5,000 to Beale's credit, thought it best that not more than twenty-five camels be taken along. Should there remain any unexpended balance from the "camel fund," however, the lieutenant might hope to have that added eventually to the total. If by that the correspondent meant whatever funds might be left after Lt. Porter returned from his second camel-buying venture, they would amount to some $10,000 more.

More important than how the camels' way should be paid remained the question as to whether that way would prove worth the paying for. It was, therefore, encouraging for Ned Beale to find that on their very first day of service and despite the fact that they had not been thus worked for some time, the camels covered sixteen miles, carrying loads of five hundred and seventy-five pounds apiece. In his journal he wondered whether the animals were being handled right, for "the only men in America who understand them, are some Turks, who came over with them, and who left at San Antonio, refusing to go on so long a journey." They were under no legal obligation to go, for the year they had contracted for at the time of leaving the Near East must already have been up. Yet some imported camel hands must have finally decided to go with the camels, for Beale mentions their presence now and again. Two of the hands—Hadji Ali and "Greek George" —were destined to become a part of the legends of the Southwest. They, like the camels, would never see their homelands again.

By July 2:

The camels are doing better today and arrived shortly after the wagons. I am very much encouraged to see how eagerly they seek the bushes for food instead of grass, which certainly indicates their ability to subsist much easier than horses and mules in countries where forage is scarce. . . .

My fear as to their feet giving out, as I had been led to believe, . . . have so far proven entirely unfounded, though the character of the road is exceedingly trying to brutes of any kind. My dogs cannot travel at all upon it, and after going a short distance run to the wagons and beg to be taken in. The camels, on the contrary, have not evinced the slightest distress or soreness; and this is the more remarkable as mules or horses, in a very short time, get so sore-footed that shoes are indispensable. The road is very hard and firm, and strewn all over it is a fine, sharp, flinty gravel . . . It is certainly the hardest road on the feet of barefoot animals I have ever known. [8]

On the following day, the camels were stirring him to poetic expression:

As our line of wagons ascended the hill, the camels appeared on the further side, winding down the steep road, and made a picture worthy of the pen of a great artist. The steep, gray rocks, the beautiful green river bottom or meadow, the clear sparkling stream, the loose animals, the wagons and teams, and then old Mahomet with the long line of his grave and patient followers, winding cautiously, picking step by step their way down the road on the opposite side. [8]

By July 23, the party had progressed to the valley of the Rio Grande near today's El Paso, Texas. The river's grand name had aroused too grand expectations, which were doomed to disappointment. Though the green of riverbottom cottonwoods was welcome to eyes wearied by desert drabness, May Stacey expressed the feelings of all "in finding the stream so small in the first place (being only about a hundred yards wide) and so muddy in the second." Fortunately, they were not to learn on that trip that the smallness could alter dramatically within hours.

The leader's description was still more explicit:

The valley of the Rio Grande is here about twenty to twenty-five miles in width . . . the mountains . . . are destitute of timber, and offer the eye naught but gloomy masses of rock where the very spirit of desolation seems to reign. Only the clear fresh green of the cottonwoods in the river bottom creates a point for the eye to rest on with pleasure; speaking to us, as it did, of a fine stream in which to bathe our weary limbs; but, like all other anticipations of pleasure, this, too, faded on nearer approach. We found the river, after groping some distance through a dense undergrowth of weeds, briars and willows, a muddy stream about a hundred yards wide; but with such a deposit of mud and quicksand that even our thirsty mules were obliged to go half a mile below, before we

could find a place where we could safely take them to water.
[8]

The party would now take a northward course along the river,
which, in addition to the fresh green cottonwoods—or, rather,
because of them—now offered scattered human habitations and a
temporary end to the monotony of desert travel. Somewhat north
of El Paso they came to the little town of San Elizario, where "our
train arrived this morning, and the whole Mexican population,
which, since our getting in, had been in a perfectly feverish state of
excitement in relation to the camels, had their curiosity gratified.
The street was crowded, and when we went on to camp the whole
town followed."

Continuing northward, they traversed "Cruces and Doña Ana"
to veer away from the river and face the ninety waterless miles of
the Jornada del Muerto—Dead Man's March. Beyond were more
Mexican towns, more excitement over the camels. This was increased by the population's discovery of Beale's wagon, "which the
taste of the builder had painted a bright red." No doubt about it,
here was a circus come to relieve the isolated monotony of the life of
a town like theirs!

"Dis show wagon, no?" asked a slouchy looking ruffian who
seemed eager to act as interpreter.

Denial must be useless, else why should a train like theirs come
to a remote town? The recent naval lieutenant took the path of least
resistance and admitted he was proprietor of a show wagon. When
pressed to say what he might have, in addition to the obvious
camels, to offer for entertainment, he replied, "Horses."

"What can do horses?" the would-be interpreter demanded
scornfully.

Make it the kind of story expected of an experienced showman—
these were Beale's thoughts as he announced soberly, "Horse
stand on head and drink wine."

That registered promptly. "Válgame Dios!" exclaimed the interpreter, "What a people these are to have horse stand on head and
drink wine!"

What Beale did to fulfil the preposterous claim, he did not
record. He and the rest of his train were enjoying the silly interlude, for all were painfully aware that such happy, carefree moments must soon end. Ahead loomed the serious business of the

trip beyond Albuquerque, where they arrived on August 10. That city was still a happy, carefree place for them all and notably for the "Turks and Greeks," who had not found "even in the positive prohibitions of the prophet, a sufficient reason for temperance." Beale prudently hurried his train on from those so tempting fandangos and pleasures. He remained behind waiting for whatever mail might arrive in the next express from Santa Fe.

A few days later he happily rejoined his train at Covero, "and no one can imagine the pleasant thing it was to get back to flannel shirts, big boots, and greasy buckskins once more. It was home to us." Here they remained while they awaited the arrival of Col. Loring, the officer who was to accompany Beale to Fort Defiance, the official starting point of his survey, where a military escort was to be picked up.

When news came that the colonel was not far off, the showman in Beale came to the fore again. The colonel must have, for the moment, questioned his own sanity when he looked up to see towering above his horse a great white dromedary topped by a man in greasy buckskins. If the colonel, like Beale, kept a journal, his comments would be most interesting to read. Ned, of course, was bound to demonstrate the value of his kind of mount.

"After a pleasant interview," he wrote, "we started back together; but finding his animal unequal to mine, I rode on to camp again alone, and arrived after an absence of three hours, during which I had ridden twenty-seven miles. 'Seid' [the dromedary] seemed not in the least tired; indeed it was as much as I could do to hold him in on my return."

On the following day, Beale sent his train on the direct road west to Zuñi while he accompanied Col. Loring in a more northwesterly direction to Fort Defiance "so as to start with my escort from that place." This time he would miss El Morro. His train would not, camping there the night of August 23.

On the 24th, the romantic mind of Stacey gave his imagination and his pen full rein:

Last night a tremendous dew fell, saturating the blankets of those who slept out. We again visited Inscription Rock this morning and entered the corral [box canyon] on horseback. It is a beautiful place, secluded and secure, fit for the echo of words of love. Here one might pour out all the tender ideas of love without interruption. Who knows but that in this same spot scenes similar to those described by the classic author of Paul and Virginia might not have occurred, and that a broken-hearted Indian youth wasted away wandering over these mighty rocks. It was a romantic spot and one we shall all remember, when years have passed and other scenes will have grown dim in the waters of memory. We parted from the place with regret, after having inscribed on the rock's soft face our names." [56]

Today, of Beale's three boys' names, only Bell's remains, along with the two party members' "T. Bolman" and "John L. Tribit."

Beale rejoined his train at Zuñi and was ready to move out on August 29. The journey was now serious, and the man most aware of it was Edward Beale, who, while at Fort Defiance two days earlier, had written so eloquently of his worries. Anyone, even without Beale's special responsibilities, about to leave behind the settled areas of New Mexico, would surely have known the same kind of anxiety Ned then felt. Three hundred years before, Coronado's men had known it and, knowing it thus, had placed reliance upon native guides long after their trustworthiness should have been questioned. Partly this may have been because to question the reliability of those guides was also to question the tales they told of fabulously rich great cities ahead, always ahead. Having risked their lives and such fortunes as they possessed in their venture and wanting to believe in the reality of those cities, the Spaniards had to believe in their guides.

Equally, the trustfulness of the usually far-from-trusting Spaniards may have been due to an unadmitted dread of the dim uncertainty that they, even more than Beale, knew lay before them. There was a kind of reassurance in the conviction that as long as they were being led by someone who had trod the same paths before and was now returning to tread them yet again, they would not reach beyond the point of no return to drop into some dark and bottomless abyss.

Every explorer, no matter how skilled, longed for such a guide. In the Southwest, the first guides would, of necessity, be Indians whom men of the intruding race had small reason not to expect to be faithless. In later years, there would be guides who had already trapped and hunted in the trackless wilderness—those mountain men like Kit Carson or Antoine Leroux, as well as less legendary ones. When the profession of guide seemed to be growing profitable, their ranks would be joined by men who, coveting the eminence and the financial rewards the appointment as guide to an expedition might mean, managed to persuade themselves, as they would persuade others, that they knew as much about the land as those less boastful, though far more knowledgeable, mountain men.

Such a man, it turned out, was the José Manuel Saavedra whom Whipple had engaged with the expectation that his knowledge should supplement Leroux's, but who managed to lose both himself and his party (being surely extricated by Leroux). What Leroux thought of the man who had edged himself in as colleague is, of course, not recorded. Leroux, letting his own actions do the speaking, was ever sparing of words.

One way or another, Saavedra was bound to profit from that trip. He'd received pay that must have looked munificent to him. Then, with pay spent and Lt. Whipple safely departed on more distant assignments, and thus not to be consulted, Saavedra could continue turning his expedition to profit.

Was he not the man who had guided Lt. Whipple on his 35th parallel survey? What might have become of Whipple without him? Must he not know the land as no other resident of Albuquerque could? Was he not, in fact, the very man to guide future parties over the same route? Stay-at-home residents of Albuquerque, easily persuaded to see it that way too, were psychologically prepared to further a fellow-townsman's interest, as also were prospective travelers, all too conscious of the dim uncertainties ahead.

That Ned Beale had several times already crossed the lands lying between Albuquerque and California could not totally relieve him of anxiety as he entered upon his special survey. Past experience, in fact, may have served to aggravate his anxiety, having taught him a just estimate of the risks and pitfalls ahead. When friends began to urge upon him the services of a man whom they believed to know the route from recent first-hand experience, he would not be inclined to reject the idea out of hand.

As with Whipple, five years earlier, Beale had let himself be persuaded to accept a guide for those days ahead when everything was unknown except the dangers—dangers which, as it eventually turned out, Saavedra could help only to increase.

11

Parallels and Politics

For Beale and his men what was commencing in earnest that August morning of 1857 was two months of "up at dawn and off at daybreak" in search of the shortest and smoothest route from Zuñi to the Colorado River and across into California. Steep slopes were to be cut down and graded with pick and shovel, holes to be filled in. Campsites must be located where there was fuel for campfires, water for men and beasts, grass to feed the great herds of cattle the emigrants were bound to drive to California. Sold at their destination, such herds would provide support for a hopeful emigrant family until the lord and master came home bringing his bucketsful of gold.

Barely more than a week after starting, Canyon Diablo opened out before Beale's party as it had before Whipple's and with similar dramatic effect. "Our trail," Beale told, "has led to the west and north for the last day or two, but for no other reason than that a cañon known as Cañon Diablo, a mere chasm in the plain, prevented the passage of wagons in a due west direction . . . This singular chasm extends for thirty or forty miles . . . which obliges us to go greatly out of our direction to pass its mouth. This is the more annoying as the country directly across it presents to the eye an almost uninterrupted plain." [8] Uninterrupted save for other such chasms, he might better have written. A bridge across just this one, he was certain, could shorten the trip materially—by some twenty-five miles, in fact.

Guide Saavedra, had he lived up to his professions, should have helped here, for he was the one who had passed this exact way before. He should have led the party to good camping places, with

120

plenty of water, and should have known how and where to avoid coming suddenly to impassable canyons.

Soon completely disillusioned with the man, Beale wrote, "We unfortunately have no guide, the wretch I employed at the urgent request and advice of everyone in Albuquerque, at enormous expense, being the most ignorant and irresolute ass extant. This obliges us to do the double duty of road making and exploring, which is very arduous, besides adding infinitely to my anxiety and responsibility." [8]

He still cherished hopes in another so-called guide named Leco, "who once passed through with Mr. Aubrey and, thinking he might be of some use, I employed him. Up to this time he has only justified my expectations by looking out for water, but now he becomes useful as a guide, and with his assistant I hope to get along rapidly toward the Colorado." Vain hope, as it soon became evident!

Being safely buried, Aubry was not on hand in 1857 to give his estimate of Leco's worth as a guide. The mere fact of having accompanied Aubry on one of his trips was an impressive recommendation. A relative latecomer to New Mexico, Aubry did not reach Santa Fe much before 1846. His was then a name to rival Carson or Leroux. French Canadian by birth, his territory really knew no bounds, for it was his temperament to keep moving, striving to open new trade routes and achieve new records. Today he would have joined the company of the astronauts.

When, during the 1840s, Aubry became a Santa Fe freighter, he scorned the usual freighter's single trip a year that left Independence in the spring to return there by snowfall. For him no less than three trips a year would do, starting out from Independence in April, September, and late December. Once he made a wager of $1,000 that he could cover the whole distance in eight days, and won the wager, arriving in Independence so stiff that he had to be lifted from his horse. After that, he was referred to as "Telegraph Aubry—the man to whom the telegraph is a fool."

The same Lt. Brewerton who published an account of his ride with Kit Carson described him: "'Little Aubrey,' like my friend Kit Carson . . . . . is (alas! that I should now say *was*) a man of medium stature, slender proportions, iron nerve, great resolution, and indomitable perseverance." And of quick temper, Brewerton should have added, for Aubry was shot and killed in 1854 during a heated argument with a publisher who had, so Aubry claimed, misrepresented his recent trip to California.

Self-made guide Leco had presumably accompanied Aubry on that trip, which Aubry undertook "simply to satisfy my own curiosity as to the practicability of one of the much talked of routes for the contemplated Atlantic and Pacific railroads," and which Lt. Whipple already had been assigned to explore. Aubry's journal shows he stopped in Zuñi on September 6, 1853, and reached Albuquerque four days later. Exactly when he camped at El Morro is not clear, probably September 7. Even though in his usual hurry, he should have left his name there for he was one of the truly great folk heroes of the 1840s and 1850s.

Though Leco should have learned much from Aubry, he must have missed the chance or else lacked the intelligence so to do. Within a few days after expressing hopes for Leco's usefulness along his route, Beale's happy faith was shattered: "Our guide retained his confident air, and assured me there was no doubt of our finding water a short distance beyond. A half mile further, he came back to tell me the distant mountain, towards which our course was directed, was not the one he thought, and he was completely lost. I ought to have killed him there, but I did not. . . . We were thirty-two miles from water in a country entirely unknown." [58] Unknown not only as to terrain and water, but as to Indians! Both guides, the leader remarked, "had proved a perfect curse to the party"—no less a curse, if a less malicious one, than the Indian who, centuries before, had deliberately led one of Coronado's exploring parties astray.

Going in search of water himself, Ned Beale found the hilly land quite as deceptive as that "uninterrupted plain" he had glimpsed across Canyon Diablo. "On our line we travelled through some low hills, and following an Indian trail came suddenly upon a most wonderful sight. This was a chasm in the earth, or apparently a split in the very centre of a range of hills, from the top to the bottom."

It was not the guides but rather his "dromedary men"—his boys, undoubtedly—who distinguished themselves at this juncture by finding

a river (the Little Colorado, I presume) about sixteen or twenty miles off, but very rough to approach. Our animals are now beginning to suffer very much, having been constantly at work for thirty-six hours without water; and one of the most painful sights I ever witnessed was a group of them standing over a small barrel of water and trying to drink from the bung hole, and seemingly frantic with distress and eagerness to get at it. The camels appeared to view this proceeding with great contempt and kept browsing the grass and bushes. . . . .

The camels were sent on [to the river] in advance, and shortly after our arrival here, although, like the rest of us, they had been on the road all night, they started back with eight or ten barrels of water for the camp at the wagons. Six of them are worth half the mules we have, although we have good ones. [8]

May Stacey's journal shows an equal disgust with Leco. "Our guide has again deceived us," he wrote. "He has brought us to this place where there is neither grass nor water, where we cannot go ahead because an impassable canyon is before us, extending both ways for many miles." [56]

As with previous expeditions arriving in the vicinity of today's Flagstaff, Arizona, they were learning what today's tourist can read from road maps. Less than a hundred miles south of the Grand Canyon, they were already in canyon country where, as Major Powell wrote,

For more than a thousand miles along its course, the Colorado has cut for itself a canyon; but at some few points where lateral streams join it the canyon is broken, and these narrow transverse valleys divide it into a series of canyons. . . .

All the scenic features of this canyon land are on a giant scale, strange and weird, the streams run at depths almost inaccessible, lashing the rocks which beset their channels, rolling in rapids and plunging in falls, making a wild music which but adds to the gloom of the solitude. [49]

Listening to that distant wild music, the young Pennsylvanian felt a new romantic excitement. "Mr. Beale, and a party, one of whom was myself," he recorded in his diary, "left camp to explore and discovered a wonderful canyon four thousand feet deep. Everybody in the party admitted that he never before saw anything to match or equal this astonishing natural curiosity . . . after de-

scending into the canyon in the hope of finding some water, we
. . . returned to camp." There the mules, he noted, "hung around
the empty water kegs, braying huskily for what they were perishing
for" while "the camels alone seemed perfectly indifferent, and, like
good fatalists, chewed their cud in cheerful contentment." [56]

Ned Beale had now become a devoted camel fan: "My admiration for the camels increases daily with my experience of them. . . .
They pack water for others for days under a hot sun and never get a
drop; they pack heavy burdens of corn and oats for months and
never get a grain; and on the bitter greasewood and other worthless
shrubs not only subsist but keep fat; withal they are so perfectly
docile and admirably contented with whatever fate befalls them
. . . I look forward to the day when every mail route across the
continent will be conducted and worked altogether with this economical and noble brute."

By early October: "I rarely think of the camels now. It is so
universally acknowledged in camp, even by those who were most
opposed to them at first, that they are the salt of the party and the
noblest brute alive." [8]

Far from being the salt of the party was self-styled guide
Saavedra: "This old wretch is a constant source of trouble to
everyone and his entire and incredible ignorance of the country
renders him totally unfit for any service, I keep him moving,
however, on all occasions, by way of punishment for putting himself off on us as guide." Lt. Whipple had done the same four years
before.

They were soon in Indian country where Beale regarded the
natives with a mixture of caution and pity. He gave his men "strict
orders to touch neither corn nor melons," without paying for them,
that is, "or to allow their animals to do any damage whatever to the
place. Poor creatures! Their time will come soon enough for extermination when the merits of this road are made known, and it
becomes, as it most assuredly will, the thoroughfare to the Pacific."

Arrived at the pass whence they could at long last look upon the
Colorado River, he

sent my boys to the summit to make fires as signals to the
Mohaves that we came as friends, and desired to trade.

It is about twelve or fifteen miles yet to the river, and from
the Indians living there, who are a fine, large, bold race of

agriculturalists, we hope to obtain corn enough to feed our animals all the way from here to California.

I shall go into Fort Tejon to recruit and refit, as we have but ten days' provisions, at half rations, left, which short fare is owing to our having been misled by the miserable Leco, our guide. [8]

To the camels, Beale assigned the task of packing the wagon loads through the pass while the men worked down the route with pick and shovel, making it safe for the passage of the wagons themselves. Until the government wagons managed to pass, it would not do to pronounce the road complete. Emigrants, accompanied by wagons, were practically breathing down the roadbuilders' necks.

At daylight we were at work," Beale wrote in his journal:

The passage of the hill which we were obliged to work down cost us nearly all morning. Once over this, we descended the dry bed of the arroyo rapidly. Here the Indians began to pour in upon us from the Mohave villages. First, two or three, then by dozens. They were a fine-looking, comfortable, fat and merry set; naked except for a very small piece of cotton cloth around the waist, and though barefooted, ran over the sharp rock and pebbles as easily as if shod with iron. We were surrounded on all sides by them. Some had learned a few words of English from trafficking with the military posts two hundred and fifty miles off, and one of them saluted me with, 'God damn my soul eyes! How de do! How de do!'" [8]

On the next day, October 18, 1857:

Camp is crowded with Indians again this morning, some bringing melons, others corn, and others beans, &c., to trade for old clothes, worn out shirts, handkerchiefs, or almost anything of ours they fancy. They are shrewder at a bargain, though, than our men, whose keen appetites cannot bear the delay necessary to a successful trade. The watermelons, cantelopes, and pumpkins, are of excellent flavor and fair size. . . .

Trading with the Indians, in a day we had secured a hundred bushels of corn and beans, pumpkins, watermelons, and cantelopes, to last us to the settlements. [8]

With understandable relief, especially in view of previous gloomy forebodings, Beale noted, "Here my journey, as far as the road is concerned, terminated, my instructions directing me, in the event of a want of provisions, to proceed to Fort Tejon and procure them there." What they had secured from the Indian agriculturalists was not sufficient to promise a safe return journey. Fort Tejón, then, must be visited, a visit that would later lay Edward Beale open to the criticism of using this excuse to push the road to the vicinity of his own property.

At the moment, though, Beale's urgent problem was how to get those camels across the river. Certainly it would never do to leave them on the east bank of the Colorado while he went forward to the settlements of California. Those Indians crowding around might seem as afraid of the huge beasts as had their ancestors when first meeting horses. Familiarity could cure them of that and perhaps suggest the camels might serve them as beasts of burden or just as food. Definitely, the animals brought thither at such great expense of energy and of money must not be left behind to the doubtful mercies of Indians.

Abbé Huc's reference book had been explicit about the fact that not only could camels not swim but that "camels having a horror of water, it is sometimes impossible to make them get into a boat . . . they would die sooner." For camels being invited into small craft, it had certainly been a matter of judgment rather than of horror. At the banks of the Colorado where there were no boats to be forced into, they "not only swam with ease, but with apparently more strength than horses or mules." To the delight of Ned Beale, this proved their crowning achievement, one that sealed the devotion which ever after, and despite the camels' active detractors, he held toward them.

The best way to discourage such detractors, Beale knew, was to keep these pets dramatically in the public's eye. On November 9, at seven in the morning, he mounted his favorite white dromedary, Seid, and, accompanied by the imported camel driver Hadji Ali on Tuili, covered the last fifty-seven miles into Los Angeles, arriving there by three o'clock in the afternoon.

At Beale's request, a friend immediately sat down to write to Mrs. Beale, eagerly awaiting news back in Chester: "The whole town is agog, everybody, man, woman and child, interested to see Beale riding in on a dromedary." While he was continuing to fill

her in on news, Ned himself finally managed to get a few moments
to compose a postscript before the letter had to be sent to the
steamer that was on the point of leaving port.

"My dearest darling," Ned's part of the letter ran, "I have this
moment dismounted from my dromedary, and the crowd of friends
around, and the necessity of shaking hands with all, keeps me so
busy that I have been obliged to get Ozier to write you." [1] Of
course there was excitement! Had not the *Los Angeles Star*
predicted a mere two years before that it could never happen!

Nearly a month earlier, on October 18, after he'd made sure his
whole party was safely across the Colorado River, Beale sat down
confidently to write a long letter to the secretary of war. "Sir," it
ran, "I have the honor to report my arrival in California, after a
journey of 48 days. It gives me pleasure to inform you that we have
met with the most complete success in our exploration for a wagon
road from Fort Defiance, New Mexico, to this State. In a hurried
letter of this kind, it is not possible that I should give you much of
the detail of our exploration. Leaving that for my daily journal to
disclose, I shall endeavor to give you an idea of the character of the
country as well as the advantages of the road I have explored." [8]

This he proceeded to do at some length, pointing out that for
travel to California it was not only the shortest and most level but
also a well-timbered and well-grassed route. Keeping as it did to a
high altitude, it was "salubrious"—suggesting he felt there was
small risk of contracting malaria along the way—and temperate,
with water holes spaced not more than twenty miles apart. Furthermore, it crossed the "great desert (which must be crossed by
any road to California) at its narrowest point . . . and although the
double duty of exploring [a dig at the incompetency of the guides!]
and marking the road has fallen upon us, we have passed through it
without an accident of any kind whatever." Quite a contrast to
those sombre forebodings that had filled him on the eve of setting
forth from Fort Defiance!

Of course his pets came in for their share of appreciative comment:

An important part in all our operations has been acted by the
camels. Without the aid of this noble and useful brute, many
hardships which we have been spared would have fallen to
our lot; and our admiration for them has increased day by day,

as some new hardship, endured patiently, more fully developed their entire adaptation and usefulness in the exploration of the wilderness . . . . Unsupported by the testimony of every man in my party, I should be unwilling to state all that I have seen them do . . . . I have subjected them to trials which no other animal could possibly have endured; and yet I have arrived here not only without the loss of a camel, but they are admitted by those who saw them in Texas to be in as good condition today as when we left San Antonio . . . .

Leaving home with all the prejudice invariably attaching to untried experiments, and with many in our camp opposed to their use, and looking forward confidently to their failure, I believe at this time that I may speak for every man in our party, when I say that there is not one of them who would not prefer the most indifferent of our camels to four of our best mules; and I look forward hopefully to the time when they will be in general use in all parts of the country. [8]

January 6, 1858, saw Beale about to start back over the route he had been surveying a scant three months earlier. Before leaving California, though, he made sure the camels should not be forgotten. The *Los Angeles Star* for January 8 helped him in this with the notice:

General Beale and about 14 camels stalked into town last Friday week and gave our streets an Oriental aspect. It looks oddly enough to see, outside of a menagerie, a herd of huge ungainly, awkward, but docile animals move about in our midst with people riding them like horses . . . . These camels under charge of General Beale are all grown and serviceable and most of them are well broken to the saddle and are very gentle. All belong to the one hump species except one which is a cross between the one hump and two hump species. This fellow is much larger and more powerful than either sire or dam. He is a grizzly looking hybrid, a camel-mule of colossal proportions. These animals are admirably adapted to travel across our continent and their introduction was a brilliant idea the result of which is beginning most happily . . . . They were found capable of packing one thousand pounds weight apiece and of travelling with their load from thirty to forty miles a day, all the while finding their own food over an almost barren country. Their drivers say that they will get fat where a jackass would starve to death. The "mule," as they call the cross . . . will pack twenty-two hundred pounds. [16]

Among the onlookers were practical businessmen who, sensing the possible usefulness of camels in many situations, began to consider setting up a camel business on their own. It took as much as a year to stir up similar enthusiasm in hoped-for investors in such a scheme—a period during which the camels again did their part in assisting another roadbuilding expedition. By May 1859, there was organized the short-lived Camel Association (officially The California and Utah Camel Association), which undertook to sponsor the importation of camels from Mongolia, two-humped Bactrians of a kind that must have carried Father Huc through the Mongolian deserts he'd described. This undertaking got off to a bad start when, of the thirty-two camels originally shipped, seventeen died during the severe winter when the transport remained icebound in the Amur River.

On July 26, 1860, the *San Francisco Daily Evening Bulletin* was begging people to remain orderly and quiet as these surviving camels made their way ashore from the ship, adding, "The camel is the last institution necessary—before the advent of the Pacific Railroad—to bend the uninhabitable frontiers of the continent into contact and annihilate the wilderness which separates the New from the Old West." Alas for that last institution! Sold at auction, a camel would bring the importing entrepreneurs a maximum bid of $475, though the owners valued them at a minimum of $1,200 each.

In 1858, however, Ned Beale was cherishing high hopes for the future of the government herd. He started back East with most he'd brought West, reaching the Colorado River on January 23. There he was amazed to find a steamer—the *General Jessup*, appropriately named after the chief of the Quartermaster Corps— "waiting to convey us to the opposite side. Here, in a wild, unknown country, inhabited only by savages, the great river of the west, hitherto declared unnavigable, had, for the first time, borne upon its bosom that emblem of civilization, a steamer [which] . . . was to lend its aid to the settlement of our vast western territory. But alas! for the poor Indian living on its banks and rich meadow lands. The rapid current which washes its shores will hardly pass more rapidly away. The steam whistle of the *General Jessup* sounded the death knell of the river race." [8]

Alas, rather, for the too vulnerable *General Jessup* in those barely navigable waters. A too large and boastful imitation of Lt. Ives's little iron steamer that had explored the Colorado, its own death knell would sound within a short time after Beale's crossing. As it steamed proudly along, it struck a rock near Fort Yuma and sank, an emblem of civilization ingloriously and emblematically sunk in the wilderness waters of an uncharted river.

Beale explained:

I had brought the camels with me and as they stood on the bank, surrounded by hundreds of wild, unclad savages, and mixed with these the dragoons of my escort and the steamer slowly revolving her wheels preparatory to a start, it was a curious and interesting picture.

The camels, immediately upon my arrival [at Fort Tejón, some forty miles south of today's Bakersfield] for the sake of testing their capability of withstanding cold, I had placed in a camp within a few hundred yards of the summit of the Sierra Nevada, and to this date they have lived in two or three feet of snow, fattening and thriving wonderfully all the while. Lately, in a terrible snowstorm, the wagon carrying provisions for the camp could proceed no further. The camels were immediately sent to the rescue, and brought the load through snow and ice to the camp, though the six strong mules of the team were unable to extricate the empty wagon. . . .

My object in undertaking the winter journey is to test the practicability of the road surveyed last summer for winter transit. [8]

On February 19, he made a brief visit to the rock he'd bypassed on the way west. "Up at 3 and off at 5 A.M. One would have to deal with superlatives altogether to describe the beauty of the country through which we have passed this morning. When at 9 A.M. we reached Inscription Rock, I was tired of exclaiming, as every hundred yards opened out some new valley, 'how beautiful.' The rock itself seems to be a centre from which radiates valleys in all directions, and of marvellous beauty. It rises grandly from the valley, and the tall pines growing at its base give out long before they reach the top of its precipitous face. Inscriptions, names, hieroglyphics cover the base, and among the names are those of adventurous and brave Spaniards who first penetrated and explored this country . . . . Those with us looked with listless indifference at the names of the great men of their nation, and who made it famous centuries ago, cut by themselves upon this rock." [8]

Those listlessly indifferent Mexican observers probably could read little either in English or Spanish, certainly not in the archaic lettering of the brave Spaniards who had penetrated and explored the land centuries before. Beale does not mention names placed there by members of this party—his three boys, Bolman, and Tribit certainly, possibly also that "L.W.W. PA 1857" since it had been in Pennsylvania that so many of his party had enlisted.

Of the four other still legible names bearing 1857 dates, Lt. McCook was an army scout who served in the Apache campaign of 1857 as well as of 1855. C. H. Fry was probably the Major Carey H. Fry (U.S. Military Army, class of 1830) who, a couple of years later, was listed among the officers stationed at old Fort Wingate, situated approximately fifty miles from El Morro. The other two 1857 names seem to belong to otherwise forgotten men.

"The rock is some three or four hundred feet in height, and the spring almost hidden in the cavity of it" Beale went on describing the place at some length, ending with, "Leaving this beautiful place with regret, we travelled up the valley some miles further . . . and encamped for the night."

His regret could not have been too poignant for he confessed himself both tired and homesick for his family back in Chester. Two days later he gladly brought his expedition to an official close since with "the main road to Fort Defiance being intersected at this point by that which I have explored and surveyed to Fort Tejon, California," he had now come full circle.

"A year in the wilderness ended!" he exulted. "During this time I have conducted my party from the Gulf of Mexico to the shores of the Pacific Ocean, and back again to the eastern terminus of the road, through a country for a great part entirely unknown, and inhabited by hostile Indians, without the loss of a man. I have tested the value of the camels, marked a new road to the Pacific, and travelled 4,000 miles without accident." [8]

On April 26, 1858, he forwarded his journals to newly appointed Virginian Secretary of War John B. Floyd. Beale's covering letter read, in part:

The journal which I send you is a faithful history of each day's work, written at the camp fire at the close of every day. I have not altered or changed it in any respect whatever, as I desired to speak of the country as it impressed me on the spot, so as to be as faithful in my description of it as possible. I have written it for the use of emigrants more than for show . . . . I presume there can be no further question as to the practicability of the country near the thirty-fifth parallel for a wagon road, since Aubrey, Whipple, and myself, have all travelled it successfully with wagons, neither of us in precisely the same line, yet through very much the same country. [8]

Old Bullion would have liked to be on hand to applaud this achievement of his young friend, but Old Bullion had died nearly three weeks before the date of this letter.

Secretary of War Floyd did not need Old Bullion's applause to convince him that "the entire adaptation of camels to military operations on the plains may now be taken as demonstrated." He urged that, without waiting for the time-consuming process of breeding and training animals, the army should immediately expand the corps to include 1,000 camels. Congress turned a deaf ear to this recommendation in 1858, as it would also in 1859 and 1860. Old Bullion should have lived a few years longer.

In 1861, southerner Floyd took his departure for the South. But before that he had entrusted twenty camels to Beale's care and for his use. These, Ned Beale watched over carefully, keeping them on his Tejon ranch until finally, some time later, he could turn a herd increased to twenty-eight over to the Army Quartermaster stationed in California.

12

"First Emigrants"

The first emigrant train that would test the practicability of Beale's new route was already on its way from Missouri in April 1858. By the time they reached Albuquerque in late June, the emigrants had had time to learn how to deal with animals, wagons, and one another. Rugged individualists though they had to be to survive both the kind of lives most had led and the kind all were now facing, they knew they were entering upon a phase of their emigration where the risks, to be survived, must be shared. How shared was a question each must decide upon.

This time, the question was particularly urgent since previous emigrations heading west across New Mexico Territory had been assigned military escorts—an assignment with an admitted duality of purpose. For one thing, no politician in Washington quite dared ignore the growing number of emigrant trains and the needs of citizens thus traveling. For another, such trains were offering a welcome excuse for those railroad dreamers and planners who, stimulated by visions of both personal and political gain, wanted to see transcontinental tracks laid down.

Instructions issued to escorting officers were specific: "The escorting of a number of California emigrants and at the same time the exploration, survey, and construction of a wagon road . . . to Santa Fe" and beyond, a wagon road, of course, being a preliminary to a railroad. This meant the assignment of soldiers under regular army officers, with an engineer officer to undertake exploration and map making. While this went on, and assuming Indians did not interfere, troops could be set to work at roadbuilding. Dilatory

133

though such troops occasionally proved, they yet offered inexperienced emigrants both a faint sense of security and a measure of
wilderness know-how.

Even though this duality of responsibility served the ends of
men in Washington, it could be a source of trouble in the field.
Who was really in charge? On whom might be fixed blame for
failure? To whom should go the credit: to the captain of an army
detachment doing the escorting or to a lieutenant of topographical
engineers doing the exploration and drawing the maps?

It might lead to smouldering resentments, as is suggested in the
book published in 1859 by Captain Randolph B. Marcy, a manual
for emigrants entitled *The Prairie Traveller*. Of the road from Fort
Smith, Arkansas, to Santa Fe, he wrote bitterly: "This route is set
down upon most maps of the present day as having been discovered
and explored by various persons, but my own name seems to have
been carefully excluded from the list. Whether this omission has
been intentional or not, I leave for the authors to determine. I shall
merely remark that I had the command and entire direction of an
expedition which in 1849 discovered, explored, and marked out
this identical wagon road." [44]

Marcy may have done all that, but his instructions specified no
more than that his assignment was "for the purpose of providing
protection to our citizens emigrating to our newly acquired territories." To engineer officer Lt. Simpson, the man who was on his
way to rediscover Inscription Rock, was assigned the "exploration,
survey, and construction of a wagon road." Whipple would follow
the route later, as Beale was about to do in 1858, each improving it
a bit here, relocating it more conveniently there.

Whatever Marcy's feelings on the subject may have become by
1859, in 1848 he and Lt. Simpson seemed able to work together
without friction. Both were highly intelligent, keenly observant,
articulate enough to record effectively what was going on about
them. Through their eyes we can get a glimpse of a typical emigrant train of over a century ago—a train that could not have
differed too fundamentally from the one which the Udells were to
join, save that in 1849, the 35th parallel route remained yet to be
explored.

In Camp 54, on June 15, Simpson undertook to draw a word
picture of the emigrants, as graphic in its way as if from the
drawing pen of artist R. H. Kern:

On account of the position of our camp [the army camp, of course] we had a good view of the emigrants . . . I here introduce them. The ground having been selected by their leader, Mr. John Dillard, the *corral*, or enclosure to secure the cattle is made as follows: the first wagon is driven up to its place and halted; the second is then driven up to the left of the first—their tongues being so near to each other that, after the mules are disengaged, they may be made to cross each other . . . [52]

He went on, telling in detail how the wagons were driven in sequence into their places, first to the left, then to the right until, when all were in place, a closed circle had been formed. With this formation completed,

the animals are turned out to graze and a guard detailed to watch them.

Now comes the busy scene of pitching tents, collecting wood, preparing food, &c. The sound of axes, the metallic ring of the blacksmith's hammer, the merry voices of children, the lowing of cattle, the braying of mules is heard. Some children are playing near the water, and under a large, shady cottonwood tree on the bank of the stream, I see a young lady who has just alighted from her palfrey, enjoying the luxury of a camp seat, after a fatiguing day's ride. Habited in her riding dress, and with a bonnet, on, a veil thrown carelessly aside, she is twirling listlessly a switch, and giving heed to the conversation of a young emigrant who is sitting contentedly at her feet. The other and older ladies are attending to their domestic concerns, in the preparation of a good meal for their families, or of a comfortable sojourn until the morrow.

At sunset the signal will be sounded for the driving up of the animals; the animals will be secured in the *corral;* the camp watch established for the night. [52]

Except for that watch, whose business it was to remain alert, eschewing all distractions, there was great merriment among the campers—flute, fiddle playing, singing, dancing to a degree that would have made old mountain hands, like Leroux or Carson or Beale, most uncomfortable.

Marcy noted:

Our friends of the emigrant camp are enjoying themselves
much this evening; they have managed to raise some music,
and are dancing around their campfires most merrily. It certainly looks as if they were determined to keep their spirits up
as they go along.

Captain Marcy, obviously an understanding man, looked upon
the civilians entrusted to his care with a kindly, almost fatherly eye
and they appeared to respond in kind. A week earlier he'd told of
moving ahead of the emigrant party because

they were detained in consequence of the illness of the wife of
an emigrant; and we have learned this evening that the result
of the detention has been an addition to the company of two
promising boys (twins), which the happy father has done
Captain Dillard and myself the honor of calling "Dillard" and
"Marcy." For my part, I feel highly complimented and if I
never see the gold fields myself, I shall have the satisfaction of
knowing that my name is represented there. [42]

Nine years later, in 1858, with a road of sorts laid out and
military escort no longer provided, emigrants were having to look
out for themselves. This would burden their leaders with grave
responsibilities and make the setting forth into the wilderness
more than a little frightening for lesser members of a wagon train.
For such a party, even more than for a man like Beale who
understood both the wilderness and its inhabitants, a knowledgeable guide would seem almost a necessity. It was over a discussion
of the particular route to be taken, of the man to guide them over
it, and the amount he should be paid (and by whom paid) that the
first really serious rift between John Udell and his party's "captain"
opened.

It had been in the books from the very beginning that pious,
improvident John Udell and the less self-consciously pious, more
prosperous, and provident chief man of the train should approach a
profound disagreement. Undoubtedly others were finding John
Udell a pious bore. In Albuquerque, as plans for continuation of
their way west were discussed, the disagreement became explicit.

"Through the influence of the citizens of this place," John
complained, "our company had, all except myself, agreed to take

Mr. Beale's newly explored route, and leave the old traveled road here [the longer way closer to the Mexican border must have been what he meant by the "old traveled" route] and to undertake to travel nine hundred miles through an altogether savage and mountainous country, all the way without any road, except the trail of a few explorers, which could not be found much of the way by a stranger." [60]

Ned Beale would surely have violently protested this slander of the road to whose surveying and smoothing he had already devoted so much thought and effort. No emigrants had yet had a chance to follow it so there were none to defend it. John, conscious of the grim tricks life always seemed to be playing on him, was genuinely convinced that Mr. Beale's newly explored route could be no more than the trail of an explorer.

"I thought it preposterous," John continued in defence of the stand he took, "to start on so long a journey with so many women and children, and so many dangers attending the attempt. A burnt child dreads the fire; I had once, in crossing the plains, come near perishing by taking a cut-off, a trail, the Indians stealing our horses and leaving us to suffer many days with hunger, and we had no women or children with us to suffer. I opposed the move at that time, and I oppose it stronger now, but it was of no avail." [60] From that *"was* of no avail," we might guess that John was letting editorial hindsight assist his boasted foresight.

"We all agreed," he went on, "we could not travel without a guide so, with other heads of families and owners of property, assembled for the purpose of hiring one. Mr. L. J. Rose and Mr. Gillum Bailey were the largest owners in the train. We all expected to participate; but as I commenced talking on the subject, says Mr. Rose, 'Mr. Udell, Mr. Bailey and I can attend to this business without your help, and after a guide is hired, you can have the benefit of him with the rest by paying what we think right.' Such an expression from a German aristocrat, caused the blood of a free-born American to rankle in my bosom." [60]

John had disliked Germans ever since some German families had moved too close to his Ohio home. John, furthermore, could not have had much personal acquaintance with aristocrats of any kind. The epithet, "German aristocrat," however, coming from "free-born" John Udell could be just about as damning as any his infuriated pious imagination could devise. Undoubtedly Rose and

Bailey had in mind equally effective epithets to apply to this overargumentative member of the train, though they forebore to express them. After bitter argument flared up, Udell pointedly enrolled himself "in Mr. Bailey's train," though in fact it could make very little difference to whose train he belonged, all having to travel together.

They were all to learn that the guide they thought they could not travel without differed from no guide at all only in that he was to receive the, to them, princely sum of $500, to be paid in advance. As fate would have it, the man they engaged was none other than the José Manuel Saavedra about whom previous and more experienced employers had found nothing good to say. In 1858, Whipple was exploring in distant parts. Lt. Beale, his last employer, was then, as Saavedra must have learned with delight, far away in Fort Smith, Arkansas, completing plans for another road survey which would not set forth before the following November. Saavedra was very much in Albuquerque, talking smoothly and convincingly to the emigrants as he must have already for months been doing to any Albuquerque citizen he could buttonhole. For emigrants, all too sombrely aware that they would soon be heading into the great unknown, someone who had already several times been over the proposed route, twice in the company of renowned explorers, must have seemed like the answer to their prayers.

Undoubtedly the emigrant company was equally an answer to Saavedra's prayers. Pickings, he was finding, were getting pretty slim for an aging, self-made explorer. His asking price had dropped considerably from the $1,200 Whipple had agreed upon. Beale, too, mentioned bitterly his guide's "enormous wages." Saavedra was well aware that no matter how much they felt they needed him, emigrants could not begin to meet the kind of wages to be extorted from government-sponsored expeditions, and, moreover, no government expeditions under new and gullible leaders were expected that way. To him, therefore, $500 looked far to be preferred to no dollars at all. To some Albuquerque citizens, perhaps, Saavedra's absence may have seemed worth something, too.

In any case, instead of letting his free-born blood rankle, John Udell would have served himself and others far better by making careful enquiries into the guide's credentials. Somewhere in the then not very large "Mexican" city, there must have been folk both aware of Saavedra's demonstrated limitations and able and willing to tell the truth about them. Admittedly, however, some of those "intelligent families residing here" had let themselves be misled either by the boastful guide's claims or by their own eagerness to benefit Albuquerque through promoting the new route that should bring their city much business.

Some citizens helpfully raised $180 toward the demanded $500. Those, of course, could not have been folk who knew Beale very well. People who had talked with him after his previous year's return from the Colorado River would have heard his low estimate of Saavedra, and some such there must have been. To ferret out the facts by a systematic investigation was not in character for an improvident man who, in his mid-sixties and accompanied by his older wife and all his property, had set out on such a trip.

So, on June 30, with Saavedra much in evidence, they "left the Río Grande with our guide before us. . . . Travel today, 20 miles."

John was soon forced to revise his unkind estimate of the new road. On July 7, he wrote: "This morning we came over the dividing ridge between the Atlantic and Pacific waters. It was formerly hard to ascend but Mr. Beale has since improved it and made it easy." [60]

That night, approximately 130 miles from Albuquerque, they encamped by Inscription Rock. Udell was impressed by the great rock, by the many and varied inscriptions, by the ruins atop the rock and, most of all, by the box canyon that could so easily be made to serve as a natural corral. Strangely, the liberal supply of water did not seem to impress him, though circumstances would soon teach him a juster appreciation.

Of course, members of that train were bound to leave their marks upon the rock, some from self-esteem, some because of the same nagging doubts that had haunted the early Spanish passersby, that there was no real certainty as to when or whether they would ever reach California. It was well, therefore, to let it be known explicitly when they had camped by the rock. For July 7: "L. J. Rose, Iowa," appears with a now unidentifiable "R. T. Barnes." Clearly recognizable are the "John Udell, Age 63, July 8, 1858, First Emigrant," as well as "Isaac T. Holland, July 8, 1858, from Mo, First. Emgt. Train."

Almost exactly three months before, in Eureka, Missouri, the Udells had enjoyed a farewell dinner at the home of Isaac Holland's father-in-law, Mr. John Daily. "We expect Mr. Daily, with his large family, will overtake us at the Missouri River and travel with us to California," Udell wrote.

What, one wonders, happened to that home in Eureka where the Udells were so hospitably entertained? Did the Dailys just walk out to leave it with scarce a backward glance as had the Udells from so many homes in so many places? Was not such ability to uproot themselves without regret the outstanding characteristic of the westward drifters? Udell, himself a drifter, could not have thought it merited comment. On April 30, as expected, "Mr. Daily, with his large family and his son-in-law, Isaac Holland and family overtook us." All would presently be overtaken by disaster, some also by romance. About six months later, in Zuñi, lay preacher John Udell was joining "a merchant residing in Zuñi, Mr. Ezra Bucknam and Miss Adaline Daily in the sacred bonds of matrimony." This ceremony took place on the return trip, but no hint of pending romance comes through Udell's entry for July 10 when they passed through Zuñi on the way west!

The undated "Hedgpeth" on the rock belongs to a member of the same train. The Hedgpeths and the Udells, as it turned out, were the first of all that group, by many months, to complete their journey to California. From that train, too, are the only names definitely identified as belonging to women, "MISS A. E. BALEY" and "MISS A. C. BALEY" (see photographic section). "P. H. Williamson, July 8, 1858" was the Paul Williamson who had begun the trip as one of Mr. Brown's hands. But on May 30, he exchanged places with a Tamerlane Davis who had started out in Udell's employ; "not by my consent," Udell explained the shifting of help, "but I hope it may be for the best." Had Tamerlane Davis, we wonder, found John Udell too piously strict? Was Paul Williamson of a temperament better able to cope with the preacher-employer?

Two young cattle hands whom Rose was grubstaking to a California they would never reach were Billy Stidger ("W. C. Stidger, '58"), aged 19, and Will Harper ("W. C. Harper, 1858"), a year older than Stidger. Within a year they would both be back in Iowa, undoubtedly sated with adventure. Will Harper soon became a teacher in a local academy, where Billy Stidger enrolled himself as a student. When the Civil War started, Harper promptly joined the first company to be raised in his county, rising to a lieutenancy before meeting his death at Fort Donelson. Stidger was luckier. Though twice wounded, he survived four years' service to emerge as adjutant of his regiment and to return to Iowa, where he lived until 1880. Others of the cattle hands would presently be fighting in the Confederate cause, one becoming a bushwhacker, who, refusing to surrender to Union forces, was shot down and killed in a running fight.

Though the young men may have spent many an hour around their campfires, arguing the pros and cons of the issues already threatening to tear their land apart, they could have had little foreboding that they might, within three years, be facing one another as enemies. In 1858, California and the fortunes they would pick up there were foremost in the minds of all. Their immediate problems involved only the handling of their grubstakers' cattle, sometimes shooting game for the people of the wagon train, always keeping their eyes open for forage for the cattle and water for all.

Three weeks and 260 miles beyond El Morro, actually well past the San Francisco Mountains, hunters were sent out scouting for game and water to return "with deer, antelope and turkeys enough for the whole company." Few knew enough to suspect that where game was so plentiful, Indians might not be far behind. The immediate availability of game was their only concern.

Most emigrants, striding or riding, passed along, gun in hand, happily taking pot shots at anything that moved, missing most of the game, so that their hunting parties had to be sent far afield. Later emigrant trains would pay the price of such trigger happiness. A double price it would be, in that they would have to seek game at greater and greater distances from the road and that Indians would resent the frightening off of game they themselves needed for survival. In this first party along that route, though, not even the presumably experienced guide had sense enough to suggest that wild animals, frightened by the incessant chatter of guns, might become scarce but that Indians certainly would not.

Saavedra, typically, was presently returning from a scouting trip to report he could find "no sufficiency of water for our stock for over seventy-five or eighty miles ahead. . . . Many of the company," John wrote, "thought our stock could not travel that distance without water, and we must remain here and wait for the rainy season. I contended that we had better travel on for, with careful and proper treatment, we could get the stock through to water, and if we remained here until the rainy season, in all human probability, our provision would be exhausted, and we should perish by starvation . . . but all my entreaties were in vain, none would agree to go on." [60]

Obsessed with the fortunes that were to be theirs in California, the men of the train could brace themselves to remain near water and live for weeks, if need be, on limited dry rations augmented by the game they were sure they could shoot. They refused to risk their cattle on an eighty-mile waterless stretch for they were relying on those cattle, and the high prices such were reputed to bring in California, to tide their families over the first lean weeks while they themselves sought and staked claims to fabulous gold diggings. Their earlier grim forebodings that the train might not get through intact to California still haunted them, as did the alternative of arriving there penniless.

Still hopeful men again went out in search of water holes and one—not, of course, Saavedra—returned presently with news he had located a small supply. Udell, ever ready with unsolicited advice, urged the train to move on in sections so that they might use even a small water hole to advantage. Suddenly becoming aware of possible Indians, though none had as yet been sighted even from afar, others adamantly refused to consider dividing the train.

John, writing of this, was bound to add his editorial comment: "As I was copying my journals of 1858 in 1859, if our company had been as fearful of separating when among Mohave Indians as they were here, where no Indians lived near, we might probably have saved a number of lives of our company, and all our property and much suffering. . . ." [60] The advice of a knowledgeable guide could have been of utmost value here, but John gives no hint that Saavedra spoke up in the crisis. Having once taken part in Indian raids on other Indians, the guide should have known where the risks were real, where imaginary. As always, though, he was living up to Beale's characterization of him as a "humbug."

When other scouting emigrants returned with the news they had located a larger water hole ahead, the whole party undertook to move on. By August 7, however, scarcity of water again threatened and the travelers turned back to trek to the previous night's camp where "our oxen, having travelled fifty-two miles without water, forced their way down into the canon, where there was some." [60]

Providentially, a week later brought "a hard shower of rain and thunder of about one hour's duration, which filled our water holes and for which I feel thankful to the Giver of all blessings. At night the men who had been out five days exploring for water returned, [it shouldn't have taken "guide" Saavedra five days to locate water holes in a country he had already traversed!] and reported they had found a large spring eighty miles ahead and five miles off our course, and there was a strong probability that the afternoon shower would furnish us plenty of water in the canons that were only half that distance, viz: forty miles ahead. This news lighted a smile on every countenance, and we had hymn-singing by excellent female voices until late at night"—conducted by John Udell, it's a safe guess.

By August 17, the emigrants had crossed those eighty-five miles to settle into camp somewhere within hailing distance of that promised spring, though not at its rim. The next morning early "we were engaged in driving our stock to the water. We had to travel over mountains, and through deep rocky canons, and huge precipices almost perpendicular, to get to it . . . It was, indeed, pleasant to us and the poor, half-famished cattle. I started for camp, with ten gallons in two kegs, on my horse, the mountain was so steep I could not carry them on my horse but had to roll them up half a mile, one at a time." [60]

Where were those two young men he was grubstaking to California? With a gallon of water weighing about eight pounds, ten gallons, without counting the weight of the keg, would come to eighty pounds. Small wonder that sixty-three-year-old John found that "I was so worn from loss of sleep and hard labor that it was with difficulty that I was able to get into camp with my water that night." One of his men (where was the other?)—was it the Paul Williamson who left his name on the rock?—"remained with the stock that night, with the others at the spring, to drive them into camp the following day. One horse and one mule stolen by Indians." [60]

This grim warning of the presence of Indians, and thus of things to come, should have suggested to the guide, at least, the urgency of getting those two separated trains back together. On August 21,

John had recorded that, to ease the strain on water resources and on pasturage, Mr. Rose's and Mr. Bailey's trains "now travel separately."

The stolen animals, one belonging to Rose, the other, with unusual poetic justice, to the guide, were presently brought in by Indians. These virtuously protested that they had had nothing to do with the removal of the animals in the first place, that they had taken great personal risks in recovering them from bad and dangerous Mojave thieves. For this unsolicited act of altruism, they promptly let it be known, they expected extravagant rewards which Mr. Rose, now uncomfortably aware that they were deep in Indian territory, unwisely gave them.

"This," wrote John Udell, "was the first annoyance we had met with from Indians . . . but they continued to annoy us from this on." A mere two days later, word came back from the Rose train in front to the Bailey train in the rear that Mr. Rose

> had seven of his work oxen stolen by Indians and his brother-in-law severely wounded by them. The Indians were frequently shooting their arrows among us from their hiding places in the rocks and brush, as we passed along, and when in camp wounding our stock; we were constantly in imminent danger, and our trouble was great, knowing that if our teams should fail, we should be sure prey for the merciless Indians. We concluded to go on as far as we could; perhaps some of our stock might live to get through, which was our last forlorn hope. We travelled all night. . . . [60]

Night travel made them less certain targets for the hovering Indians whose attentions, they agreed, could not be avoided by an about-face so late in the game. Those Indians—the very ones Beale's party had found so fat, merry, and friendly the previous year—were certainly clever enough to realize that here was no military group with its expert and disciplined marksmen, but a lot of greenhorns who, to their eye, provided legitimate and easy prey. Surely they were by now beginning to realize that more and more strangers would come, leaving less and less space for the natives. That "death knell of the river race" was beginning to be heard and the river race was getting the message.

On August 27, Mr. Rose's train had reached the banks of the

Joel Hedgpeth (1809–75) and Jane Hedgpeth (1808–59)

Hedgpeth Family Members on the 1858 Wagon Train

These photographs of members of the Hedgpeth family were taken in 1858 in St. Joseph, Mo. After the wagon train disaster at the Colorado and the return to Albuquerque, Thomas went back to Missouri and remained there. The parents (Joel and Jane) went on to California under Beale's protection, during which trip Jane had her adventure in Mud Springs. She died in Visalia, Calif., shortly after settling there. In the 1890s an Indian depredation suit was filed in behalf of Joel's estate by his son William Pleasant Hedgpeth. Like other such suits, it was unsuccessful. *All portraits courtesy Joel W. Hedgpeth*

Thomas Riley Hedgpeth (1830–87)

Lewis Hedgpeth (1837–1917)

William Pleasant Hedgpeth (1843–1928)

Elizabeth Hedgpeth (1845?–?)

Edward Fitzgerald Beale when a midshipman. Copyright 1954 National Trust for Historic Preservation. Courtesy National Trust for Historic Preservation.

Beale in the costume he wore when crossing Mexico, carrying with him the little sack of gold. Copyright 1954 National Trust for Historic Preservation. Courtesy National Trust for Historic Preservation.

Nancy Funderbunk Baley, William's wife, 1893

Sarah Margaret Baley Simpson, 1893. She was probably one of the "Misses Baley" whose name appears on Inscription Rock.

Three Women of William Wright (Right) Baley's Family

Dolly Baley Parker and her husband, the Reverend Mr. Parker. Though she was one of the many Baley girls who traveled in the wagon train, she was too young then, according to the usage of the times, to be referred to as "Miss." The date of this portrait is uncertain.

All portraits courtesy Mark S. Simpson

Inscription Rock today. *Dick Kent photo*

The lithographs on the following pages are from sketches made on the spot by artist R. H. Kern. The first six are from Lt. Simpson's report, the last three from Capt. Sitgreaves's. The inscription is only a small section of a long plate in Simpson's report. The view of the "Cascade of the Little Colorado River" gives some idea of the abrupt canyon walls. The "Mohave Indians" seem to be more than a bit romanticized.

Drawn by R.H. Kern from a Sketch by E. M. Kern.   P. S. Duval's Steam Lith. Press Philad.ª

VIEW OF THE PLACER OR GOLD MOUNTAIN, AND SANDIA MOUNTAIN

Drawn to accompany Lt. Simpson's report of the Arkansas route by R. H. Kern. Copied in the Topographical Bureau.

P. S. Duval's Steam Lith Press Phil.

VIEW OF SANTA FE AND VICINITY FROM THE EAST.

R. H. Kern delt.

P. S. Duval's Steam Lith Press Philad.

PUEBLO OF JEMEZ
from the East Aug 20.

R. H. Kern delt. P. S. Duval's Steam lith Press Phila'd.

PUEBLO OF ZUÑI.

R. H. Kern del. P. S. Duval's Steam lith. press. Phi.

NORTH FACE OF INSCRIPTION ROCK.

y cap.n gen. de las pra.s del nuebo mex. Por el Reyno, e Paso por aqui debuelta delos pue
blos de Zuni Allos, 29 de Julio delaño de, 1620, los puso en paz a supe dim, pi
Prendiole su fabor com obos Allos desu mag. y denuebo diezon la obdiencia. toddoqual
hiso conel agasaxe selo yprudencia como tan christianisimo———o, tampartica
lar zy gallar do soldado dem acobable yloada mem or———

Diego Nuñez Bellido

Alje/sapata Bartolomen arrso

CASCADE OF THE LITTLE COLORADO RIVER, near Camp 13

MOHAVE INDIANS [Big Colorado River N.M.

FIRST VIEW OF THE BIG COLORADO RIVER
from summit of mountain between Camps 31 and 32

Colorado, with California, the promised land, now within reach. While they awaited the arrival of the rear train, they saw Indians boldly stealing stock and driving it into the river. The rear party was lagging behind, working on road improvements that should make those last miles easier for their creaking wagons to negotiate.

Already in the previous April, Lt. Beale had made a point of warning the secretary of war of the dangers awaiting emigrant trains at the river crossing: "I regard the establishment of a military post on the Colorado River as an indispensable necessity for the emigrant over this road . . . The temptation of scattered emigrant parties with their families, and the confusion of inexperienced teamsters, rafting so wide and rapid a river with their wagons and families, would offer too strong a temptation for the Indians to withstand." [8] Though he liked those Indians, realist Beale understood only too well what such temptation could do to even quite friendly Indians. His own party, kept under strict discipline, had had no women and children to guard, no large herds with which to tempt agriculturally inclined Indians.

Not even the self-conscious wisdom of John Udell had ever suggested that the emigrants might have eased their problems by getting rid of part of their stock, at least. Stock was both food and capital and they would have greeted such a suggestion as might bank depositors of our day the idea of blowing up the bank holding their deposits. By August 31, in any case, the emigrants were left no choice in the matter.

"This day," wrote John Udell,

> all who were left alive of Mr. Rose's party came into our camp, bringing melancholy intelligence. I will here relate the whole story as it was reported to us by the party when they came in: Soon after our men arrived at the river and were nearly ready to drive our stock up to our wagons, the Indians rushed in from the brush in every direction, to the number of three or four hundred, and closed up around Mr. Rose's camp, and commenced shooting their arrows into it, like a shower—intending, as was supposed, to massacre all in a few moments; but our men had so many rifles and revolvers loaded for their reception, that they soon retreated a little and took shelter behind trees and brush. The battle continued

nearly two hours, they thought, until the Indians had
succeeded in driving the cattle into the river and out of reach;
they then left—and for twenty or twenty-five men (one half of
them badly wounded) to pursue so many, would be throwing
away lives for naught. Mr. Brown was killed . . . one of his
daughters was also badly wounded . . . Eleven of the men
were wounded, and Mrs. Jones and Mr. Brown's daughter,
making in all thirteen wounded (some badly) and eight killed.
Seventeen cattle and eight or ten horses were all that were
saved, and they by being near camp, the majority of them
were the property of Mr. Rose. These they hitched to one of
Mr. Rose's wagons and a light buggy, loaded with as much
provisions as they could haul . . . ; and commenced retracing
their steps, leaving the awful battle ground, but not without
fear of being pursued." [60]

Though many owners of stock were in Bailey's train, they'd sent
this stock ahead to the river with the stock of the first train for more
convenient watering while they lingered making road repairs.
Thus, even the families that escaped the bloody fight were involved in severe personal losses.

Guide Saavedra does not come in here for even the slightest
mention, so it's a safe bet he did nothing to distinguish himself
during the fight. Of course, he managed to survive.

Says Udell,

Here we were left in the midst of merciless savages, thirsting
for our blood, some sixty women and children, several infants,
and none except Mr. Rose had a team sufficient to move the
families and the little provision we had from the spot . . . I
was in the worst situation of anyone in the company who had a
family—my wife being sixty-five years of age, and so feeble
that she was not able to walk, and I had not an ox or a hoof
left, except an Indian pony which I had kept at my wagon, and
he so worn down he could scarcely travel or stand. The other
families had an ox or two each, which they could have put
together to haul their little ones who could not walk and the
small quantity of provisions they had left, which they finally
did, but there was not one half enough provision in the
company to sustain us until we could reach the white settlements." [61]

There remained for them all no alternative but to return to those "white settlements." So that there might be no mutilation of the dead, they consigned the bodies, weighted with the now useless wagon chains, to the river. Then they buried their valuables, hoping somehow to recover them later. Finally, a silent and depressed company, they turned their back on most of their possessions as well as the river and the unreachable promised land beckoning from the far side, and started the long, long walk back to the settled part of New Mexico.

13

Emigrants' Return

Fortunately for the despondent travelers, however unfortunate it might prove for other emigrants, several more trains had already started west along "Beale's route." Inscription Rock reveals that three weeks after Rose's train camped there, another train remained by the pool for three nights, at least. That train's proprietor, Bradford Caves, seems to have disdained to leave his mark there, but the men who cut two of the five inscriptions dated July 28, 29, and 30, were presently to be singled out by Udell as belonging to Caves's train. All inscriptions bearing the same dates would have belonged to the same train since, in an Indian-conscious time and land, groups arriving so close together must have joined forces.

After leaving there, Caves's group moved ahead more rapidly than Rose's, possibly because encumbered with fewer families, possibly because they were luckier in the matter of water holes. Though also harassed by Indians, who had managed to run off with much of their stock, Cave's train was, by September 1, but a few days behind the other. By the time the miserable stragglers from that emigrant train ahead began arriving in the camp of the new group, problems with Indian horse thieves had already psychologically prepared them to turn back. Fortunately they still had enough provisions to help eke out the pitifully small supply the other group had started back with.

The morale of all improved somewhat five days later when they were successful in holding off an Indian attack. They camped with "Indians showing their heads over the tops of the mountains, menacing us, but dare not come down in reach of our guns."

Two weeks after the massacre and some eighty miles along the return journey, a third emigrant train turned up—the one responsible for the records on El Morro dated August 23. Of the men in the train, the "R. J. Hamilton, Ind. August 23rd, 1858" was, according to John Udell, "an intimate acquaintance of mine . . . . John Hamilton is the gentleman's name; to him I repaired immediately for assistance for my old lady and myself—at least to carry our provisions for us . . . . The generous-hearted man said: 'Yes, come, you and your old lady, and go with us; you shall fare with my family as long as I have an ox left, or anything.' Mr. Hamilton had lost two-thirds of his stock for lack of water and hard driving to reach watering places. He had left [behind] four out of five of his wagons, not having oxen or horses left to haul them. He was illy able to haul his own large family, yet his sympathy prompted him to take us in—while his companions in travel refused to take any except Mr. Rose and his men, although some of them had plenty of horses, mules and cattle to take the whole company—but Mr. Rose was a monied man." [60] Some of these stock-owning men, John had neglected to say in his bitterness, had been friends of Mr. Rose in Iowa. Perhaps they had also known John Udell well enough to discount his complaints or to wish to escape listening to them for the next two months.

Actually, all the returning emigrants were in desperate straits, Rose hardly less than Udell. "Those of our company who had no team," Udell recounted, "suffered much in travelling fifty or sixty miles until we met another train, of more generous-hearted men. Women and children had to walk and carry their infants, and the men had to carry their provisions on their backs, until they had worn their feet to raw sores—many without shoes—walking through the thick, short, thorny greasewood and sage brush, in the night; for it was so hot in the daytime that we travelled much at night." [60] A year before Beale had written, "It is certainly the hardest road on the feet of barefooted animals I have ever known."

John's matter-of-fact account continues, "I walked, and my old lady rode my pony, and Mr. Hamilton carried our provision as long as it lasted . . . until we met another train—the Indians almost constantly annoying us, shooting their arrows among our stock, from their hiding places in the high rocks, by the side of the narrow canons which we had to pass through. One arrow was shot through the back part of the tree of my saddle, when on the horse, but, fortunately, no one was riding at the time." [60]

Soon yet another train, this one from Illinois, met them. This, with "five hundred head of cattle, with horses and mules, and forty-three men—no women or children" immediately gave west-ward-minded John Udell a change of heart. He thought "as we were now one hundred and eighteen men strong, we could go on to California . . . but a majority of those who had turned back represented the road as horrible and the Indians so numerous and warlike, that certain death to all was almost certain to ensue. I argued that if twenty-five men had succeeded in driving the Indians from them, when the Indians had completely surrounded them in the brush, and had every possible advantage of them—if twenty-five men could do that, I thought that with one hundred and eighteen men and any kind of precaution, we could achieve the victory without the loss of one life." [60]

The others did not think so and were not to be persuaded by an argumentative old man. "Messrs E. O. and T. O. Smith," proprie-tors of the new train, "took a vote of their men as to whether they should turn back, and, also, as to whether they were willing to give up their seats in the wagons to the suffering emigrant women and children, and to divide their provisions with us. All but two or three voted in the affirmative." [60]

So all turned back. Still, for some days, they would avoid marching during the hot hours of the day by moving at night, which had an added advantage in that they could thus escape too continuous attentions of Indians. Cooler weather coming on and Indian country left behind, they could again travel during daylight hours. Camping at night, however, had its own drawbacks for most of them had only cold, damp ground for a bed "with nothing but clouds and one quilt over us," as Udell wrote. Nights in that high country could be penetratingly cold.

Within five days of starting on that return trip, the Messrs. Smith had to butcher some of their cattle to feed the tremendously enlarged train. "They killed their best for us," John wrote appre-ciatively, "but they were all lean and feverish, in travelling so far and suffering so much for want of water and food. Twenty or twenty-five of the young men concluded to steer two hundred miles south, through the wilderness, and strike the South Mail Route . . . into California" [60] the route that approximated the 32nd parallel of latitude.

Supplied with jerked meat from several of the best beef cattle remaining, and "after several pathetic and eloquent speeches," the adventurous youths set out, guided by hope alone. Ten days later,

> three of those men who left us to go to California a few days since, returned and said they supposed the others had all perished for want of water. They travelled together, finding no water, until some of the party became so famished they could travel no further. They then started in different directions to find water. Three of them succeeded, and returned to inform their companions. On their return they found guns, ammunition and provisions strewed along, but found no men . . . We all supposed the other twenty had perished. [60]

Another three days later, that twenty who had thus panicked straggled back, sobered and wiser, to the train, "much emaciated, their visages thin and wan."

Meanwhile Udell, getting news of yet another wagon train ahead that just might have flour to spare, set forth alone to beg some "for my old lady, as she was becoming sick from living on feverish beef" (more likely, we may guess, from lack of vitamins).

Arrived at his destination, John found that Mr. Rose, whom he was bound to cast as the villain of his tale, seemed to have cornered the very limited market without setting any aside for the party behind. A few sympathetic ladies contributed flour from their own store and with this John returned grouchily to his vitamin-starved wife.

Too obsessed by his own worries, Udell could not perceive that even the monied Rose was having plenty of troubles. Rose himself, as he admitted in an account he wrote later in Albuquerque, was close to complete exhaustion. Yet he was still leader, still saddled with responsibility for others in his company, still nagged by complainers. Nearly everyone was now walking most of the time. Mrs. Rose's mother, Mrs. Jones, was one of the severely wounded who must be cared for. Mrs. Rose herself, having worn through the soles of her shoes, had now to continue barefoot across that congealed lava, bits of which strewed the ground, and cut the feet of unshod animals.

In Rose's company was the so-recently widowed Mrs. Brown, who had now lost her husband's horse so that she, too, must walk most of the time. Her mind was filled with worries about her severely wounded daughter, Sallie Fox, and with thoughts of her husband's body, one of those committed to the river, as well as of the young son who had sickened and died along the way to be buried in an unmarked grave lest the Indians mutilate his body. Years later she would tell of how, like Penelope of ancient legend, she determinedly kept her hands busy with knitting, unravelling, reknitting the same stocking as she dragged her weary feet across the harsh ground or took her brief turn in the wagon. Few in this forward train could have had energy to spare for concern over the worries of folk in the part of the train that was following somewhere in the rear.

On October 20, Udell wrote,"We all arrived safe in Zuñi, in starving condition. My wife and I had suffered much with cold, from lying on the ground in freezing nights, before we could get a room from the Indians. We soon obtained some corn meal and flour, ground between two stones . . . it makes very good bread. We also got some beans and pumpkins from them—all of which we ate so greedily for several days that we made ourselves quite unwell." [61]

"Mr. Bucknam, the merchant here" promptly cast an interested eye on Adaline Daily. By October 23, he'd "hired a large room from the Indians for Mr. Daily's family, and permitted my wife and me to go in with them"—with an eye, perhaps, to John Udell's services—"and we are now quite comfortable. We have to remain with these friendly Indians until Mr. Smith comes up with his whole train. Mr. Bucknam is an American from the Eastern States, and is quite an intelligent man—a trader with these Indians. He acts in the capacity of interpreter for us." [60]

On October 31 there arrived at Zuñi "two large government teams from Albuquerque, laden with provisions for us poor sufferers," thanks to the efforts of some of the young men who had pushed ahead from the main group for just this purpose. On the following day, all celebrated the joining in the holy bonds of matrimony of Adaline Daily and the intelligent Mr. Bucknam, with preacher John Udell performing the ceremony.

November 2 saw the Smith train catching up.

The whole train, alive and well . . . . He was now done sacrificing his cattle to sustain over one hundred poor starving human beings. We had subsisted on his cattle over thirty days, for which he could have no hope of ever receiving but very little compensation, some few who had money paid him. Such philanthropy is seldom met with as the Messrs. Smith manifested toward us. The Government provision was immediately divided out to every person alike, children and all, and we had enough to make us comfortable to Albuquerque. We, who arrived here first, were with the Zuñi Indians fourteen days. [60]

The next day all left Zuñi "in good spirits; the two empty wagons were again loaded with women and children. We made slow progress but we were comfortable."

Within the following week, they must have camped at Inscription Rock, but this time, with all eyes focused upon distant Albuquerque, no mention at all is made of the days and nights between November 3, when they left Zuñi and November 10, when they paused in "Lagoona." There "Elder Gorman again preached to us in the evening—a discourse very applicable to our misfortunes and present circumstances. Mr. Gorman also contributed to us in money, flour, clothing, and vegetables, to the amount of twenty-five or thirty dollars. We arrived in Albuquerque on the 13th of November. Here we met good American citizens, and we now know how to appreciate their society, having been four months and fourteen days suffering in a savage country." [60]

In Albuquerque, "the chief officer in command had granted to all returned emigrants (nearly two hundred of us) thirty days' rations each." This was no negligible grant from a military post so far removed from its own sources of supply!

That winter, which would long outlast the thirty days of grace thus granted the emigrants, was already upon them, forcing them, each according to his nature, to find some means of keeping alive. Only the young cattle hands, now purged of their great desire to reach California, could afford to live from hand to mouth without making immediate plans for the future. Finally, after about seven months of such living, most of those remaining in Albuquerque took employment with the U.S. government, engaging to drive teams that hauled supplies to forts or to scouting parties or, as they had learned, to distressed emigrants. By the end of another year, most of these youths had drifted back to their homes.

The Masonic Order in the city took care of the Mason's destitute widow, Mrs. Brown, and her surviving children. These would again take to the road to California the following year when those kind and generous Messrs. Smith, who had so notably succored Rose's train, started out once more—and this time reached their destination.

Mr. Rose himself, having owned the biggest part of the herd appropriated by the Mojaves, had suffered the greatest financial loss of all. One of the young cattle hands later surmised that he would have been forehanded enough to keep some cash in reserve. That this was really the case is suggested by the fact that he presently moved to that trading center, Santa Fe, where he started a business of his own and promptly began accumulating more cash. Only when the Civil War was making New Mexico an uncomfortable place for any outsider of uncertain loyalties did he again start for California. Having settled near Los Angeles, he became, according to his well-established habit, a prosperous and prominent citizen.

It was upon the elderly Udells, of course, that was focused much of the sympathetic attention of Albuquerque citizens. "When we arrived here, " John recorded on the day of his arrival, "My wife and I found a nice comfortable little room fitted up for our reception by our good friend, Judge Henry Winslow (he being apprized of our coming by forerunners), in his own house. He also fed us at his own well provided table, and furnished each of us with a good suit of clothes out of his store." [60]

Though, obviously, John Udell's self-esteem was flattered by this attention from a prominent citizen, the same kind of sturdy independence that had kept him moving in search of an illusory better life, rebelled at living indefinitely on anyone's bounty. None of the kind of hand-to-mouth living that satisfied the footloose young cattle hands would do for him either. Within ten days of his arrival, he had "engaged to herd and feed the Government beef cattle, for fifteen dollars a month and a soldier's rations of provisions. We thought that with this we could support ourselves through the winter and not trespass on Mr. Winslow's hospitality any longer. Accordingly, we hired a comfortable room and moved into it, with the few articles which had been presented to us, for housekeeping, by the generous citizens and officers." [60]

Forty-two years earlier, in Ohio, the Udells had started life together with no more—"But we were both stout [i.e. strong] and healthy," he'd written of that start, "and we thought we could labor and get a home." Now, many homes later and in their sixties, the Udells were still hoping. Unfortunately, "soon after we moved, my old lady was taken very sick, so that I was confined to her bedside most of the time for two weeks." For five days, while she hung between life and death, John remained there at her side, helped by the kind ladies of the city and by "Mr. Gillum Bailey's daughters— the same kind Misses who, back in July, had happily left their names on Inscription Rock.

December 2 saw John at last able to absent himself sufficiently to begin herding cattle though "high wind and cold rain, mixed with hail" made the work "quite uncomfortable for an aged man, but necessity compels me to do it." And pride, and self-respect, he could have added. However obvious his shortcomings, however irritating his complaints, no one could ever deny him the cardinal virtue of an invincible determination to live by his own efforts.

By the end of January, John still keeping at his work through snow and cold, the Udells received letters from their son, now established in California, together with a check for fifty dollars which "we much needed and were thankful for it." He continued working into early March, continually noting with almost naive surprise "the cold climate for the 35th degree of latitude." It was the mile-high altitude, not the latitude, that made for such cold.

On March 4, John could make the happy entry in his diary:

> Finished my labor of herding cattle for the Government. Lt. Beale having agreed to take my wife and me and Mr. Hedgespeth's family through to California, and we gladly embrace the opportunity to leave this unpleasant, half civilized, half savage country, not having means of our own to carry us away. I have labored three months and four days, through storms of snow, hail and rain, and not lost a day. In the meantime, I have chopped my firewood and helped my wife to cook and wash at night, after my day's work was done, and preached to the Americans a number of times at night. [60]

Having mailed letters to their children in Ohio, Missouri, and California, they started on March 8 with Mr. Beale's train—"Mr. Beale's business being to improve that route under the instruction or employ of the United States Government. We came five miles and camped."

Thus began a return to California under auspices quite different from those that marked the previous undertaking. It was fortunate for those two emigrant families that Mr. Beale was in Albuquerque, having left Fort Smith, Arkansas, to improve the road all the way thence to the Colorado River, on almost exactly the same day those weary and discouraged emigrants had left Zuñi for the last miles of their return to Albuquerque. Now Lt. Beale, ever thoughtful and generous, had—at his own personal cost, undoubtedly, though John Udell would not have been aware of that—"prepared for Mr. Hedgespeth's family and us a team and a wagon." Thus they were on their way once more on what, for the Udells, would be their last long trek.

14

Arkansas
to Albuquerque

Though in Fort Smith the uncertainties ahead looked less dimly threatening and gave the now more experienced leader less concern than had those of eighteen months before, there had remained plenty of problems. For one thing, not far beyond Fort Smith the party would be entering the country of Indians quite as hostile as any to be met with at the banks of the Colorado.

Two weeks out from Fort Smith, this was brought home to all when, as Beale told, they encountered "R. Frank Green, Esq., with his mail stages awaiting my arrival, intending to take advantage of my escort to pursue their way to New Mexico. Mr. Green has been waiting nearly a month, the late fight of Major Van Dorn (United States Army) and the hostilities consequent thereon making it impossible for him to pass the Comanche nation unescorted. This is a most unfortunate matter, as he has prepared himself at great expense and trouble to carry out a contract which he entered into with the Postmaster General to carry mail from Neosho, Missouri to Santa Fé." [9] What was a mere month's delay in the delivery of mail that otherwise might never reach its destination!

The next most urgent problem Beale had to face at that outpost of civilization was the high cost of grain purveyed by government contractors. Beale wrote bitterly of this in his journal, pointing out that such graft had already driven most of the emigrant trade from Arkansas to Independence, Missouri, then across the river from Independence to Westport Landing, Kansas. Soon, he felt, trade would dry up altogether and the dreamed-of 35th parallel route would die aborning. To make sure the allotted funds should cover all his expedition's expenses, Beale avoided those government contractors, finally securing the supplies he needed from an unofficial source at more reasonable rates.

On the credit side, Beale had managed to secure the services of that truly skilled guide whom Whipple had failed to enroll in 1853 because of the man's private business commitments. This guide was the half-breed Scotch-Cherokee (Creek) Jesse Chisholm, after whom a great cattle trail of the Southwest was to be named. Chisholm, carrying a map of the country in his head, also knew his way among the Indians.

This bit of luck was all but cancelled out by the behavior of the officer of his military escort, Lt. Steen, assigned to guard the expedition from the Indians. Like too many of his kind assigned to such duty, he seemed to believe in keeping the party he was to escort waiting upon his personal convenience, which meant his unpredictable whim. Though a military career man, or perhaps because of it, he had no yearning to win military glory by risking his life in the chancy undertaking of protecting mere explorers or lesser stage drivers.

Beale waited for some time at Fort Smith for Lt. Steen to be ready to accompany him. Then, all too painfully conscious that the season was becoming dangerously far advanced, he started. When he did this, he left explicit instructions for the escort to follow and overtake the exploring party, a not too onerous undertaking since Beale's forward party was bound to be slowed by his obligation to construct bridges across streams and smooth out the many rough places in the road. Nevertheless, by the time R. Frank Green, Esq., joined him, he was still without military escort and, like Mr. Green, facing the country of hostile Indians just ahead.

William Floyd, one of the civilian doctors accompanying Beale's party, told of all this in his lively penciled journal, composed in the dim light of campfires and obviously never intended for publication. Three weeks after leaving Fort Smith, he recorded that a letter had come to Beale from Lt. Steen. "He has a justification," Floyd wrote indignantly, "of the delay of himself and escort on what he says was a request of Mr. Beale that he would remain ten days at Fort Smith after the party left." [3]

What had actually happened was that Beale had made not a request but a sympathetic suggestion. "Knowing that Steen had buried his child two or three days before he intended to leave and that his wife was lying in bed, 'Old fellow,' he said, 'wait ten days and then you can overtake me,' supposing that Steen would take it as intended, not applicable to his command, but to himself alone . . . what the deuce has delayed him up to this time, I should like to know."

Steen, of course, had plenty of excuses. In addition to those ambiguous orders, there was the "loss of his beef cattle. He was told before he made the purchase that they were wild and could not be driven, but his wagon master is his brother-in-law, Eliason is his relation. He sold Steen the cattle. . . ." Graft on the frontier again where there were few to check the goings-on!

Floyd commented sarcastically on the recent letter to Beale from Steen, who

> modestly inquires if his services as escort will be needed by Beale. I wonder if he started from the City of Washington without knowing the nature of the duty he was going on, very remiss of the War Department. Or does he hope to be discharged by Beale whose patience is, as he trusts, worn out by this time . . . One thing is certain, if Steen can travel no faster than he has averaged since leaving Fort Smith and Beale stays with him, we are likely to pass our time this winter *subfrigido* zone on the 35th parallel. Beale sick and I with a headache which I hope is nothing more than cold and exposure to the glare of sunshine on crusted snow. [3]

On exactly the same day, Beale was expressing himself on the subject.

> We are getting disgustedly tired of waiting for our escort. Considering they waited idly at Fort Smith for six weeks we can see nothing to detain them. The worst part of the business is that having started with only sixty days' provisions we are in great danger of being on mule meat before we get in. On a neat calculation, the escort has traveled on an average of five miles and a half a day. This snapping turtle speed will ruin us, I am afraid. [9]

Clearly the only thing that was fast about Lt. Steen was the bucks he seemed intent on making before he returned safely to the civilized East. It was yet another five days, November 26, to be exact, before he would finally catch up with the party he had left Washington long before to escort.

When Steen's party arrived, Dr. Floyd had the privilege of meeting his opposite number, military surgeon Duval. His acid comment was: "Had Dr. Duval of the command (Steen's) with us last night. Wonder why Army Surgeons have done so little to advance medical science. Is it that certain pay of a fixed amount paralyzes a man's mental as well as his physical exertion and he becomes content to do just what is required of him and then stops?" [3] The only professional man, Floyd said, he had ever heard of admitting this frankly was old Judge Tyler, the President's father, who once confided to a friend that he never read law any more because, "The legislature made me judge and pays my salary for what I do know. If they will pay me more, I will read more." This, Floyd surmised, must have been Duval's sentiment, too.

In the evening of the same day, Floyd wrote, Beale's troubles were aggravated by word that "Breckinridge had gone to hunt and had not returned. He is lost, now it is dark and bed time. I trust no accident has happened to him. Beale proposes a search for him in the morning." [3] The lost youth, member of a prominent Virginia family, was P. G. Breckinridge, whose initials had earned him the sobriquet "Peachy" though his behavior had clearly not justified the name, save in irony.

On the following day, Beale was feelingly confiding to his journal comments he would prudently delete from the part published later in the final government report on his explorations of that year:

> Of all the annoyances in the world to the Commander of an expedition of this kind, are these trifling lazy boys whose friends have influence enough to get them on parties of this kind where they invariably become a burden to themselves and everybody connected with them, the result is they go home disgusted and humiliated to see how badly they compare with men infinitely beneath them in birth and fortune, in all that makes *a man* upon the plains, and unwilling to attribute their failure to their own lazy blood or utter worthlessness. They satisfy their revenge by pitiful anonymous attacks on all who have had command of them. [1]

All this sounds as if Beale had had previous bitter experience of the same kind. Was it a byproduct of the 1857–58 expedition, or one of the earlier ones? And who of the various expedition members was he recalling with so much bitterness? In any case, two days later on Sunday, November 28, and 263 miles out from Fort Smith, Beale noted that "that man Breckinridge" had been found, adding impatiently, "so much for these greenhorn annoyances, if they would only stay lost, one could put up with it." [1] That exasperated comment with the strangely twentieth-century ring was something he would also delete. He must have been all too painfully aware that he already had all the detractors, known or anonymous, that he could use.

"I laid by today," he wrote for the published record, "and intended to have hunted up Breckinridge, who had been lost since night before last. Two Delawares and two Shawnees"—Indian hunters engaged to keep the party supplied with game—"left camp a mile or so hunting for him, where they found him and brought him into camp; he had wandered in a bewildered state over about forty miles, and was in a wretched, dilapidated condition; the merest chance had directed his footsteps towards our camp." [9] Floyd's comment was that he hoped it "would be a lesson to him and all the other deadheads in camp."

In that November of 1858, Peachy was extraordinarily lucky. Just a few days previous the party had encountered its first buffalo bull. The deadheads, of course, would have missed the message that Indians could not be very far behind. Beale knew quite well that "it is generally the case that when buffalo are on one side of a hill, an Indian is on the other." Peachy could have lost his scalp to such an Indian. Or, had he remained lost a bit longer, he could have frozen to death, scalp and all. So much for Beale's trivial lazy boy. Within five years, however, a no longer trivial Breckinridge would die in a skirmish at Kennon's Landing, fighting for his native Virginia and the Confederacy.

This winter of 1858 was turning out to be exceptionally cold, as Jesse Chisholm averred, and in such matters Chisholm generally knew whereof he spoke. In the high country, even a mild winter was no trifling matter. Udell was finding the winter equally hard many miles to the west near Albuquerque. Beale's diary entry for December 3, is practically identical with John Udell's for the same date. "The night past has been a hard one," Beale wrote. "A stiff northwest wind, accompanied by hail, rain and snow, has rendered it a most unhealthy one for animals and men. This morning looked so threatening that I determined to remain in camp."

The rugged camp life still offered its compensations, thanks to the prowess of the hunters, amateur as well as professional (though not of amateurs of the stamp of Peachy). On that day of bitter cold, Beale added a note. "We dined today on buffalo, fat raccoon, venison, and marrow bones. On our wagon was wild turkey, and oppossum and side of bear, and Mr. Baker this evening killed a good bunch of rice birds. . . . The President himself could not sit down to such a table."

The following day saw the party standing on a high bank of a typical creek, looking down at the usual boggy bottom. "I immediately set out to bridge it which we accomplished by sundown. All the creeks we have passed for the last three days will require permanent bridges of iron, so that the Indians cannot burn them. . . ." Briefly and uncharacteristically, for he rarely recorded purely personal troubles, Beale added: "suffered intensely all day with rheumatism."

For his part, Virginian Dr. Floyd would not imagine what anyone, even Indian natives of the area, could want with the kind of country they were passing through: "The country poor and broken . . . The whole country is nearly a desert and if the Comanches would be quiet, the country might well be left to them." On the next day, December 15, the outlook seemed a trifle less forbidding to Floyd, though not to all others of the party. Dick, the Delaware Scout and hunter, reported an Indian trail on the north bank of the river. As with Beale's boys of the previous year, "It was strange how the report made Indians to be seen in every hollow and behind every rock. They, and at least 100 ponies were said to be visible by some of the party. I saw none, neither with my eyes nor with a glass nor do I believe any were seen by others. I had rather trust my eyes than any man's say-so, more especially when marvels more than their neighbors can see, are to be seen." [9]

Another Indian hunter, Shawnee Little Axe, reported on the next day, "having seen the head of someone peep over one of these points and draw back. He thinks it was a man and his thoughts on such subjects are very apt to be facts." Clearly the difference between the visions of nervous greenhorns and the observations of experienced scouts had already become evident to Floyd as, years earlier, it had to Beale when seven men of his first command defected in Santa Fe. Greenhorns, unfortunately, did not always know enough to defect.

Lt. Steen, with the accompanying escort, would not wait to

reach Albuquerque or Santa Fe to defect. When, on December 18, just about three weeks after he had caught up with Beale's party, he heard Little Axe point out that they were passing through a former camping place of "Kioways," he was sure he'd had enough. Not admitting this explicitly, he excused his party on the grounds that his mules were getting worn out.

On the next day, Floyd confided disgustedly to his diary:

Lieut. Steen has determined to stay a day and rest his mules . . . and we would now . . . had we not been delayed in the first place by waiting for the escort, [have] been in Anton Chico. The escort has been inefficient and discourteous. It may be army regulations but they are curious to one who thinks that when a man undertakes to do a thing, he should do it. Our escort stopped just in the heart of the Comanche country to rest mules. What was the commander doing for two months at Fort Smith that he did not procure corn and transportation for it to feed his mules during the trip? Or why did he not feed half portions to his stock and thus enable them to go through as Beale and Green are and have been doing for a month? But enough of their inefficiency! Steen refused to furnish Beale 25 men under the command of his second officer unless Beale would wait a day until the papers were made out, transferring the Government property to Beale, as it would take a day to make them out and this he did, knowing Beale had but 3 days rations of flour for his men in camp, and that this condition was brought on by waiting for him before he overtook us and waiting on his slow movements after he had done so. [3]

Beale's comment—to be deleted from the published journal— was: "We left our escort this morning although we have seen more fresh Indian [tracks] at our late camp than at any place on the road and are now in Kioway and Comanche range but so far they [the escort] have proved only an embarassment as Mr. Steen says his mules are broken down so that he was desirous to lay over and recruit them—doubtless we shall do better without them." [1]

Beale, knowing that his journal must meet the scrutiny of the War Department before achieving publication among government Executive Documents, was wise to cross out his indignant words. Floyd's more explicitly angry comment was confided to a very private diary that would remain private for a century. Undoubtedly, quick-tempered Beale felt at least as strongly as the doctor who was the kind of associate he could invite to go exploring with him after supper, when they might bag some game and, best of all, talk out their frustrations safely beyond earshot of the camp.

Christmas was looming close ahead. The natural deep freeze that had so aggravated Beale's rheumatism would now offer one real compensation. Those wild turkeys in the wagons had kept well and could provide a feast, which, though necessarily lacking some of the traditional fixings, must have been almost as memorable, if less fiery, than had been Whipple's of five years before. Dr. Floyd wrote of it happily: "We had, as a Christmas dinner: wild turkey, raccoon, antelope, venison, prairie dog, wild geese and beef, bacon and mutton, a few pies of peach or apple compound, altogether with a bright sky and keen appetites. We are more than content for once."

This sense of contentment was increased by the realization that they were now close to the end of the first stage of their proposed journey. On December 27, at Hatch's Ranch in Taparito, Ned Beale could at last sit down to write a long letter—and an overdue one—to his wife in Pennsylvania:

My darling, I have been in the saddle almost constantly since half past three o'clock this morning, and now nearly nine at night and am just sitting down to tell you of my safe arrival. As usual, I have brought *all* my men through without the loss of a single one, nor have I abandoned a wagon on the road. Some two hundred and fifty miles back I left my escort, and came on with my own men, which may be censured, as we travelled through the worst part of the country with a diminished force. Never mind—"Success, after all, is the test of merit." Harry will be able to guess why I left the escort—ask him. [1]

Awareness of such possible censure may have restrained Beale from airing more specifically in his official journal his irritation with Lt. Steen. For a certainty, he sensed trouble ahead, even at the start of the trip when Harry Edwards, Mary Beale's brother, was along. A not very robust young man, Harry had soon had to accept dismissal from the brother-in-law who, nevertheless, remained burdened with the unwanted presence of politically important trivial lazy boys.

"I am now," Ned wrote on, "at Mr. Hatch's ranch at a town not very far from Santa Fé, where I shall remain to recruit my animals and men." Comfortably lodged there, he expected his train to catch up with him the following morning. Meanwhile he had sent grain back to relieve the nearly famished mules. Of Fred Kerling, a relative of Mary's who seemed to be some kind of foreman on the Beales's California ranch, Ned had as yet "heard nothing . . . I send this [to you] by express to intercept the mail which leaves Fort Union tomorrow. Tell Harry he was in luck when I sent him home. We have not slept on beds of roses since he left." [1]

Floyd found at the ranch "very comfortable quarters, plenty of provender and house room in his adobe walls. It is a strange kind of architecture, but taken all in all, the most convenient, cheapest and best for farming purposes of a structure I have ever seen. Mr. Hatch says that money can be made and that fast and sure in this country. At all events, he has made it in the last ten years." [3]

Before setting out from Fort Smith in the previous November, Beale had written his "darling Mary" instructions which she was to relay, by steamboat, of course, from Pennsylvania to Fred Kerling in California: "Let Fred take Jordan and come and join me [in New Mexico]," he wrote (Jordan being a former slave whom Beale had purchased to emancipate). "Or he can let the camels come to me by the Gila so that people can see they *are in use,* and he can come on in the mail [coach], leaving Jordan to bring them on. I want Jordan to be prominently connected with the camels—*mind that.*" Was this to underline his own support of the camels or was he anticipating a rewarding career for Jordan in connection with the new venture in transportation? Of his motives, however, he says nothing, only that, "Altogether I would very far prefer . . . for Fred to come and meet me, and let Jordan bring the camels to Albuquerque, so as to show they are doing something for their feed."

Fred had arrived as directed for, on January 12, Beale again wrote his Mary from Hatch's Ranch: "You see we are still at this place. Fred and myself will probably start for Santa Fé tomorrow, he to return to the Rancho [in California] and I to hire teamsters and laborers for my work to the westward of Albuquerque. Fred will be at home in about 16 or 18 days after starting in the stage, whilst it will occupy me some three or four months to accomplish my journey to the same place." [1]

Ned then expressed his delight with the news Fred had brought from the California ranch whence generous profits were now accruing. Soon, he guessed, the Beale family might look forward to less strenuous days together. A quiet, happy year abroad, perhaps, was something they now might dare plan for.

Continuing this happy theme in his next letter home, he wrote lightly: "As for me, I change for the worse, and every one out here is laughing at my grey hair and weatherbeaten appearance. It is certainly no improvement to one's looks, these long journeys and hard times. I . . . feel that I am too ugly to be loved by any one unless their eyes had been touched by poppy juice." This from an ancient man of thirty-six! After again enlarging upon the success of their ranch, he added, "I expect you were wondering what such a rich widow would do with herself before my letter arrived to assure you the Indians had not scalped me." [1]

"You need be under no apprehension," he assured her in yet another letter, "as I travel too cautiously ever to be taken by surprise, which is the great secret of safety among the Indians." [1]

Whether the camels had arrived under Fred or Jordan's care was not mentioned. Some camels, certainly, were on hand by the time Beale was ready to start out on the second leg of that roadbuilding expedition. In the meantime, during the month of January, he was "making an official visit to Santa Fé and a social one to my old and esteemed friend, Kit Carson," at his home in Taos, some sixty miles north of Santa Fe.

On February 3, Ned was writing Mary from Santa Fe: "I returned here yesterday from Taos, where I had a most pleasant visit with my old companion, Kit Carson. We were two days going over the mountains between here and Taos, which were covered with snow and ice, but did not suffer at all from the cold, and enjoyed the journey very much. Kit determined to come down here on a visit, so that we started from his house together." This time, despite the cold, Ned's rheumatism did not seem to bother him.

Beale continued on from Santa Fe to Albuquerque where he had to busy himself with details of the arrangements for the continuation of his trip and the completion of his survey. Most of the rest of his party were remaining at Hatch's Ranch, about which, on February 26, Dr. Floyd wrote, "We left the Ranch today, having been two months, lacking two days, stationary there. The delay has been caused by the necessity of recruiting the mules after their winter's trip across the plains on half rations of corn and but dry grass for roughness. Their condition was miserable to the last degree. They are now quite recruited and will make the remainder of the journey in fine style." [3]

On March 3, Floyd joined Beale at the "famed town of Albuquerque," a "Mexican adobe town" that he thought inferior to Santa Fe. The fact that it was apparently for the most part "taken up by the military" implied that labor and rations for the remaining part of the survey might be obtained there. Wagons must be repaired, more animals purchased, supplies secured from whatever sources, military or civilian, might make them available.

Inevitably, Ned Beale was told much about the troubles encountered during the previous summer by those first emigrants along his route. Perhaps, in arranging for the purchase of government beef, he met herder John Udell who, though certainly never reticent about his own hard luck, had yet kept doggedly at work. Officers' talk informed Beale of how desperately ill Emily Udell had been after their return to Albuquerque and of how determined both Udells had shown themselves to remain independent while younger men hung around for the easy out. John had kept on herding cattle throughout the bitter winter, ever since that first week of December when "my wife's health so improved that she is able to wait on herself, which is a great relief to me." [60]

Kindhearted Beale could not have listened to the tale without the profoundest pity, as well as admiration, for the Udells' unswerving struggle to keep body and soul together without accepting alms from anyone. What a contrast to those trifling lazy boys whose presence had been forced on him! Nevertheless, unless the Udells were, before another winter, helped to reach their children in California, the outlook for them must be grim indeed.

The destitute and weary cattle herder, occasional preacher, may have approached Beale in forlorn hope of employment on the survey, or Beale might have offered assistance without being thus approached. In any case, John could, on March 8, confide happily to his journal that the Udells and Hedgpeths were setting out for California with Mr. Beale's party—the same Beale whose road he had scorned less than a year before.

It may not have been quite according to government rules to take such unofficial folk along on an official, government-sponsored expedition, even though the leader himself bore all their expense, as was undoubtedly the case. Neither in his report to the secretary of war nor in his daily journal—which was eventually to meet official inspection—did Ned Beale ever acknowledge that addition to his train. The emigrants, of course, assumed their government was taking care of them as it was of the construction of the road they were to follow.

15

Escort
for Emigrants

In March 1859, indomitable John Udell was headed west for the fifth time. Headed west for the second time was John's "old lady," still seeming little more than a pious, self-effacing drudge. Actually, she must have been considerably more than that just to face again, after the disasters of the previous year, the risk of encountering more of the same. She could not have entirely believed that even a Lt. Beale could stand between her and a possible repetition of Indian attacks. Perhaps her over forty years of marriage to John had taught her that, having no real choice in the management of her life, she must somehow make the best of what she had. What she had this time was a place in an emigrant wagon in a train that, according to John, consisted of "nearly fifty men, fourteen wagons, and probably one hundred mules and horses." Not even a whisper of the camels!

The winter's bitter cold was already letting up. Not so, however, the typical season's "strong wind blowing fine sand in every direction, but mostly in one's eyes." By March 12, they were making camp beyond the Pueblo of Laguna where the country, as described by the doctor, "is one of much fertility. At this point there are quite large masses of lava, apparently having run down the valley . . . All the mountains here are bare and look as if they had been thrown up from beneath and scattered from above." [3]

For March 19 and the five following days, the party would remain near Agua Fria where "the road, just as you ascend to the top of the Rocky Mountains" needed working over by the road hands. Floyd occupied himself with exploring the vicinity, visiting the crater of a long extinct volcano. The weather, though cool, was beginning to show promise of spring, while patches of snow remaining here and there bore witness to the heavy fall of the previous winter. Floyd estimated them still to be "from one foot to fifteen inches deep."

At their encampment near Agua Fria, the Rocky Mountains may have looked rocky but hardly very mountainous. Here were no sheer and dramatic heights such as a stranger might expect of the divide between two great and distant oceans. Beale wrote, "It is the last stream or spring we shall see flowing towards the Atlantic until our return, as the back-bone of the mountain divide of the western waters flowing to the Pacific, and those going to the Atlantic, is within a mile of it . . . the ascent is a gradual inclined plain, so that although a great altitude is attained . . . one does not perceive it and only the test applied by instruments would convince a person of the fact." [9]

On March 16, while they were "lying by to work the road," Beale decided "to despatch two wagons to the Indians at Zuñi, in hope to find corn there, and the Indians in a selling humor. They either sell readily and for little or nothing, or not at all, and are as capricious in their dispositions as possible."

Five days later, Dr. Floyd, seeing El Morro for the first time, recorded, "after a most windy, somewhat cold and very disagreeable day of it, we made the celebrated camping ground known as Inscription Rock. It has many names, some of them as early as 1639 and from that down to the present day. Those of the early Spaniards are mostly well done, those of the Americans mostly scrawl, many with obscene remarks attached, thus perpetuating as far as they could their blackguardism." [3]

No such obscene inscriptions remain to excite to amusement or indignation today's visitors to the rock. Some well-meaning Victorian must have removed them, leaving those smooth areas whence inscriptions have, obviously, been deleted. What else they deleted we cannot know.

Presently Floyd was accompanying Ned Beale "and four others," which number included the Shawnee, Little Axe, and the Delaware, "to explore the valley and find other waters than the small spring at Inscription Rock. In this we were completely successful." They also hunted, visited a ruined and deserted pueblo, and made it back to the rock by March 25.

When they arrived there, they found the face of the rock enhanced by three of the most professionally incised inscriptions that were ever to adorn it. None of the journals kept by party members so much as mentions the presence of a stone cutter, a professional obviously skilled and experienced in cutting names on monuments. Definitely not an amateur, he must either have carried his patterns with him from the start or have known them so well as to need none.

With time on his hands during the wait, he would have offered his services for a consideration, we guess. The first name to be cut, in sharp, square letters, would be that of Beale's second in command—"F. ENGLE JR. NEW JERSEY 1859." Not to be outdone in a bid for immortality was "P. GILMER BRECKENRIDGE VA. 1859"—that trivial, lazy boy whom Beale had once angrily wished could stay lost. Finally, in a distinctive, beautifully flowing script, came "E. Pen^n Long Baltimore Md." In the loop of the "L" the cutter left a clear but, unfortunately, unidentifiable mark. Though this last inscription bears no date, E. P. Long's name is several times mentioned in Beale's journal. Was he, we wonder, another of those trivial, lazy boys? Might he have been the stone cutter? Hardly, we think, for if he were, Beale would have mentioned it.

John Udell was finding inscriptions on that rock an old story. He improved his time by investigating the ruins atop the rock and the artifacts still to be found there in quantity. We would prefer he had been moved to remain below near the tank, to remark solemnly on the silly vanity of youths so preoccupied with fancy inscriptions and, perhaps, to mention the name of the man who cut them. After John was safely back from his hilltop expedition, he showed no impulse to add either a postscript or his wife's name to his earlier record.

On March 22, when camped with his little party some miles north of the Rock, Ned Beale was writing home, expecting to send the letter by some courier to Albuquerque, whence it might proceed by post:

> I continue my letter at a distance from camp . . . We are now at our noon camp, Dick the Delaware, Little Axe, Ab and myself . . . Tell the children I left at camp quite a number of Indians who had been over to a neighboring tribe to purchase *children*, and if they don't behave, when I come out again, I will bring them out and trade them off. As for Trux, we shall

have to trade him anyhow." [Then, dropping his playful threats,] "You must tell Truxie, how coming along through the woods this evening, father saw a great big catamount . . . and shot the ugly fellow . . . and we skinned him, and father put his skin by for his little boy. [1]

Four days later Ned and his party were back with the main party and George Beale, Ned's brother, was back from Zuñi with the gladdening news that he'd been able to purchase plenty of corn from the Indians. The roadbuilding detail had completed its assigned task so all could now move ahead to make another camp beyond Zuñi village.

Ned recorded:

This day was very disagreeable, with a high wind blowing dust in every direction, reminding us of Washington City in a winter gale . . . The old [Indian] met me in town with many compliments and congratulations, and bearing in his arms a box containing my "artificial horizon," which I had left with him in passing last winter. He told me the charge had been a great burden on his mind, and he was glad to be rid of the responsibility . . . I left town after giving some things to the Indians and trading for some corn meal, and through the dust, which was almost blinding, we rode to camp. [9]

Anyone who has resided in New Mexico will recognize this merciless wind as an inalienable part of the New Mexico spring. Floyd, to whom it was a relatively new experience, described it in greater detail than did his commander: "We left camp this morning at six o'clock. The morning was still and clear, after travelling some six miles it commenced blowing and such a day of wind and sand I never saw. It was a perfect *sand storm* and in looking at it with your back to the wind and the sun shining through the sand, it presented the appearance of the lurid glare of a large fire." [3] He might have added that the only possible way to look at it was with one's back to the wind. Facing it, the blowing sand fills and blinds one's eyes.

"We passed through the village of Zunia [sic] today," he went on. "It is situated in a wide and beautiful valley, but the soil seems to be poor. The Zunians however manage with irrigation to raise moderate crops of corn and splendid crops of wheat. Will time and cultivation by bringing up the sand make this country a desert?" [3]

Overcultivation, with wind erosion removing the top soil thus cultivated, seems to have been a recognized problem long ago.

Still four days later—on March 31—Floyd made practically the only mention of both the camels and the emigrants that had been with them all the way from Albuquerque. Beale's journal mentioned the emigrants not at all—for reasons already suggested —and, in contrast to his previous trip, seemed to take the camels altogether for granted.

Floyd's journal for that date indicated that they were camped about 40 miles west of Zuñi at Jacob's Well, also called Navahoe or Mud Springs.

> They are most curious [he went on], surrounded by a range of low hills or rather a basin in the great plain. They run all year and several of them apparently force up mud along with the water until their rims are several feet, from three to four, above the level of the basin or the other running springs. The mud is very deep, a camel was mired in one over his hump and had to be drawn out with ropes. This morning they were frozen over and Mr. Beale, in attempting to walk over one of them, broke in up to his waist. I was near and gave him a helping hand. Scarcely half an hour afterwards, an old woman, Mrs. Hedgepeth, with the curiosity of a *woman* and the gawkyness of a green one, popped into the same place. She screamed *painter* and Tucker pulled her out. She never would have got out without help. [3]

Beale's diary omitted most of the picturesque details, perhaps not quite happy to present his mud-covered image to the public that might be reading the House Executive Documents. "Travellers," he warned of the springs, "should be cautious not to approach them in the night, as there are places where a man or beast falling into the mud springs . . . would be entirely lost. I myself stepped incautiously too near, and though on the brink sank instantly to my waist, and but for being so near the brink could have gone out of sight as quitely as in water. Emigrants approaching it should place a guard at each to keep stock from getting in, as the ground to the very edge of the quagmire is firm, and one step would occasion the loss of man or beast." [9]

April 1 still had high wind but this time with snow. The country, Floyd noted, "is one vast undulating plain, with but little wood or water at this season of the year, though some emigrants who are in our company say these are plenty in July and in the fall. They are part of the party defeated and driven back from the great Colorado last fall by the Mohave Indians." [3] The emigrants seemed to have forgotten the past year's problems with locating water holes.

The emigrants certainly could not have forgotten those bitter nights of late October and early November when they'd had to compose themselves for sleep on the frozen ground, covered by no more than one thin quilt and the clouds. Now, in early April, there was wind as well as snow, a continued handicap for the party, with night time temperatures hovering below freezing. In the relative comfort of the wagon Mr. Beale had so kindly provided for them, the Udells and Hedgpeths must have thought often of those miseries of six months before.

Even on April 13, the morning showed ice "frozen to a thickness of two inches; old snowbanks in places three feet deep—in others, within a short distance, it is dry and dusty." Soon it would all be dry and dusty, for spring was really on its way, even in the high country.

April 17 turned out to be a pleasant day after a night of "only light frost." The next day, even pleasanter, brought no frost at all as well as all-too-welcome reinforcements to the camp at Leroux's Spring, named after the scout who had so successfully guided so many expeditions across that land. The springs were situated some 350 miles west of Albuquerque, 250 east of the Colorado River, happily well past the halfway point.

"No frost," Udell entered in his journal. "We came four miles to a spring where we met Mr. Samuel Bishop, Mr. Beale's partner, from California; he had brought with him provisions and about forty men and Mr. Beale's camels." [60] For a man who had only during the past few weeks learned to value camels in action, John Udell was taking the arrival of additional ones strangely for granted. In the Southwest, we may conclude, camels were no longer altogether novel. Besides, what concerned the Udells increasingly was just how the much battered Udells were to reach their destination. That critical crossing of the Colorado was yet ahead, though looming ominously closer each day. Thus, with the new arrivals, it would be not the camels but the men and the tidings they brought with them that the emigrants must find of the greatest interest.

"Our fears of the Indians were dispelled," John wrote in happy relief. "Mr. Bishop, with forty men had fought his way through the Mohave Indians, after being surrounded by them, and effected his crossing of the Main Colorado without the loss of a man. See what men of composure and courage can do! I wonder what our one hundred and eighteen men will think when they hear this." [60]

The forty men had been a picked lot—the one hundred and eighteen mere chance associates, some brave and wise, many not. It still rankled in Udell that against his urgent and explicit pleas, those hundred and eighteen had not had the pluck to turn back west toward the Colorado and to make a valiant attempt to fight their way through to California, a fight he could never persuade himself would not have met with success.

Ned Beale could not have been too surprised at the arrival of Bishop's train, though the instructions he'd sent out from Fort Smith had not urged the trip on Bishop. Fort Smith was over a thousand miles to the east and nearly six months past and much could have happened to convince Ned's "very good friend and partner" that it was wise to push on to meet the expedition on the, to him, far side of the Colorado. One decisive factor was the definite likelihood of troubles with Indians who were ever alert to perceive the weariness, and hence weakness, of a travel-worn party. There was also that plea for provisions that Beale had sent ahead from Albuquerque—where, remember, he'd arrived on very short rations, thanks to Lt. Steen.

So it was a happy leader who, at Leroux Spring, somewhat west of today's Flagstaff, looked up when he

heard exclamations of surprise from the men, and looking down the valley saw two men approaching rapidly on drome-daries; I recognized at once the white Egyptian dromedary, my old friend of last year [this would have been Seid, the dromedary Beale had ridden to his rendezvous with Colonel Loring of Fort Defiance]. As they came nearer I saw that one of the men was S. A. Bishop esq., and the other was Ali Hadji, who accompanied me on my former expedition; they had glorious news to tell me; I had sent my clerk, F. C. Kerlin [from Albuquerque] by El Paso, to California, to say that I should take only provisions to last me to the Colorado, and expecting Colonel Hoffman with the troops to pack my camels with provisions, and meet me at the crossing of that river. [9]

Mr. Bishop apparently knew enough not to take anything for granted with the military. "Colonel Hoffman had gone to the river to reconnoitre, but the Indians having attacked him, he returned to the settlements for reinforcements; Mr. Bishop knowing I would be at the river at about the time set, and that Colonel Hoffman with his seven hundred troops could not get there in time to meet me . . . fitted out an expedition of forty men, and boldly came on to the river; here he was met by a thousand warriors flushed with their successes over the emigrants, and rendered confident by their skirmish with the troops." [9] Such a defeat, any fighter would know, concerned not alone the defeated men but the men who would later have to deal with the overconfident victors.

As for Bishop's party at the river, the Indians

> immediately attacked him, but did not calculate on the character of the men he had, nor the deadly efficiency of the frontier rifles in the hands of frontier men . . . in a brilliant battle, he completely routed them; then he crossed the river and remained in their village a number of days defying them, then so completely was the spirit of this formidable tribe broken, that he divided his party, sending back twenty, leaving a strong garrison of six at the river, and with the remainder came on to meet me. [9]

So much appeared in Beale's published journal. Not for publishing apparently, was his sarcastic comment, "It is to be hoped that the gallant seven hundred under Colonel Hoffman will find no great trouble in subduing the tribe which has been so badly beaten by the forty men and boys of my command." [1]

For Beale, the camel fan, there was special delight in Bishop's story that

> as he approached the Colorado River, four men of the mail party, which had been making fruitless attempts for nearly a year to get the mail over the road [year-old letters still were better than none!], joined him, but on seeing the number of Indians, their hearts failed them and two turned back to the Colorado. The mail was brought on my camels and delivered to the agent, Mr. Smith, who was traveling with my party; and having no means of sending back the mail he brought and

as the camels after meeting me, turned back to the Colorado [with me] it was transferred to the back of one of them, and now returns with us. Thus the first mail of the 35th parallel was brought on my camels both ways, and never would have come until the establishment of a post, as the men who accompany it affirm, but for Bishop coming under my direction to meet me. [9]

When writing Bishop's instructions (via Mary Beale in Chester, Pennsylvania) from Fort Smith, Beale had left the decision open: "If Bishop has determined to come over, then the camels . . . must come with him, and something must be done *to tell upon the road.* Either the Colorado mountain must be made *good for wagons,* or . . . a tank containing a very large amount of water constructed." [1]

All the camels, despite Beale's "my camels," were still government camels, though some had been confided to Beale's care. This matter of the first post was dramatic enough to attract general attention to the disputed camels and just might turn the scales in favor of those animals when their future was being argued by politicians in faraway Washington. Why, then, had he not mentioned them before, those he had been anxious to have brought to Albuquerque in such a way as to demonstrate they were earning their keep? Soon after Bishop's arrival with the camels, Beale was commenting quite freely, "Our camels with their solemn faces make our camp look like old times." [1]

John Udell made little note of this addition to the party. He was finding it more interesting that on the following day, three antelope were killed and the camp now had "fresh meat aplenty." Floyd mentioned the camels quite casually, as might a man who had been in their company for weeks.

For all in the party, the approaching meeting with Indians was a matter of concern. Ten days after Bishop's arrival and when still some forty miles east of the river, Indians in the full light of noon stole one mule and shot another, which "belonged to the two mail men traveling under my escort, this mail being carried on my camels."

Such insolence must not be overlooked. If worse were not to follow, as it had with the emigrants of the year before, the Indians must be taught a lesson in their own language. Beale planned action something along the lines Kit Carson had used twelve years before.

A bit earlier than usual the train settled, with conspicuous weariness, into camp. The men were cooking and eating, in no apparent hurry, in full sight of the invisible Indians they knew to be watching. This finished, they doused their fires and threw themselves on the ground as if to sleep, though it was not yet fully dark. Like the Indians, though with different emotions, Udell was watching the coolly planned ruse: "Left our camp at dark," he wrote, "and moved five or six miles. The men lay concealed all night, watching the mule," the one the Indians had killed. "At daylight, four Indians made their appearance, three of whom our men killed" (the men who had remained in ambush, of course).

This was repartee Indians could understand, for it was of a kind they themselves indulged in. Had they not been thus warned, greater slaughter both of Indians and of road builders must have resulted.

Ned Beale was taking no further chances. "Preparing for a descent on the Mohaves," he noted on April 30, "all hands getting ready their arms, I shall take with me thirty-five men and three days' provisions on three camels. The men will go on foot, so that we shall not be encumbered with mules to guard while we are fighting; as for the camels, they will pack our provisions and require no guarding, as they will feed when tied to a bush." [9] Indians had not acquired the trick of stampeding camels, if indeed they could be stampeded. Another score for Beale's pets!

On the following day:

> We marched the twenty-five miles in six hours. On our arrival at the river we saw some Indians, and the men, as soon as they had drunk, started out to get a shot. Whilst they were hunting them through the thick undergrowth, which fills the bottom, and about three hours after we arrived, we were surprised at seeing three or four white men coming up the trail. These informed us that the troops were encamped on a bend of the river a few miles below, and that Colonel Hoffman had made a treaty with the Indians; so that we immediately called in our men, much to their diasppointment and intense disgust. [9]

Even pious John Udell found it hard to accept this peaceful end to his warlike plans for revenge. "We were all disappointed, for we

were prepared and willing to punish these savages for their outrages on us emigrants last year." For Indians, a lesson deferred for
a year could have had little meaning.

For the emigrants, the shock and misery of the 1858 outrages
were freshly revived when the Udells and the Hedgpeths "walked
over the mountain to where we left our wagons and effects last
year. We found the irons, the wagons and effects were burnt and
destroyed by the Indians. Even valuable property that had been
carefully buried by some of the emigrants, had been dug up and
carried off." [60]

Poor helpless emigrants: How well they could have used the
experience and wisdom of a Kit Carson or Antoine Leroux or Ned
Beale, rather than a Saavedra, to guide and counsel them, to teach
then how to deal with Indians as well as such small details as to how
valuable effects might be successfully cached. Had they themselves piled their useless wagons over their buried valuables and
set them afire before leaving, those buried valuables just might
have been found again.

On May 4, all moved camp three miles down the river to where
the soldiers were camped. Though protection should no longer be
necessary, in view of the recent treaty, it was well to take no
unnecessary chances. In the military camp, the emigrants should
remain safe for a while.

"Lieut. Edward Beale, his brother George Beale and Mr. Bishop took some of the best mules across the river," Udell wrote, "to
go to Los Angeles, to send back supplies for his men, as this river
was as far as the government had employed him to improve the
road, intending that we emigrants should go to California with the
train that brings his supplies. His animals are so worn down and
the current so strong that it was not safe for his teams to cross the
river." [60] The *General Jessup*, alas, had long since lain in her
watery grave.

The Udells and Hedgpeths remained in one another's company
in the military camp while "all Mr. Beale's men, except a few to
herd the animals, returned to the mountains to grade the road so
that a fast running stage can glide easily over them, which they can
do in thirty days." [60] Thirty days for the road building, of course,
not for the fast running stage across the mountain!

Udell now had time to record his amazement at the polyglot
origins of the roadbuilding party: "Americans, English, French,
Germans, Irish, Mexicans, Greeks, Turks and Indians from several

different tribes and several different languages spoken. Notwithstanding, there are so many men thrown together so promiscuously, from so many different countries, and have remained together so long, since I came among them, perfect peace and harmony has prevailed." [60]

Was this wonder due, in part, to a remembered lack of harmony in the emigrant train? Had the man who once so resented the "German aristocrat" now learned the hard way that when men who are thrown together begin to differ over small things, cherishing small resentments, small things become big and the gap grows wider the longer they remain together? Might he now, having learned the value of a strong leader able to reach quick decisions and prepared to put them into prompt action, have come to re-evaluate the man Rose he'd so abhorred the year before? Perhaps this was too much to expect of any human being—yet his appreciation of Ned Beale was unqualified.

"Lieut. Beale," he recorded almost wonderingly, "is a kind, affectionate, persevering man; he possesses a spirit of endurance and dreads no hardship or fatigue, and is very faithful to his trust. Mr. Samuel A. Bishop, his partner, is much like him; they both treated us emigrants with much attention and respect during all the time we were with them, nonwithstanding we were altogether dependent upon them in getting through to California—for which I shall ever owe them a debt of gratitude. [60]

"Faithful to his trust" and promise, in less than thirty days, "Lieut. Beale's supplies came in on a train of pack mules, driven by Spaniards. With this train, we are to go to Los Angelos [sic], California, three hundred miles . . . Mr. Beale was kind enough to purchase two ladies' saddles for our two aged ladies, and send them in with the pack train."[60]

Mr. Bishop was coming along somewhat behind that train of pack mules. On June 14, the train, already headed back on its return trip to Los Angeles, "met Mr. Bishop's party, on their way back to assist in improving the road . . . Mr. Bishop gave me a check in behalf of Lieut. Beale for fifty dollars, which paid the expenses of my wife and myself to the end of the journey." [60] Mr. Bishop went on to the river where he was to continue supervising road improvements until his partner's return.

So, finally on June 30, 1859, possibly somewhat wiser, definitely much older, though hardly much richer than when they had set up housekeeping in Ohio, John Udell and his "old lady" were able to take up their residence in California. Surely, though, a creeping sense of frustration must presently have begun to set in as he came to the bitter realization that here, at long last, he'd arrived at an insuperable barrier to his further westward trekking, that henceforth all such traveling must be done in retrospect.

For this, of course, he had that diary he had kept during all the trials and dangers of the emigrant train and which he had borne back with him all those weary miles of the return trip to Albuquerque. Ten years later, this account was issued by the same Ohio press that had published the earlier book. However many fascinated folk may have purchased the little paperbound book, few must have cherished it enough to preserve it. Today only five or six copies are known to exist. Exactly how many years John outlasted its publication is also unknown. The last known record of John Udell is in 1872, in California.

Perhaps understandably obsessed with his own problems, John Udell had recorded little to do with the other families of the wagon train. His journal makes no mention at all of the many children, some quite young, some in their teens and old enough to share in the daily chores. Boys over twelve were certainly active in helping to herd the many cattle, girls in helping their mothers and in keeping an eye on younger sisters and brothers. One of the twelve year olds was Sally Fox, stepdaughter of the train's foreman, Alpha Brown, who was killed at the Colorado. John Udell does note that little Sally was wounded at that time.

One learns from other sources and with surprise that there were two Baley families: Gillum's and that of his brother, William Wright—or "Right"—Baley and that between them they were accompanied by nearly a score of offspring. Of these, there were twelve girls, ranging in age from about five years or younger to the early twenties. Exactly which were the ones who left their names—initials, rather—upon Inscription Rock is not certain, but a descendant of one believed the "MIS.S.A.E.BALEY" stands for "Misses Sarah and Ellen"—cousins of about the same age—or possibly "Misses Sarah and Elizabeth Baley," the latter being Ellen's sister and a daughter of Gillum Baley. Actually, from census returns taken in California somewhat later, it would seem that Elizabeth would have been the one, since at the time of passing Inscription Rock, she was more of an age when she might properly be referred to as "Miss." Whether it was the same Misses Baley who helped care for the ailing Mrs. Udell after the return to Albuquerque is not known.

More is ascertainable about some of the wagon train families after they reached California. Sarah, William Wright Baley's daughter, not too long after reaching California married John G. Simpson, who had come to the state during the gold rush and was to be the first assessor of Fresno County, a long time County Supervisor, and one of the founders of the subscription school at Academy on Big Dry Creek. A great-grandson of that couple writes: "There is a little beautiful Alpine meadow in the mile deep fork of the King's River in King's Canyon National Park called 'Simpson Meadow,' where John G. and Sarah M. grazed sheep in the 1870's and 1880's. I think that type of thing is a fitting memorial to them."

Shortly after reaching his destination, Gillum Baley moved his family into spacious quarters in what had once been the blockhouse of Camp Barbour and there, during the following January (1861), his daughters Rebecca and Elizabeth were married, with cousin Sarah Margaret Baley Simpson and her husband in attendance. Rebecca, seventeen years old on her arrival, had promptly been appointed school teacher in Fresno County, where, the newspaper reported, Gillum Baley "with his wife and family of two sons and seven daughters" had recently arrived. Gillum, incidentally, was presently to become the last county judge of Fresno County and city treasurer of Fresno City.

Neither Gillum nor William Wright Baley forgot the harrowing experience they had undergone during their first attempt to reach California and much later Gillum, on behalf of his deceased brother as well as himself, was to enter an Indian Depredation Claim against the U.S. government in the hope of recovering losses, claimed to amount to a total of about $8,000, sustained by both of them through the attack of the Mojave Indians. That claim, Number 8214, was not filed until 1891 or 1892. It states that Gillum was then eighty years of age, having at the time "no particular occupation, am at present keeping a hotel," and gives an eyewitness account of the attack such as John Udell could not, since John was, at the time, some miles from the Colorado River. It constitutes an interesting document, if a futile one, since according to William Wright's descendant, it was a "loser."

Also a loser was Indian Depredation Claim Number 8378, filed at about the same time by "William P. Hedgpeth, Administrator of the Estate of Joel Hedgpeth, deceased, vs. U.S. and Mohave Indians," which claimed losses totalling $4,340; interestingly, this includes $100 for books lost. This suggests an intellectual slant that persists in the present generation of Hedgpeths, one of them, Dr. Joel Hedgpeth, being a noted oceanographer.

Why, one wonders, did these people wait until the 1890s to file such claims? The answer, one suspects, is that about then the one-time wagon train leader, Leonard J. Rose, was urging that such claims be filed in order to give support to his own claim for considerably greater losses. Rose had not waited until the 1890s to seek redress. Already in 1872, his petition for compensation had been considered by the Senate Committee on Indian Affairs and reported adversely in the Senate on May 23, 1872 (see Appendix A). Nothing daunted, Rose continued to petition again and again. The file on this is long and detailed, including testimony from everyone Rose thought might help his cause, some of the depositions having been taken in 1858, as soon as the people of the train returned to Albuquerque. Though futile, Rose's Claim Number 2176 (see Appendix B) filed on June 3, 1891, makes interesting reading. It includes a list of property lost and the original costs, the total coming to a hefty $27,936.76, the highest single item being a Morgan stallion for which Rose stated he had paid $2,500. The extent and kind of these losses suggest that Leonard John Rose was an unusual man, unusually interesting to contemplate in the perspective of a century. From his own later reminiscences, published in a California journal, a biographical sketch by his son, and another published by a bank in Rosemead, California, named after him, we may gather a picture of an able man, a gambler whose haughty manner, we suspect, led John Udell to dub him a "German aristocrat."

German he was, having been born in Bavaria, near Munich, in 1827. But he was hardly an aristocrat if being of a titled line is implied by that word. When young Leonard was eight years old, his family was immigrating to New Orleans, where his father established a store. Presently they were moving to Illinois, where the elder Rose, apparently a classic German disciplinarian, and his son came to a parting of the ways. A year later, Leonard had a store of his own in Iowa, where, three years later, in 1851, he married Amanda Jones, who was presently to accompany him on his trek to California. In 1857, Leonard Rose had sold his business, and the sum he realized therefrom, plus money derived from what his son called "speculations," amounted to $30,000. Most of this was, within the year, to be invested in the trip to California where Rose hoped to realize his dream of owning a racing-horse breeding ranch. [65]

The disaster at the Colorado put only a temporary stop to the realization of that dream. Soon after his return to Albuquerque, Rose moved on to Santa Fe where, using his own now skimpy bankroll and money lent him by a brother-in-law in Illinois, he purchased La Fonda, then a rundown Mexican style inn that was to prosper sufficiently to clear the new owner, after two years, a neat $14,000. With this, he would again set out for California. A "first-class poker and seven-up player," according to his son [65], Leonard Rose did not profit exclusively from room renters and meal buyers.

The gambler in Rose was to take him far and to his fate, through running a winery on a princely estate he called Sunny Slope. When sold some years later, it netted him a cool million dollars. [66] He was also to realize that dream of owning a stable of thorough-breds. But he gambled once too often—on real estate in a falling market, as it turned out. In 1899, at the age of seventy-two, unable to face poverty or arrange yet another rise to affluence, Leonard Rose died by his own hand, leaving his futile depredation suit to be continued by his wife and executrix, Amanda Jones Rose.

And what of the "River Race" whose passing Lt. Beale sadly thought he foresaw and whose depredations were never to be paid for? Sarah Baley Simpson's great-grandson, who has dedicated much time and effort to pursuing the survivors of the Rose-Baley (or Baley-Rose?) wagon train, writes from California: "A few years ago my wife and youngest son and I set out on a trip to follow the route of the wagon train, which roughly parallels Highway 66. When we arrived at the Colorado River, we were greeted by a large sign that said WELCOME TO THE MOHAVE INDIAN RESER-

VATION AND AGRICULTURAL CORPORATION. Those Indians own all that fine river bottom land and are growing cotton, soy beans and all those other money crops. They live in modern mobile homes, own motor boats and campers and all drive pick-up trucks or Buicks." Unless he were more than human, no descendant of people of the shattered wagon train but must have had at least a momentary urge to begin evening old scores of stolen property, burnt wagons, and slaughtered comrades by driving off a Buick or two.

16

The Colorado Crossed

Possibly relieved to be free of his commitment to the amateur travelers whose needs he had so generously seen to, Ned Beale passed a month or so at Fort Tejón and inevitably at his nearby ranch. He arrived back at the Colorado River on June 26, "having been absent since the 4th of May, busy in procuring and packing out provisions for my camp." On June 27 he "commenced crossing our packs and provisions; the river very high" (snows were melting in the mountains), "and nearly a quarter of a mile in width, with a rapid current." The crossing was completed in a day.

On the east bank of the river, Beale was delighted to find the camp in fine order and all the men in good health. "Two months had made a vast change in the road over the mountain; an ordinary six-mule team may now easily go through John Howell's Pass, hauling thirty-five hundredweight." At about the same time, Beale's second in command, the Frederick Engle whose well-carved inscription is so conspicuous on El Morro, noted in his own journal, "we crossed the mountains by the most excellent road, which had been built by Mr. Bishop's party during our stay at the river." [9] Thus successfully had Mr. Bishop fulfilled his partner's hopes and justified his trip to join Beale at Leroux Spring.

Camp could not be moved at once. There were dry and difficult weeks ahead between them and Albuquerque, even though there was now a wagon road to make those weeks less gruesome. Wagons that had stood for nearly two months in the blazing sun needed special attention. In that heat, wooden wheel spokes and rims had shrunken as they dried, iron tires had become loose. "The party was

186

engaged in preparing harness, &c., for a start. Soaked the wagon wheels in the spring, and set up a forge to repair iron work." [9]

Once on the move, they found that all the streams were now swollen, like the main Colorado River, and some previously dry ravine crossings had become filled with swiftly running rivulets. Typical of river crossing problems was the one they had to deal with when back on the banks of the Little Colorado: "This morning we started at five A.M., and in a short time we reached the river crossing. On our arrival we found that the water had risen during the night, and that scarcely a trace of the work done there the previous day was left. We turned out the mules, and after breakfast, the bank was cut down, and we crossed our wagons and stock with but little trouble." [9]

Some days after this, they reached Inscription Rock, where they stopped briefly to water their stock and undoubtedly themselves. The men had seen the rock before. What the weary roadbuilders now wanted was to see Albuquerque and the end of their long journey, which they did on July 29. The return trip from the Colorado River, even including the time spent in repairing harness and wagons, had taken exactly a month. This was a considerable improvement over the two months that the first emigrant train had needed to cover the same distance.

Beale, whether he had planned it or not, had fixed his name on the whole route to the exclusion of embittered rivals. The West was now the stuff of which legends were made and Ned Beale the man to fit such legends, for newspaper reporters, bound to satisfy the curiosity of stay-at-home Easterners, needed some definitive personality with whom to associate their accounts.

"I have seen Santa Fé traders taking Beale's route as far as it would take them to their destination," a reporter calling himself "Wanderer" wrote for the *Philadelphia Press* in 1859. The Santa Fe Trail was a wagon road that left the Missouri River near Westport Landing, across from Independence, and angled southwest toward the city whose name it bore. Santa Fe traders, rough and picturesque, had long been driving their laden wagons along that route. To Wanderer, the Santa Fe Trail, being identified with Beale's Route, started from Fort Smith, Arkansas. To eastern readers, it didn't much matter exactly where that route ran. They had heard of Santa Fe and they'd heard tales of Ned Beale's exploits, and it all added up to something legendary and romantic.

In Albuquerque, on July 30, a Ned Beale who would not have recognized himself in the legend was at last able to write his wife. His roadbuilding had been completed, he told her, and now he hoped the War Department would not withhold its seal of approval for his accomplishment. The return trip, he added, had been wet and depressing, in part because of unusually rainy weather, in part, we guess, because the route could no longer offer the kind of challenge it had formerly held for him. "Tell my babies," he added in postscript, "every night when father gets into his wet blankets in the mud and water on the ground, he thinks of them and of their dear mother, and forgets in dreams of them all the discomforts of the camp." [1]

For Edward Fitzgerald Beale, this 1859 trip was a sort of requiem for his exploration of the wilds. Though as owner of homes both in Washington, D.C., and in California, he would many times span the continent, he would never again lead a party of the kinds he had guided west during the past three years. Age and rheumatism—the latter briefly mentioned in letters and journals—may have had a small part in this. A bigger part must have been that, in very truth, that particular undertaking had been completed. Biggest of all would be external forces beyond the control of any one man—those war clouds gathering so blackly over all the great land.

Meanwhile Beale had yet to complete his assignment with the submission of his report to the War Department. This he accomplished in Chester, Pennsylvania, having reached there via the Santa Fe Trail to the Missouri River, proceeding thence by riverboat and railroad. From Chester, on December 15, 1859, he was ready to write the secretary of war: "Sirs: I have the honor to submit herewith the report of my last expedition from Fort Smith, Arkansas, to the Colorado River, from which I have lately returned." [9]

Ned Beale was somewhat reluctant to admit that any expedition could be his own last. Sometime before sending his report to the secretary of war, he contacted the Navy Department with an offer to make a reconnaissance for the Department in Panama, in the region of Chiriquí and Golfito. Though the Department was already eyeing the general area with a possible canal in mind, Beale received a cool reply that the Department "will accept your services . . . but upon condition that it is not to be subject to any expense thereby and that you are to have no claim upon it for compensation." With this, apparently, the matter was dropped by both parties.

By the time the report of his second roadbuilding expedition reached the War Department, it was 1860. Once Fort Sumter was fired upon and the nation was split into two warring parts, the road to California became of less importance to politicians of both sides than the hopes of each section of attaching to itself a California of doubtful loyalties. It then became very important for the Union to send there appointees of recognized character and unquestioned loyalty. Thus, when Beale wanted to volunteer for military service, President Lincoln asked him to accept the post of Surveyor General for California and Nevada, a post he retained throughout the war.

When peace came in 1865, Beale was at last able to retire to the Tejón Ranch he had purchased so many years before. Situated as it was at an altitude of about 500 feet above Bakersfield, Beale later described it to a friend as having "a refreshing atmosphere of perpetual spring which never becomes close summer."

For nearly thirty years, Beale would be spending time there and in the home he presently purchased in Washington, with an interlude for diplomatic service abroad. It is as a rancher, though, that we like to think of him whose modest inscription on El Morro is one of the few reminders of the man who devoted so much of his life's energies to making clear a pathway in the wilderness.

"Our host," wrote author Charles Nordhoff in 1872 when he visited Tejón,

> is a sparkling combination of scholar, gentleman, and Indian fighter, the companion and friend of Kit Carson in other days, the surveyor of transcontinental railways and wagon roads and the owner today of what seems to be the most magnificent estate in a single hand in America.
>
> The rancho from which I write, the Tejón as it is called, the home of General Beale, contains nearly 200,000 acres and lies at the junction of the Sierra Nevada with the Coast Range . . . The Tejón Pass, a narrow defile, separates them and gives egress from the valley into Los Angeles County.
>
> The Tejón is devoted to sheep and here I saw the operation of shearing: eight or nine weeks are required to shear the whole flock. [16]

That flock, numbering over 100,000, was a kind of California gold mine, growing and renewing itself each year, which would have appealed to medieval alchemists as well as to the man who had carried the little sack of real gold to Washington.

Author Nordhoff, whose grandson won fame in our time as coauthor of *Mutiny on the Bounty*, went on to give a fascinating account of his visit with the Tejón's owner:

> "This country is quiet now," said the General one evening in a reminiscent mood, "but when I first came into it it contained some rough people. The head of the famous robber, Joaquín Marieta, and the hand of his Lieutenant, 'three-fingered Jack' was brought into my camp but a few hours after the two scoundrels were shot. Jack Powers and his band used to herd their bands of stolen horses on my ranch as they drove them through the country . . . Mason and Henry, the worst of all road agents, used to go through Kern County, waylaying and robbing; and in those days a man had to be careful not only of his money but of his life." [16]

And who better equipped to take care of both than Edward Beale!

Living in the midst of those wide acres and the great flocks of sheep roaming there, Ned Beale still retained the old loyalty to the great beasts who had so well served him and of whose services he had foreseen so great use. So, when the government herd was put on the auction block, he acquired some of his own to use for his private ventures.

When grown to manhood, his son, the Truxie for whom he had destined the catamount skin acquired not far from El Morro, would recall proudly riding to Los Angeles beside his father in a sulky drawn by a team of camels, harnessed tandem. Throughout the ride, his father carried on a private conversation with those camels in "Syrian" which, with typical energy, he had taught himself for the sole purpose of communicating with them.

17

Camels' Last Camp

The camels that had not gone to California with Beale, would, by virtue of their residence on Texan soil, become Confederate spoils of war. They might have performed yeoman service for the Texan Confederates, had men and officers been willing to take the ridiculous-looking beasts seriously. As always, the conservative military mind, which then thought in terms of infantry and horse-borne cavalry, could see no future in the animals that had fallen into their hands. Camels were to them only a source of embarassment, not exactly to be destroyed outright because some fool superior officer might hold the destroyers responsible for alienating government property, yet hardly to be assigned stable space and forage needed for mounts of troops already more than occupied with the grim business of war. The thought of using the camels to further that business never entered their heads.

An exception was one General Sterling Price, who managed to acquire one of the camels and who used it throughout the war as a baggage train. Onto one camel was piled all his company's baggage. Many a time, while his company was on the march, a local resident would be startled to see the animal swinging along under a small mountain of carpet bags, frying pans, cooking pots, blankets, and whatever other items members of Price's company may have tired of carrying. No one has recorded the ultimate fate of that particular camel.

Most of the Confederate camels passed the war years in unproductive idleness. Jefferson Davis, now President of the Confederacy, had more urgent matters to preoccupy him than the fate of these alien beasts that had once so interested him. Fellow

Southerner Major Wayne would become an officer in his Confederate Army, where that handsome major would meet his death. Already before the start of hostilities, he had seen the handwriting on the wall as far as his own relationship with the dreamed-of camel corps was concerned.

In December 1856, he was conscientiously writing Secretary of War Davis:

> Sir: As the political changes of the coming year may terminate your official connexion with the War Department . . . I have thought it advisable to make a few suggestions at this early date, that if you agree with me a system may be organized, that the matter may be left to your successor in as complete a form as possible. My observation of and experience with civil employees in Texas, satisfies me that the accomplishment of your views for the use of the dromedaries and the burden camels can only be attained through military responsibility and accountability. [25]

Behind these quiet words, we may guess that Wayne must have had many a frustrating experience and must have foreseen many more.

Wayne went on to suggest to Davis that responsibility for the animals be assigned to "an intelligent regimental officer" with authority to make the men under him learn how to handle camels efficiently. For his own part, Quartermaster Officer Wayne felt, "The prejudices of regimental officers against the exercise of command . . . by an officer of the staff, precludes me from the control of enlisted men. I have no desire to hold a questionable position. In making the proposition, I sacrifice personal wishes to what I conceive to be a necessary duty."

After pointing out that, for the doubting Thomases, some years would yet be required to prove the camels' real value, and suggesting the names of possible officers to carry on where he was leaving off, Wayne added a last paragraph to underline his own conviction that "the usefulness of the camel for all military purposes, and its economy, I hold to be fully shown already."

Two months later, at Davis's suggestion, Wayne was sending Quartermaster General Jessup his own helpful suggestions as to how the camels should be handled. Of course, nothing would come of this. Wayne himself was on the point of departing from Valverde for Washington, in response to his own request for transferral and possibly in response to General Jessup's growing irritation with the importunities of the camel enthusiast.

The new Secretary of War, John Floyd, a Southerner, was entering upon his manifold duties with much personal enthusiasm for the new experiment in transportation, but apparently with little means of persuading politicians to share it. At least twice he would submit plans for a camel corps that was to be one thousand strong, and as many times Congress would turn a deaf ear to his pleas that funds be appropriated for the purpose.

Less anticamel in sentiment than residents of most other areas, Californians were prepared to give the beasts a try in places for which they seemed particularly adapted. When, early in 1860, plans were being made to run a survey along the boundary between California and Nevada, a line that must, in part, traverse Death Valley, it was inevitable that the use of camels should suggest itself to the surveyors' minds.

Camels were to be obtained from the government corral in Los Angeles as well as from the group Secretary of War Floyd had assigned to Beale's care nearly three years earlier. In March 1860, an officer of the survey party wrote in a newspaper article: "The camels which were ordered for our use were at first four, but one was killed by another, so only three remained to us."

Alas! that the camel thus killed should have been Ned Beale's pride and joy, that great white dromedary Seid, which he had ridden so proudly on so many occasions: when meeting Colonel Loring on the way to Fort Defiance and when, at the end of his 1857–58 expedition, he, with Hadji Ali on Tuili, made those last fifty-seven miles into Los Angeles in eight hours, arriving there to the open-mouthed astonishment of all viewers.

Seid and Tuili were males, and at the time of setting forth of the border survey, it was rutting season, when no male camels could be expected to be friends. New camel handlers, like those involved in the survey, had perhaps yet to learn that in such a season, male camels should be kept apart. Seid, in any case, managed to get loose and, becoming the aggressor, attacked his fellows. Tuili turned on him in a furious fight, which no bystander dared interfere with. When Seid fell, Tuili, quick as a flash, finished him off with a blow from those heavy camel feet. Seid lay dead in a pool of blood that flowed from his crushed head. Ironically, this ignominiously defeated beast is the only one of whom anything survives today—a whitened skeleton in the Smithsonian Institution of Washington.

So the survey started with its three camels. "They are certainly very useful beasts," the newspaper article continued:

> strong . . . gifted with wonderful intelligence and docility, [when not in the rutting season, of course]. Their jaw is very strong [as the so-recent fight amply demonstrated], and I should not like to have its power tried on me, wherefore I kept a respectful distance for a while, but I soon gained their friendship by some bribes of bread which they eat with evident pleasure.
>
> When they see a friend approaching, they stretch their necks forward, stick out their upper lip and make a kind of whistle. When angry or tired, they make a sound similar to the creaking of an ungreased cart wheel. If their pack galls them, they groan and turn their heads toward the pack.
>
> In consequence of the peculiar form of the animal, much attention and practice is necessary to pack them well.

Not only was the peculiar form to blame, but the fact that the peculiar form, being where the animal stored its fat against lean days to come, was changeable in size. When the animal was in a high state of nourishment, its hump would be large and firm. When times were hard, the hump might flop over like an empty sack. Mule skinners would never learn to be patient with animals that could find no more convenient way of storing nourishment, even though such storage was what made them particularly useful during desert journeys. No one was prepared to devote to packing of camels that necessary "attention and practice."

On the border survey, the value of camels soon became evident to the surveyors in charge, one making, on February 8, a diary entry that might have been written several years before by either Lt. Beale or Maj. Wayne: "Our well-burdened mules came straggling in wearily, and it was really piteous to see the anxiety they manifested in . . . jostling one another at the short trough into which water was drawn from the well. . . . Their impatience and suffering presented a strong contrast to the placidity and quiet indifference of our huge Arabian beasts."

A Paiute Indian presently visited camp to stare unbelievingly at the strange beasts. "The camels filled him with amazement," a party member wrote, "and evidently overreached his powers of classification; it was far from clear to him whether they were birds or beasts." [62]

Bird or beast, it was destined to remain an outcast in both categories, despite all the efforts of camel-minded Californians like the San Francisco merchant Otto Esche, who had sponsored the importation of camels from Manchuria. He saw them as destined to carry freight from California into Nevada and Utah, returning to California laden with the products of the mines they would serve. Few entrepreneurs shared his vision, for when he put his imports up for auction, they brought less than they had cost him, and still could prove no bargains for purchasers who failed to use them wisely or well.

The camels Esche had imported, as well as some of those auctioned off in 1864 from part of the government herd remaining in California, would be seen until about 1877 in the vicinity of Virginia City or Carson City in Nevada. Along mountain roads, they packed salt, mining machinery, all manner of other supplies. There, as elsewhere, few took trouble to learn how to care for them. Denied even the kind of care a good mule might expect, the camels became an increasingly sad sight—unkempt, galled by ill-fitting saddles, their sores aggravated by salt that trickled out of their packs, cordially hated by practically everyone, even the men they served so well and unprotestingly.

Already by June 1864, the *Reese River Reveille* (Nevada) carried a report that efforts were being made to deny camels passage through the streets of that town. By February 1875, camels had become a statewide problem, so that an anticamel bill was introduced into the state assembly, as reported by the same Reese River paper: "The Senate devoted a large portion of the morning session to a little fun over the Assembly bills to prohibit camels from travelling the public roads and highways in this state. A motion was made for its reference to the Committee on Public Morals, to which an amendment was offered that it be to the Committee on Indian Affairs. A discussion ensued in which some jokes were cracked about humps in general."

Jokes or not, the bill passed promptly. It stipulated the penalty for an owner of an offending camel of "a fine of not less than twenty-five (25) dollars, or by imprisonment of not less than ten or more than thirty days, or by both such fine and such imprisonment."

The first prosecution under that anticamel ordinance took place in the following September, when the *Reese River Reveille* announced, "Like the poor 'droms' the citizens of Walker River Valley have got their backs up and want the unsightly animals properly restrained. Nothing is safe from these voracious critters, as they will bolt down a Murphy wagon, four rods of rail fence, a Yankee stone boat or anything else at a single meal. As pack animals across the desert they can't be beat, but when it comes to a bump of destructiveness, they have one as big as a Brooklyn preacher!"

That Brooklyn preacher—undoubtedly Henry Ward Beecher—must have been to the writer equivalent of today's antiwar demonstrators. Whatever special incident that phrase recalled, it was self-evident that the camels' destructiveness might have been abated had they been offered more regular and acceptable feed. "Things that no other animal will touch," Abbé Huc had said, "to it are welcome; briars, thorns, dry wood itself, supply it with efficient food"— particularly when the animals are especially hungry. Certainly none of the expedition commanders whom they served ever mentioned their destructive taste for wagons or stone boats.

Camel problems were not confined to Nevada. In 1879, four years after the Nevada law was passed, the *Arizona Sentinel* announced:

A herd of camels was driven here from Nevada nearly two years ago. Finding no profitable work for them, their owners turned them loose along the Gila, to the eastward of Yuma. There they have been living and breeding, looking sleek and fat all the time [no wagons or rail fences mentioned, but, of course, there were plenty of thorny bushes]. For a while they were in danger of extermination. Whenever they put in their appearance along the wagon road, they frightened mules and horses beyond control of the drivers. They soon earned the everlasting hatred of the teamsters, some of whom acquired the habit of shooting camels on sight.

Since, however, the railroad has been delivering freight at Adonde, the road along the Gila has been comparatively abandoned, and the remaining animals have a good chance to show what they can do in the way of propagation.

The heart of any enterprising circus owner who came upon that article was bound to leap with excitement. Camels actually to be picked up free in the American Southwest! Camels that otherwise might serve as objects for target practice! No more need to go to the expense of importing the animals from the Orient! Just catch yourself one along the Gila River—catch a dozen or so, then stage an oriental camel caravan in action! That should draw the crowds!

Not surprisingly, a year or so later a newspaper of Flagstaff reported: "A carload of camels captured by Indians in the vicinity of Gila passed through Flagstaff last Wednesday. There were 7 large ones and 2 small ones in the car consigned to a circus in Kansas City . . . The price was said to be trifling. Indians were glad to get rid of them . . . A large number are still in that vicinity." Of course a large and curious crowd was on hand at the depot to see the camels off.

Had there been on hand anyone able and willing to indoctrinate such crowds and persuade them there was money to be made by experts in camel lore, the animals might yet have served their adopted country long and well. Though by then railroads had spanned the continent, there still remained great open spaces between railroads, spaces that had to be reached by some kind of transport. Well into our present century auto drivers were being warned that in such areas they should take along extra cans of water to cool both their cars and themselves. Here was a situation made to order for camel transport if only the owners of competing horses and mules could have trained their animals to accept camels as, presently, they were to accept those frightening horseless carriages. It was the motivation of the men, of course, that was inadequate.

Despite predatory circus owners and trigger-happy teamsters, camels long continued to roam free in the Southwest. The sight of such a great beast suddenly looming through windblown dust may well have helped sober—temporarily, at least—the most confirmed of alcoholics. Even to an entirely sober small boy, living with a father stationed at Fort Selden, New Mexico, it was a never-to-be forgotten sight, one that the boy would recall seventy years later when he had become the world famous General Douglas MacArthur.

The camels, which no one wished to claim, were bound to

become something of a legend. For years, people were catching glimpses of one or more in remote spots. Many more people believed they'd been vouchsafed the sight of camels. As years passed and the actual number of surviving camels dwindled to the vanishing point, tales grew taller and taller, more and more tinged with the kind of romanticism that became increasingly associated with episodes of southwestern history.

Where was the very last camel seen? By whom? An elderly resident of Tucson, one Arturo Carillo, was convinced that it had been he, when a lad of sixteen years, who had caught the last live camel. While carrying mail over a little traveled road, he suddenly saw a great beast towering in his path. At first he'd thought it might be a buffalo but then, recalling circus posters he'd seen, he was sure that here was one of those camels that a circus might pay well for. Using the lariat he always carried with him, he roped the animal and then, with the greatest of difficulty, dragged it after his team into town. No one there wanted the beast. Finally Arturo persuaded a friend to take care of the camel but as the feed bill mounted the boy grew disenchanted with his catch and made a gift of it to his friend. What the friend did with it is not recorded.

What became of all those others: the eighty-odd from the two importations that still remained in Valverde when the Confederates took the camp over? Those Ned Beale purchased when government camels were auctioned off? Those set loose along the Gila and the young they there produced? Since no truly final accounting ever could be made, all joined the legendary caravan stalking the great deserts of the Southwest. There never quite died the exciting thought that somewhere, somehow, sometime a great beast might come looming out of the past to bring to mind the men its fellows served and the paths they trod together.

What, too, became of those men who were persuaded to leave their homelands to care for and pack and drive the camels? Some, when the year of their contracted services came to an end, were returned to their homelands as had been stipulated in the original agreement. Others chose not to return, perhaps feeling that life would be freer, more exciting, and more rewarding in the New World than it could be for them in the Old. Like their original charges, most of them disappeared, aliens merged with other aliens in a land that had seemed to promise much while in reality offering them very little.

Of all the original camel drivers, the ultimate fate of only two is known. One, called "Greek George," lived to an old age and now lies buried in the cemetery in Whittier, California. The other is the man who rode beside Ned Beale into Los Angeles on that memorable November 9, 1857, and who accompanied Beale's partner, Bishop, when he brought the camels and supplies to Leroux Spring. This was Hadji Ali, sometimes called Philip Tedro, but whether either was his real name no one ever discovered. No one ever really knew much about him. What is certain, though, is that the soldiers at Camp Valverde, finding "Hadji Ali" alien to their tongues, were soon calling him "Hi Jolly." Hi Jolly he would remain for the rest of his life though still, like the "Hadji Ali," as alien to the land as the animals that arrived in his care.

Like most aliens, Hadji Ali had thought to find fortune and happiness in the land of his adoption. Like too many, he lost identity. If he was truly literate, and no one was certain he was, he kept no revealing journal, left no inscription on the rock.

Throughout the Civil War he served his new land well by carrying dispatches back and forth from New Mexico territory to military posts on the Pacific Coast. Did he, we wonder, ride camels on any of these dispatch-bearing missions? They would have been fleeter, better able to live off the land than other mounts, but surely they'd have been far more conspicuous. In any case, the thought of a one-man camel corps is highly appealing.

Prospecting for gold and other minerals when and as he could, Hi Jolly continued in government service as a scout and chief packmaster until the end of the campaign against the raiding Apaches. When Geronimo surrendered in 1886, Hi Jolly, then over sixty years of age, was entirely on his own, scraping a bare living with his prospecting. By 1899, when he was approaching eighty and his health began to fail, he finally decided that the time had come to apply for the pension he understood the government had promised him when he gave up his chance to be repatriated along with those other camel drivers. By 1899, unfortunately, few were left who remembered events of the 1850s and the promises then made or implied. No written contract or record of such a promise was to be located in government files. In the days when it should have been drawn up, Hi Jolly was a new and inexperienced alien from a land where governments were expected to be both paternalistic and arbitrary, never in any case to be committed in binding written contracts.

Colonel George Sanford, under whom Hi Jolly served during the Apache campaign, did his best to help him. The colonel wrote strongly in his onetime packmaster's behalf, stating that it was always understood that the United States government had agreed to take care of Hi Jolly as long as he lived. As for indebtedness, the colonel stated, "The government has had few more faithful servants during the last half century, as many officers still living will testify." They must have testified in vain, for the faithful servant's claims to a small pension were flatly rejected.

Of course Hi Jolly would have been better advised had he not waited to enter that claim until he was old and impoverished with stark necessity knocking at his door. He should have started a couple of decades earlier while men under whom he'd served—Beale, Bishop, officers of the Apache campaign as well as those for whom he had carried so many important messages during the 1860s—were young enough to recall incidents that might move the mind of official Washington. By 1899, the few who were still alive had lost much of the influence they once might have had. A new century was dawning. Camels and camel trains belonged to ancient history.

Proud and independent, Hi Jolly had been reluctant to claim assistance, like a beggar from the Orient, for services he rendered. So, when he might have entered his plea with better chances for success, he kept busy prospecting, always expecting to strike it rich, always knowing there was that promise to fall back upon should he continue to strike it poor. In the end he was reduced to the ultimate indignity of serving as a driver of mules. Finally, he had to accept the charity of a friend in Quartzite, Arizona, in whose house he died in 1902.

Since the friend himself told of this, it is undoubtedly the literal truth concerning the circumstances of Hi Jolly's death. More true than the truth, however, is the legend which has grown up about that alien's passing. In December 1902, so the story goes, an old prospector walked into a Quartzite bar, his eyes wide with amazement. When asked what he had seen, he told of meeting with a great red beast somewhere out in the desert. At first he'd thought that in the thickening twilight his eyes had been playing tricks on him. Then, suddenly, the thought had come to him that here must be a camel. Thought they'd all gone years ago, but this had been one, never a doubt of it!

As he finished, an elderly man rose from a corner table and walked up to the speaker. In accents still tinged with the foreign tongue familiar to his youth, the man asked the new arrival just where he'd seen the vision. After listening closely to the reply, he walked out without further word.

A few days later, some Quartzite prospectors came upon him in the desert, arms linked about the neck of an old red camel, joined in death to this last relic of a never quite forgotten homeland neither would again revist in the flesh. Thus, according to the legend, Hi Jolly died.

Proper dramatic climax demands that this should also have been the last of the camels. Unfortunately for drama, reports of camels would continue to crop up, one being of a camel, showing a clear U.S. government brand, appearing nearly five years later in the midway of a San Antonio circus.

As for that last camel driver, today is he commemorated by a stone pyramid, topped by a small metal camel silhouette, erected near Quartzite, Arizona, in 1935. One is bound to suspect this tribute owes more to the publicity value of the camel legend than to an impulse to pay tribute to a long neglected public servant.

"The Last Camp of Hi Jolly," it reads, "Born somewhere in Syria about 1823, Died at Quartzite, December 16, 1902. Came to this country February 10, 1856. Camel driver—packer—scout. Over thirty years of faithful aid to the U.S. Government."

Born "somewhere," about some date, and like his camels rejected by the government both served, Hadji Ali and they now lie in alien soil. Surely though, all are now at home among the ghostly throng that, for the perceptive, will never cease to stream past El Morro.

18

The Roster Closed

With the 1859 surveying trip, not only were Ned Beale's most adventurous days passing, but the greatest days of Inscription Rock and of the road past it were approaching an end. That rock, which had guaranteed a sort of immortality to so many passersby, could do nothing at all for the route by which they passed. The year 1858 had seen added to its roster about twenty-five inscriptions with identifiable dates, though many undated ones clearly belong to that year. By 1859, and even including the fancy inscriptions left by some of Beale's company, the total was less than half the previous year's.

Personal and emotional considerations started this downward trend, practical and political considerations would prevent its reversal. Emigrants, whose collective needs provided the excuse for surveying a wagon road, had cut on the rock records each secretly dreaded might be his last. When, for some, it turned out that they were in very truth the last, the shock of that reality left the minds of survivors reeling. Many a month must pass for those "first emigrants" to recover emotionally from the massacre described by John Udell. It would take many more months for the recovered ones to summon courage to start out again for the far West.

Moreover, by the time the memory of that disaster began to lose the sharp edge of newness, many a would-be emigrant was staying put, the men involved directly or indirectly in the cataclysm of the Civil War. Even those who, because of proddings of conscience or concern for personal safety, refused to become directly involved, would know enough to avoid a southern route where, if they escaped the attentions of Indians, they were almost bound to encounter troops of one side or the other, possibly to end by drawing down upon themselves the kind of antagonism fighters so often feel toward nonfighters. In any case, emigrants who were being encouraged by Union authorities to add the weight of their numbers and votes to the California whose allegiance might be uncertain would not then take their way past El Morro.

By the fall of 1860, the sad and ominous issues were becoming more and more clearly defined. Men who had been friends drew apart and the whole atmosphere became darkly threatening. Nowhere would this show itself more clearly than in military outposts staffed by men who had been educated at the same military institute and who had long lived together in warm comradeship. Men who had trod wilderness trails together and side-by-side fought off Indian attacks knew they might soon be facing one another as enemies.

At Fort Smith, whence had started "Beale's Road" (or Marcy's? or Simpson's? or Whipple's?), the buildup of hostilities was watched by Captain of Cavalry David Sloane Stanley, the same who, as lieutenant, had done quartermaster's service on Whipple's 1853 expedition.

"As officers of the army, from the North or South," he recounted in his memoirs,

> we were for the Union, and anything done to injure that sentiment, either North or South, met our disapprobation . . . We could daily see the Union cause growing weak amongst our neighbors and secession getting stronger . . .
>
> Finally South Carolina and other states seceded and officers from the South began to talk of resigning their commissions . . . Some few resigned cheerfully, but many, even from South Carolina, resigned with bitter tears. It was sad to see men we had lived with as warm friends become cold, then offensive, and finally avowed open enemies.
>
> My captain, James McIntosh from New Jersey . . . coolly calculated his chances of promotion, thought them better in the Confederacy, was made a brigadier general and later was killed at Pea Ridge. Some of the these foolish officers had so little idea of their duty as to insist if they fought for the

Confederacy and failed, they would be entitled to resume their places in the army. [58]

Some of those foolish officers tried to persuade Stanley to accept a colonelcy in an Arkansas regiment. By declining, Stanley knew he was making his position in that southern outpost most difficult, if not downright risky. He knew also, fortunately, that there were others similarly threatened. In May 1861, he and a fellow Union sympathizer, a Capt. Sturges, undertook to escape north together. Accompanying them were troops who shared their sentiments and a large quartermaster's train numbering fifty-six mule teams. Powder and ammunition beyond what this train could carry, they rendered useless by dumping it in the river.

This was no happy adventure along the Santa Fe Trail. In fact, they avoided known trails, relying on their own previous knowledge of the country through which they must pass. It was a truly hazardous trip, but they made it all the way to Kansas. There, in October, Stanley became a brigadier general, opportunities for promotion in Union forces being apparently as good as coolly calculating Col. McIntosh found them in the Confederate. A broken leg soon incapacitated Stanley but by the following spring he was back in active service where he remained until, in 1864, he received a painful wound that ended his fighting in that war.

From the very beginning of the conflict, New Mexico Territory was officially on the Union side—partly because the Confederacy endorsed slavery, partly because her hated neighbor, Texas, endorsed the Confederacy. In that remote area the struggle was of brief duration, the New Mexico Volunteers triumphing over the Texas Confederates by March 1862. Though troops from both sides would, at one time or another, have camped by El Morro, there are no positively identifiable inscriptions for the years 1861 and 1862. As during the period of Mexican domination, there were very good reasons for not leaving records.

After their victory of March 1862, New Mexican troops under the command of Maine-born Brigadier General James Henry Carleton were trying to tame the roaming Navajo and Apache Indians who made life a nightmare for settlers all the way down into old Mexico, and for the settled Pueblo Indians as well. It would be 1886 before the last of the raiding Apache bands under

Geronimo surrendered. The Navajo problem, however, seemed to have been settled by the fall of 1864.

Troops involved in these undertakings moved back and forth by El Morro and, knowing the information could be worth little to Indians who had other signs to read, some added their names to the roster. Nearly fifteen now identifiable names are dated 1863, with a smaller number for 1864, most belonging to soldiers and officers in the command of Colonel Christopher Carson. One inscriber saw fit to add that "Christopher Carson, 1863," now removed.

An equally famous name for that year, which disappeared about 1924, belonged to French-born Bishop Jean Baptiste Lamy, whose personality and enduring influence later moved novelist Willa Cather to write *Death Comes for the Archbishop.* Bishop Lamy stopped by the rock in 1863 while on a horseback trip from New Mexico to California, as had been Juan de Oñate over two and a half centuries earlier.

With peace finally coming in 1865, soldiers of the disbanding armies could start their long treks home. Three such were the 1866 inscriptions ascribable to California Volunteers.

Peace also was making it possible to resume the long-deferred plans for completion of transcontinental railroad surveys. Parties again took to the field—this time rather to cover wide areas than narrow strips along specified parallels. Less imbued with that sense of being first comers, only a few of the surveyors' parties left their names on the rock. The only such name now positively identifiable as belonging to a government-sponsored survey of the 1870s is that of photographer T. H. O'Sullivan who, like R. H. Kern of 1849, was keeping a pictorial record of the survey he was accompanying—records that unfortunately are now untraceable.

In the end, ironically, the railroad whose planning had sent so many explorers and roadbuilders past El Morro and Zuñi, was to bypass that valley to take a somewhat longer route up the easier grades of a valley to the north. Had the original planners foreseen the desirability of this location, how much poorer would the records now be, how much poorer we of another century.

Enmities and rivalries long since buried, those flesh-and-blood beings who left their marks on the great rock will ever continue to pass in shadowy array—the races for whom the petroglyphs had meaning, conquistadors and conquered, North Americans of infinitely varied background, explorers and trivial lazy boys, heroes and blackguards, the lucky and the unlucky. And with them pass the tamed beasts whose presence alone made possible the continued passing of so many of the humans they served.

The lives of the members of this motley throng are subtly, inextricably, eternally intertwined. All belong to the record for, in a real sense, it is a way all the world has streamed: facing and conquering hostile environments, striving to bring their dreams to realization, dreams of opening a way through an uncharted wilderness, of treading ground their fellows have not yet trod, of grasping the pot of gold at the rainbow's end, and always of leaving some enduring mark upon an indifferent world.

Appendix A

42d Congress,   SENATE.   Report
  2d Session.   No. 207.

IN THE SENATE OF THE UNITED STATES:

May 23, 1872.—Ordered to be printed.

Mr. Buckingham, from the Committee on Indian Affairs,
submitted the following

REPORT:

*The Committee on Indian Affairs, to whom was referred the
petition of Leonard J. Rose, for compensation for losses
sustained by Indian spoliation, submit the following report:*

In the year 1858 Leonard J. Rose, a citizen of the United States,
left the State of Iowa for California by way of New Mexico. The
party consisted of men, women, and children, to the number of
about sixty, many of whom joined the party after he left Iowa. He
took with him horses, mules, cows, and young stock, wagons, corn,
flour, and a variety of other valuable property. On or about the 31st
day of August, while west of the Colorado River, the party was
attacked by a large number of the Mohave Indians, and after a
battle, which lasted about two hours, they destroyed and carried
away property belonging to him which he values at $27,639.76.

The petitioner presented his claim for compensation to the first
session of the Thirty-sixth Congress, which was referred to the
Senate Committee on Indian Affairs, of which the Hon. W. K.

Sebastian was chairman. There was some correspondence upon the subject between the committee and the Commissioner of Indian Affairs, but no facts were brought to light to justify the payment of the claim by the Government, and on the 19th of February, 1861, the committee was discharged.

No new testimony has been introduced, and as those Indians have no annuities or other moneys due from the United States, and as the Government cannot be justly liable for spoliations committed upon those who remove from one section of the country to another, your committee report adversely upon the petition.

Appendix B

UNITED STATES COURT OF CLAIMS.

LEONARD J. ROSE, Claimant,

v.

THE UNITED STATES, Defendant.

No. 2176.

Indian Depredation Claim.

PETITION.
Filed June 3, 1891—J. R.

Your petitioner respectfully represents:

On or about April 1, 1858, petitioner left Van Buren County, Iowa, for California, via Albuquerque, New Mexico, with his wife and two children, Mr. and Mrs. Jones and E. C. Jones, the father, mother, and brother of Mrs. Rose. Also Mr. Brown, wife, and five children; Mr. Bentner (who joined a short time afterward), with wife and five children, and seventeen other hands to drive team and loose animals.

Mr. Brown was major domo or overseer over train and stock. Besides these there were about sixty immigrants who joined in Kansas, most of whom were women and children. Outfit was all of the best and selected, and consisted of two hundred and forty-seven bulls, oxen, cows, and heifers, one very fine Morgan stallion, one large bay fast-trotting gelding, two young matched Morgan mares, ten other good mares and geldings, mostly mares, two sorrel matched large Kentucky mules, six wagons, one carriage with harness, and other things thereto pertaining, and the wagons were loaded with goods, clothing, provisions, tools, and other outfit for the journey. Train arrived at Albuquerque, New Mexico, without any serious accident or loss of stock. At the advice of the Government officers and citizens of Albuquerque they started from there for California over the new route which Lieutenant Beal had lately explored, on or near the thirty-fifth parallel of latitude. The people of Albuquerque were so anxious that this route should be taken that they paid one hundred and fifty dollars ($150) of the five hundred dollars ($500) paid for a guide.

They left Albuquerque, June thirtieth, eighteen hundred and fifty-eight, after procuring Jose Manuel Savedra as guide and Petro as interpreter. Saw no Indians and had no trouble until they arrived at Peach-tree Springs, about one hundred and twelve miles east of the Colorado River. There they saw some Indians of the Cosninos tribe, who stole a mare from petitioner and a mule from Savedra, and two men pursued them for one day, and while going through a narrow cañon some of the Cosninos Indians shot arrows at them from a high mesa. The next evening Savedra saw some Indians on a mountain side, and by speech and sign induced them to come down. They voluntarily spoke about the mare and mule, and said the Mojaves had stolen them, and they (the Cosninos) had retaken them and would return them. Petitioner treated them kindly and fed them, and when they got to Indian Springs, about twenty-five miles from Peach-tree Springs, about twenty-five Cosninos Indians overtook them with the mare and mule. Petitioner gave them all dinner and supper, and some other things, and about fifteen remained in camp all night. Thirty or forty more joined them in the morning. About noon they began to leave in parties of from three to five. After dinner, three oxen, two heifers, and one steer were found missing, and the men following their trail found four of the cattle killed. From Indian Springs to Savedras Springs, forty-five miles east of the Colorado River, nothing of importance occurred, although Indians were constantly watching their movements. Near Savedras Springs, E. C. Jones was shot at with arrows by Cosninos Indians, and two arrows struck him and three arrows struck his horse. One other horse was shot, but both recovered and one other was lost. From Savedras Springs to Colorado Mountain Springs, some cattle were shot, but not seriously, and a mare stolen. No other stock was lost by the Cosninos.

On the west side of the Colorado Mountains, the Mojaves made their appearance and at first were very friendly, but on approaching the Colorado River their numbers increased, and they became very insolent, and killed some of the stock and drove some away, and laughed at any attempt of petitioner or his men to interfere. That day petitioner moved camp to the river bank, and there two Mojave chiefs, with about three hundred warriors, visited him. Petitioner gave them presents and the Indians said they were satisfied, and no more cattle would be stolen, and showed them the road, but petitioner had a strict watch kept.

The next day and the third day that they were on the Colorado River (August 31, 1858), petitioner sent some men out to cut logs for a raft, some to herd and watch the animals, and others staid in camp. There were about thirty men in camp, well armed with rifles, shot-guns, and revolvers.

About 10 A.M. three hundred or more Indians were seen crossing the river above the camp. Petitioner felt frightened, and had the animals herded near camp. After dinner one of the men reported many Indians were near the camp, but hidden by the brush, and one of them had told him a steamboat was coming up the river.

About 2 o'clock P.M. the Indians, perhaps three or four hundred strong, who had surrounded the camp, made an attack, but as petitioner had had some warning they only succeeded in driving off the stock. About twenty or twenty-five Indians were probably killed.

Some of the oxen were frightened by the Indians up to the wagons, and so saved. There were saved seven oxen, five horses, one wagon and its load, and one carriage. All the other wagons and contents had to be left behind. On returning, petitioner met Messrs. Caves, Jordan, Perkins, Davis, and party on the east of the Colorado Mountains. Petitioner and some of his party arrived in Albuquerque October 24, 1858, with one wagon, one carriage, and four horses, the cattle and one horse having died.

That by reason of the said depredation above set out, petitioner lost the following property purchased and owned by him, viz., the amounts stated being the prices paid therefor by petitioner:

Four thorough-bred short-horn Durham bulls, at $500	$2,000 00
One thorough-bred short-horn Durham heifer	400 00
Nine full-blooded short-horn cows and heifers, at $200	1,800 00
Fifty-one graded short-horn cows and heifers, at $100	5,100 00
Thirty-one yoke oxen, at $125	3,875 00
Four two and three-year old steers, at $30	$120 00
One hundred and one selected cows and heifers, at $50	5,050 00
One Morgan stallion	2,500 00
Two matched Morgan fillies, at $350	700 00
Seven mares and geldings, at $200	1,400 00
Two match carriage mules, at $250	500 00
Four wagons, covers, etc. 2¼ iron axle and spindle, at $150	600 00
One wagon, covers, etc. thimble skane	120 00
Four axes, $6; scythes and sickles, $3; ropes and halters, $40...................................	49 00
Ox balls and rings, $5; ox whips, $12; dried fruit, $42 .	59 00
Twenty-four chains, at $3.75; medicine, $79; tools, $84.60...	253 60
Indian goods, $233.70; saddles, $112; bells, $5	350 70
Meal, $19; flour in St. Louis, $90; flour at Albuquerque, $140	249 00
Twenty-four bushels beans, $48; buckskins, $17.50; ferriage, $43	108 50
Ox and horseshoe nails, $21; lariats, $9; three tents, $60	90 00
Wagon grease, $4.90; side meat and hams, $367.25 ..	372 15
Extra ox bows, $6; chopped rye and wheat, $75	81 00
Thirty sacks corn at Albuquerque, $60; one set harness, $45	105 00
Bedding and clothing, $300; one Sharp's rifle, $30 ...	330 00
Three stoves and utensils, stools, knives and forks	75 00
Brass and tin ware, churns, tubs, irons, etc.	150 00
Tobacco and five gallons brandy (left at Colorado River)	90 00
Sugar, coffee, tea, rice, crackers, lard, vinegar, soap,	

candles, cheese, hominy, salt, citric acid, soda, oysters, preserves, spices, fish, raisins, figs, canned peaches, and tomatoes, &c 1,154 81

Paid Savadera as guide and Petro as interpreter 250 00

$27,932 76

From the foregoing account the $43 and $250 paid to Savadera as guide is deducted 293 00

Total amount claimed $27,639 76

That in the year 1858 sworn petition of claimant was transmitted to the Department at Washington, D.C., verified by the affidavits of numerous witnesses; that report thereon was made to Congress, but no appropriation was made to pay any portion of said claim; that in 1873 petitioner refiled his claim with the Interior Department, and on or about June 22, 1875, the Commissioner of Indian Affairs recommended to the Secretary of the Interior allowance of the claim for $13,819.88, being one-half the amount claimed; and on January 5, 1876, said Secretary transmitted such report to Congress; that on October 20, 1886, said Commissioner again reported the claim to the Secretary of the Interior, recommending disallowance thereof upon the sole ground that at the time of said depredation the Indians committing same did not hold treaty relations with the United States, and said report was transmitted to Congress on March 11, 1886.

Therefore your petitioner prays judgment against the United States for the sum of twenty-seven thousand six hundred and thirty-nine 75/100 dollars ($27,639.75).

That no assignment of said claim or any part thereof has been made. The said claimant is justly entitled to the amount herein claimed from the United States, after allowing all just credits and offsets; that petitioner came from Germany when twelve years old, and was naturalized in Waterloo, Monroe Co., Ill., and has at all times borne true allegiance to the Government of the United States, and has not in any way voluntarily aided, abetted, or given encouragement to rebellion against the said Government.

L. J. ROSE.

DISTRICT OF COLUMBIA,
City of Washington, ss:

Leonard J. Rose, having been duly sworn, says that he is the claimant named in the foregong petition, and that all the statements of fact therein contained are true.

Subscribed and sworn to before me this 22d day of May, A.D. 1891.

[SEAL.]   HOWARD S. REESIDE,
Notary Public.

Post-office address of claimant, Los Angeles, California; of attorney for claimant, A. T. Britton, No. 624 F St. N.W., Washington, D.C.

Bibliography

Material consulted in writing an account like this of El Morro falls into a few rather clearly defined categories. First and foremost are the journals of men who took that route. Many of these journals reached publication in Government documents. Others have come out individually, many, much, much later, sometimes with editorial comments that add very little. John Udell's journals, published over a century ago, have been all but lost in the intervening years. Others have remained, but are almost as hard to locate. A very few are still unpublished documents, available through the courtesy of the libraries owning them. One wishes there were more to be had, since it is from such, as from material in the possession of the Library of Congress (notably some Beale letters and journals) that the truly interesting personal comments may be derived.

Except for the unpublished material, I have run all into one alphabetized list that includes an account of El Morro, painstakingly researched, and the titles of some books and articles that contribute some special knowledge or add some special interest. Of necessity, there are many more works, which, having little to add to a bibliography save length, are omitted altogether.

Unpublished

[1] Beale, Edward Fitzgerald. Letters and original of 1858–59 journal, on Library of Congress microfilm.
[2] Cheney, J. W. The story of an emigrant train (ca. 1920?), 24 pp., in Huntington Library.
[3] Floyd, Wm. P. A diary kept on Beale's 1858–59 expedition, pencilled in small notebook, in Huntington Library.
[4] Rose, L. J. Account (without title) dated Albuquerque, N. Mex. Oct. 28, 1858, 11pp., in Huntington Library.
[5] Stanley, David Sloane. See reference under published material.

Published Works

[6] Abel, Annie H. *The Official Correspondence of James S. Calhoun, While Indian Agent at Santa Fé and Superintendent of Indian Affairs in New Mexico.* Washington, D.C.: Office of Indian Affairs, 1915.
[7] Barth, A. W. "New Notes on El Morro." *Art and Archeology* 34 (1933):146–56.
[8] Beale, Edward Fitzgerald. "Wagon Road from Fort Defiance to the Colorado River. Letter from Sec'y of War Transmitting Report of Mr. Beale . . ." U.S. 35th Congress, 1st sess. Vol. 13. H. Exec. Doc. 124:1–87, 1859.
[9] Beale, Edward Fitzgerald, "Wagon Road from Fort Smith to the Colorado River. Letter of Sec'y of War Transmitting the Rep't of Mr. Beale . . ." U.S. 36th Congress, 1st sess. Vol. 6, H. Exec. Doc. 42:1–91, 1860.
[10] Beckwith, Edward Griffin, "Report by Lt. ———, Third Artillery, Upon the Route

Near the Thirty-eighth and Thirty-ninth Parallels, Explored by J. W. Gunnison, Corps of Topographical Engineers." In *Pacific Railroad Reports*, vol. 2. Washington, 1855.

[11] Bieber, Ralph P. *Southern Trails to California in 1849.* Glendale, Calif.: Arthur H. Clark Co., 1937.

[12] Bloom, Lansing B. "A Glimpse of New Mexico in 1620." *New Mexico Historical Review* 3:(1928)357–80.

[13] Bolton, Herbert Eugene. *Coronado, Knight of the Pueblos and Plains.* Albuquerque: University of New Mexico Press, 1949.

[14] Bolton, Herbert Eugene, ed. *Spanish Exploration in the Southwest, 1542–1706.* New York: C. Scribner's Sons, 1916.

[15] Bolton, Herbert Eugene and Thomas Maitland Marshall. *The Colonization of America.* New York: Macmillan Co., 1920.

[16] Bonsal, Stephen. *Edward Fitzgerald Beale: A Pioneer in the Path of Empire, 1822–1893.* New York: Putnams, 1912.

[17] Brewerton, George Douglas. "A Ride with Kit Carson." *Harpers New Monthly Magazine* 7(1853):306–34.

[18] Brewerton, George Douglas. "Incidents of Travel in New Mexico." *Harpers New Monthly Magazine* 8:(1854)577–96.

[19] Brewerton, George Douglas. "In Buffalo Country." *Harpers New Monthly Magazine* 25(1862):447–66.

[20] Camp, Charles L. "Kit Carson in California." *Quarterly San Francisco Historical Society* (October 1922).

[21] Carroll, Charles C. "The Government's Importation of Camels, a Historical Sketch." *Bur. Animal Ind. U.S.D.A. Circ.* 53(1904):391–409.

[22] Consejo de las Indias. *Collección de documentos inéditos relativos al descubrimiento, conquista y organización . . . de América y Oceania.* Madrid: Imprenta del Hospicio, 1871. Reprint Mexico City, 1966.

[23] Cooke, Philip St. George. "Rept. of Sec. of War Communicating . . . a Copy of the Official Journal of Lt. Col. Philip St. George Cooke from Santa Fé to San Diego . . ." U.S. 30th Congress, spec. sess. Sen. Exec. Doc. 2:1–85, [1847] 1849.

[24] Davis, Jefferson. "Rept. Sec. War." 32nd Congress, 2nd sess. House Exec. Doc. 1:2:8, 1854.

[25] Davis, Jefferson. "Rept. Sec. War." U.S. 34th Congress, 3rd. sess. House Exec. Doc. 1:1–404, 1856; Sen. Exec. Doc. 62, 1857.

[26] Domenech, Emmanuel Henri Dieudonné. *Seven Years Residence in the Great Deserts of North America.* 2 vols. London: Longman, Green & Roberts, 1860.

[27] Emmet, Chris. *Texas Camel Tales . . .* San Antonio, Texas: Naylor Printing Co., n.d.

[28] Emory, William H. et al. "Notes on a Military Reconnaisance from Fort Leavenworth to San Diego . . . Made in 1846–47 with the Advanced Guard of the Army of the West." 30th Congress, 1st sess. Exec. Doc. 41:7-134, 1848.

[29] Floyd, John. "Rept. Sec. War. US. 35th Congress, 2nd sess. House Exec. Doc. 2:2:1–669, 1859; U.S. 36th Congress, 1st sess. Sen. Exec. Doc. 2, 1859.

[30] Fowler, Harlan Dewey. *Camels to California . . .* Stanford, Calif.: Stanford University Press, 1950.

[31] Fremont, John Charles. "A Report on the Exploration of the Country Lying Between the Missouri River and the Rocky Mountains . . ." U.S. 28th Congress, 2nd sess., 1844–45; Sen. Exec. Doc. 174:1–294, 1845.

[32] Goetzmann, William H. *Army Exploration of the American West, 1803–1863.* New Haven, Conn.: Yale University Press, 1959.

[33] Grant, Blanche, ed. *Kit Carson's Own Story of His Life as Dictated by Him to Col. and Mrs. D. C. Peters About 1856-57, and Never Before Published.* Taos, New Mexico: n.p., 1926.

[34] Gregg, Josiah. *Commerce of the Prairies* . . . 1844. Reprint (2 vols). Philadelphia: J. B. Lippincott Co., 1962.

[35] Gunnison, Capt. John W. "Report of the Expedition of Capt. John W. Gunnison Through Colorado." U.S. 33rd Congress, 1st sess. House Exec. Doc. 18; 2nd sess. Sen. Exec. Doc. 78.

[36] Hartz, Edward L. "2nd Lt., 8th Infantry. Rept. Sc. War." U.S. 36th Congress, 1st. sess. Sen. Exec. Doc. 2:vii:422–41, 1859.

[37] Heap, Gwinn Harris. *Central Route to the Pacific* . . . *Journal of the Expedition of E. F. Beale . . . and Gwinn Harris Heap . . . in 1853*. Philadelphia: Lippincott Grambo & Co., 1854.

[38] Huc, Evariste R. *Recollections of a Journey Through Tartary, Thibet and and China During the Years 1844, 1845 and 1846*. New York: Appleton, 1852.

[39] Hughes, John T. "Doniphan's Expedition; Containing an Account of the Conquest of New Mexico . . . by John T. Hughes A. B., of the First Regiment of Missouri Cavalry." U.S. 63rd. Congress, 2nd sess. Sen. Doc. 608. 22:1–202, 1914.

[40] Ives, Joseph Christmas. "Report on the Colorado River of the West, Explored in 1857 and 1858 . . ." U.S. 36th Congress, 1st. sess. House Exec. Doc. 90:1–131. 1861.

[41] Kearney, Stephen Watts. "Report to the Sec. of War." U.S. 30th Congress, 1st. sess. Sen. Exec. Doc. 1:513–16, 1847–1848.

[42] Marcy, Randolph B. "Report of a Route from Fort Smith to Santa Fé." 31st. Congress, 1st sess. Sen. Exec. Doc. 64, 1850.

[43] Marcy, Randolph B. *The Prairie Traveler* . . . New York: Harper & Bros., 1859. Reprint Williamstown, Mass.: Corner House Publishers, 1968.

[44] Marsh, George P. *The Camel, His Organization, Habits and Uses, considered with Reference to His Introduction into the United States*. Boston: Gould & Lincoln, 1856.

[45] Möllhausen, Baldwin. *Diary of a Journey from the Mississippi to the Coasts of the Pacific* . . . London: Longman, Brown, Green, Longman & Roberts, 1858.

[46] Parkhill, Forbes. *The Blazed Trail of Antoine Leroux*. Los Angeles: Westernlore Press, 1965.

[47] Peters, DeWitt C. *The Life and Adventures of Kit Carson* . . . New York: W. R. C. Clark & Co., 1859.

[48] Pike, Zebulon Montgomery. *The Journals of Zebulon Montgomery Pike with Letters and Related Documents*. Edited by Donald Jackson. Norman: University of Oklahoma Press, 1966.

[49] Powell, John Wesley. *The Exploration of the Colorado River and Its Canyons*. 1895. Reprint New York: Dover, 1964. Original Title: *Canyons of the Colorado*.

[50] Quijada Cornish, Beatrice. "The Ancestry and Family of Juan de Oñate." *Pacific Ocean in History*. Pan-Pacific Congress, 1915.

[51] Schiel, James. *The Land Between* . . . *Account of the Gunnison-Beckwith Expedition Into the West, 1853–1854*. Translated and edited by F. W. Bachmann and W. S. Wallace. Los Angeles: Westernlore Press, 1957.

[52] Simpson, James Hervey. "Report and Map of Route from Fort Smith, Arkansas to Santa Fé, New Mexico." 31st Congress, 1st. sess. Sen. Exec. Doc. 12:1–25, 1850.

[53] Simpson, James Hervey. "Journal of a Military Reconnaissance from Santa Fé, New Mexico to the Navajo Country . . ." U.S. 31st. Congress, 1st. sess. Sen. Exec. Doc. 64:55–168, 1850.

[54] Sitgreaves, Lorenzo. "Report of an Expedition Down the Zuñi and Colorado Rivers." 32nd Congress, 2nd. sess. Sen. Exec. Doc. 59, 1853.

[55] Slater, John M. *El Morro, Inscription Rock, New Mexico* . . . Los Angeles: Plantin Press, 1961.

[56] Stacey, May Humphries. *Uncle Sam's Camels*. Edited by Lewis B. Lesley. Cambridge, Mass.: Harvard University Press, 1929.

[57] Stanley, David Sloane. "Personal Memoirs of Major-General David Sloane Stanley." *Military Historian and Economist* 2 (1917):Suppl. 1–272.

[58] Stanley, David Sloane. "Diary of Lt. David Sloane Stanley, of an Expedition from Fort Smith, Arkansas to San Diego, California." In Library of Congress holdings, c. 1935.

[59] Udell, John. *Incidents of travel across the great plains* . . . Jefferson, Ohio: Sentinel Office, 1856.

[60] Udell, John. *Journal of John Udell Kept Druing a Trip Across the Plains, Containing an Account of the Massacre* . . . *by the Mohave Indians in 1859.* Jefferson, Ohio: Ashtabula Sentinel Steam Press. Reprint. Jefferson, Ohio: L. A. & N. A. Kovach, 1946.

[61] Whipple, Amiel Weeks. "Reports of Explorations and Surveys to Ascertain the Most Practicable and Economical Route for a Railroad." U.S. 33rd. Congress 2nd. sess. House Exec. Doc. 91:1–175, 1854.

[62] Woodward, Arthur. "Camels and Surveyors in Death Valley, the Nevada-California Border Survey of 1861." *Death Valley 49ers Publications* 7(1961):1–73.

[63] Wyman, Walter D. "F. X. Aubry, Santa Fé Freighter, Pathfinder and Explorer." *New Mexico Historical Review* 7(1932):1–31.

[64] Jones, Dana. H. L. J. Rose and the founding of Rosemead First State Bank of Rosemead, 1953.

[65] Rose, Leonard J. Jr. L. J. Rose of Sunny Slope 1827–1899. Henry Huntington Library and Art Gallery, 1959.

[66] Rose, Leonard J. Cross-country reminiscences, *The Californian* 3(1893):114–22.

Index